The Chicano Experience in the Northwest

Editors:
Carlos S. Maldonado
Gilberto Garcia

KENDALL/HUNT PUBLISHING COMPANY
4050 Westmark Drive   Dubuque, Iowa 52002

Copyright © 1995 by Kendall/Hunt Publishing Company

Library of Congress Number: 94-74405

ISBN: 0-7872-0437-4

All rights reserved. No part of this publication may be reproduced, stored in a retrieval system, or transmitted, in any form or by any means, electronic, mechanical, photocopying, recording, or otherwise, without the prior written permission of the copyright owner.

Printed in the United States of America
10   9   8   7   6   5   4   3   2   1

Contents

Preface v
Introduction vii

1 An Overview of the Mexicano/Chicano Presence in the Pacific Northwest 1
Carlos S. Maldonado

2 A Demographic Profile of Chicanos in the Pacific Northwest 35
Guadalupe Friaz

3 Organizational Activity and Political Empowerment: Chicano Politics in the Pacific Northwest 67
Gilberto Garcia

4 Vivemos de la Tierra: Agricultural Workers in the Pacific Northwest 93
Carlos S. Maldonado

5 An Educational Mode for Teaching Chicano Students in the Pacific Northwest 119
Ricardo Garcia ◆ *Anita Ordonez*

6 A Cultural Profile and Status of Chicanas in the Northwest 153
Luz E. Maciel Villarroel ◆ *Sandra B. Fancher Garcia*

7 Chicanos in the Pacific Northwest: A Bibliographic Essay 183
Estela Elizondo-Radovancev

Preface

This anthology provides information and analysis of the Mexicano/Chicano community in the Northwest, including the States of Washington, Oregon and Idaho. The need for such anthology arises from the dearth of materials focusing on Mexicanos/Chicanos in the Northwest. The intent of this anthology is to provide the reader a historical and contemporary reference source focusing on one of the largest and fastest growing Latino subgroups in the Northwest region. The anthology is a collaborative project. This collaboration was possible because of an emerging cadre of Chicano/a scholars in the Northwest. It was critical that Chicano/a scholars from Washington, Oregon and Idaho join together and provide insights about the Mexicano/Chicano community in their own home state and offer a comparative analysis of Chicano communities in other states in the region.

Since this anthology is the first of its kind examining the Mexicano/Chicano community in the Northwest, it is hopeful that it will serve as a spring board for other future works focusing on the Mexicano/Chicano community in the Northwest.

We thank our colleagues that joined us and worked diligently in their respective chapters. Their expertise and contributions were critical to the succes of this anthology.

We thank the numerous individuals interviewed by our colleagues; various state agencies we contacted to obtain goverment generated data on Mexicanos/Chicanos, library staff members whom we visited throughout the Northwest and others who indirectly assisted in producing this anthology.

We also thank Rachel Maldonado, whose listening and feedback helped us significantly in the editing phase of this anthology. Lastly we thank Guadalupe Martínez Cannon, for the significant work she contributed in producing the manuscript for this anthology.

Introduction

In March 1993, the Bureau of the Census issued the report, "The Hispanic Population in the United States: March 1993," in which the bureau estimated that the Hispanic origin population in the U.S. was about 22.8 million or 8.9 percent of the total U.S. population.

The Mexican descent community represents the largest of the population subgroup under the Hispanic rubric. According to the Census Bureau the Mexican descent community comprises 64.3% of the 22.8 million of the U.S. Hispanic population.

Hispanics are the largest and fastest growing community in the Northwest. Hispanics number 214,572 in Washington, 112,707 in Oregon and 52,923 in Idaho. Mexicanos/Chicanos represent the bulk of the Hispanic population in the Northwest.

The past twenty-five years have witnesssed a significant and growing body of literature illuminating the Mexicano/Chicano experience in the U.S. Much of this body of literature has been premised on a southwestern context where Mexicanos/Chicanos are demographically concentrated. This has been reinforced by significant works focusing on the Mexicano/Chicano experience in the U.S. Among these works include Leo Grebler, Joan Moore, and Ralph Guzman's *The Mexican American People* (1970); Rodolfo Acuña's *Occupied America* (1972) and a host of other more recent works.

Some authors have argued that since Mexicanos/Chicanos constitute a national community, the proverbial southwest regional approach to examining the Mexicano/Chicano community has major limitations. Including Mexicano/Chicano populations beyond the southwest into Chicano Studies, Chicano Studies research and mainstream publications about the Chicano community, would prove useful in more fully illuminating the Mexicano/Chicano historical and contemporary experience in the U.S.

This inclusion would be helpful in amplifying the unique historical and social experience of Mexicano/Chicano communities beyond the southwest. Additionally, researching Mexicanos/Chicanos in the various regions of the U.S. would enhance regional comparatives, and expand the "national" presence of Mexicanos/Chicanos.

Chicano and non Chicano scholars have recently begun to document the historical development and presence of Mexicano/Chicano communities beyond the southwest. Resulting publications have familiarized us to Chicano communities in the Midwest and Pacific Northwest.

Felix Padilla (1985) Gilbert Cardenas (1976) Luisa Año Nuevo de Kerr (1975) and others have contributed to the literature highlighting Chicanos in the Midwest. Additionally, Aztlan; The International Journal of Chicano Studies Research (1976) and the Mexican American Studies and Research Center (1989) at the University of Arizona have both produced special issues focusing on Midwest Chicanos.

A limited but growing number of references focusing on Mexicano/Chicano communities in the Pacific Northwest are emerging in the Northwest. Among these include Erasmo Gamboa (1990) Richard Slatta (1979) Carlos Maldonado (1992) and others. A small pool of Masters and Doctoral theses have also contributed to documenting the Mexicano/Chicano Northwest experience.

The absence of a comprehensive anthology about Mexicanos/Chicanos in the Northwest has been acknowledged for some time. Yet, no such publication has emerged to fill the informational void.

It is hoped that this particular anthology will proivide a comprehensive profile of Mexicanos/Chicanos in the Pacific Northwest. This volume will in part serve as a general reference source about Northwest Mexicanos/Chicanos.

In Chapter One, Carlos Maldonado provides an overview of the historical presence of Mexicanos/Chicanos in the Northwest. This historical sketch begins with the early exploration efforts made by the Spanish to the Northwest. The Mexicano link to the Spanish exploration and settlement is highlighted. The overview is premised on the notion that today's Mexicano/Chicano presence came about through a "Viaje al Norte", a series of historical northward journeys to the Northwest.

In Chapter Two, Guadalupe Friaz provides a demographic profile of Mexicanos/Chicanos in the Northwest. Her demographic analysis based on the 1990 U.S. census provides information useful in making interstate comparison among Mexicano/Chicanos. The chapter also points out social economic realities illuminating the status of the Mexicano/Chicano in the Northwest.

In Chapter Three, Gilberto Garcia highlights the presence of organizational activities within the Mexicano/Chicano community during the past five decades. Garcia also presents an insightful discussion using demographics and voting records to indicate the level of political participation by Northwest Chicanos. Garcia also points out some political issues confronting Mexicanos/Chicanos in the Northwest.

In Chapter Four, Carlos Maldonado provides a profile and status of agricultural workers in the Northwest. The chapter also identifies and describes the various organizations that address farmworkers needs in the three state area. The chapter concludes with a discussion focusing on selective critical issues facing Mexicano/Chicano agricultural workers in the Northwest.

In Chapter Five, Ricardo Garcia and Anita Ordoñez provide an educational proposal to effectively teach Mexicano/Chicano students in the Northwest. The author focuses on K to 12th schooling needs of Mexicano/Chicano students. Considering the poor educationl status of education among Mexicanos/Chicanos. The authors' educational proposal is timely and useful in addressing the need of effective schooling among this population group.

In Chapter Six, Luz Villaroel and Sandra Fancher-Garcia provide a cultural profile and status of Chicanos in the Northwest. The authors highlight some significant barriers which have historically burdened Chicanos from progressing in the educational, employment and political areas. Much of the data used in writing was generated by interviews conducted with Chicanos throught the Northwest.

The anthology's final chapter authored by Estela Elizondo Radovancev provides a detailed bibliographic essay focusing on materials which examine the diverse experiences of Mexicanos/Chicanos in the Northwest. The author's discussion provides information about monographs; masters and doctoral theses, articles, state and federal documents, newspapers, videos and other material illuminating the Mexicano/Chicano Northwest experience.

It is hopeful that this anthology will serve as a general reader informing individuals, regardless of disciplinary interest, about the Mexicano/Chicano experience in the Northwest.

1

An Overview of the Mexicano/Chicano Presence in the Pacific Northwest

Carlos S. Maldonado

Many people assume that People of Mexican descent are geographically restricted to Mexico and the American Southwest. Mexicanos/Chicanos reside in every state of the U.S. Mexicanos/Chicanos constitute the largest ethnic community in some regions outside the southwestern U.S. The Mexicano/Chicano presence in the Pacific Northwest can be seen as being predicated on the notion of *"Nuestro Viaje al Norte"* (Our Journey North). This notion of a northward journey permeates our national and regional history as Mexicanos/Chicanos. The initial *"Viaje al Norte"* or early presence of people of Mexican descent in the Pacific Northwest is linked to the Spanish exploration of the area during the late 18th century. Most people remain generally unfamiliar with the Spanish presence and the Mexican link to the age of Spanish exploration of the Northwest. The Mexicano/Chicano presence in Oregon, Washington and Idaho is superficial or non-existent in most people's knowledge of Northwest history. This chapter will provide an overview of the Mexicano/Chicano presence in the Pacific Northwest. The overview will follow the theme of the Mexicano/Chicano *viaje al norte* as a unifying element. The chapter will end with a discussion about recent developments and issues confronting the Mexicano/Chicano community in the Northwest. The author hopes that this chapter will illuminate the Mexicano/Chicano Northwest experience which has historically been absent or at best marginalized in the U.S. and Northwest materials.

Spanish Presence in the Pacific Northwest During the Late 18th Century

Spanish expeditions northward from México begin in the mid 1700's. Initially the exploration and settlement was confined to California. Subsequent efforts moved northward to the Pacific Northwest. In the 1770's Spanish captain Juan Peréz anchored at Vancouver Island. Bruno Heceta and Juan de la Bodega went on shore on the Olympic Peninsula soon after. Early Spanish settlements on Washington's coast included a site off the Nootka Sound at Vancouver Island and another site on Neah Bay. Bruno Heceta had already pinpointed the location of the great Columbia on the Oregon coast.

Informed readers of Northwest history and geography associate numerous Spanish place names such as Heceta Bay, San Juan Islands, the Straits of Juan de Fuca and a host of other place names that link the Pacific Northwest Coast to the age of Spanish exploration. Spanish ships coming to the Northwest at times departed from Mexican ports. Some of these ships were built, provisioned, and staffed with Mexican crew members. The Spanish ships *Sutil* and the *Mexicana* which visited the San Juan Islands in 1792, as part of the Juan Francisco de la Bodega y Quadra expedition to the Northwest, were built in San Blas, México.[1] The Mexican link to the Spanish presence in the Pacific Northwest is also evident in the persona of Jose Mariano Moziño, José Maldonado and Atanasio Echeverría. Moziño and Maldonado were two highly trained Mexican botanists while Echeverría was a skilled artist who did illustrations of the plant and flora in the Northwest expedition. Moziño's visit to the Northwest resulted in a reference resource describing the social customs, political organization, economy, history, and music of the indigenous people of the Nootka area. Moziño also contributed a dictionary of the Nootkan language in his resource reference.[2]

Even though the Spanish presence was brief, geographical place names in the Pacific Northwest still reflect the original names given by the Spanish mariners. The Spanish and Mexican presence predates Lewis and Clark's trek to the Northwest. There exist much work to document and make more visible the Spanish and Mexican presence in the Northwest during the early exploration period. The Mexican link to the Spanish presence in the Northwest also needs to be highlighted to illustrate the contribution of goods, personnel, and knowledge critical to the success of the Spanish exploration efforts to the Pacific Northwest.

The Mexican/Chicano Presence in the Northwest During the Mid 19th Century

The period between 1850 and 1900 marks the second Mexicano/Chicano *"Viaje al Norte"*. This subsequent journey grew out of the expansion of cattle ranching, trade transportation, mining, and other economic activities associated with the settlement and formation of the Northwest territories.

In the territory later to become the state of Oregon, early settlers established the initial efforts of the cattle ranching industry. Oregon ranchers including Peter French, John Devine and Herman Oliver established and developed their own cattle ranching operations during this period. Mexican *vaqueros* from the southwest played a central role in the early development of the cattle ranching in Oregon. Peter French began ranching operations with the help of *vaqueros* who drove an initial herd of 1,200 from California to eastern Oregon. Mexican vaqueros including Juan "Chino" Berdugo, Primitivo Ortego, Vicente Ortego, Juan Ortego, Juan Charris, Jesus Charris, Francisco "Chico" Chararataguey, Juan Rendon and others remained in Oregon and worked as skilled ranch hands.[3] Some like Juan Rendon served as lead *vaquero* for rancher John Devine in Harney county in 1869. Primitivo Ortego also serve as a lead *vaquero* for another well established rancher. Primitivo was one of the vaqueros who ran his own herd as well. The Idaho Statesman newspaper reported in 1870 that an estate sale will be held to auction the belongings of Miguel Soto. Items included in the estate were horses, *aparejos*, and other things.[4] The Mexican *vaqueros* who journeyed north helped establish ranching in eastern Oregon and southwestern Idaho brought with them the long standing *vaquero* culture, tools and skills honed for many years in the southwest.

During the same time period Mexicans were also involved in other economic enterprises including trade or mule transportation in the Northwest. Similar to the developing cattle ranching efforts in eastern Oregon which required skilled individuals, trade or mule transportation called for skilled mule pack drivers. Mexicans coming from the Southwest to the Northwest as mule pack drivers had honed their skills to a high level after years of work in the Southwest. Mule pack drivers needed to have upper body strength, knowledge in the use and care of livestock, familiar with travel requirements in rough and isolated terrain, skillful in the art of efficient packing and knot making techniques, and other skills critical in mule trade transportation.

James Watt who was engaged in mule trade transportation in the 1860's discussed his experiences and contact with Mexican mule drivers in eastern Washington. Watt recollects in his journal that " Most of our packing terms were Spanish, picked up by the Forty-niners from the Mexicans in California.

Quite a few of our packers were Mexicans brought up from California, and employed on account of their special experience and skill in such work".[5]

James Watt's accounts of mule packing are colorful and insightful. His mule packing territory included Oregon, Washington, Idaho, and other areas. A number of these Mexicano mule packers such as Ramon Meras (Idaho 1880 census) have become part of the historical record of mule packing transportation.

Much of the need for mule trade transportation was created by the surge of new or mining settlements in the 1860's in Oregon, Washington, and Idaho clamoring for goods and materials. Mexicans were also involved in this quest for gold and other precious ore. An article appearing in the Idaho Tri Weekly Statesman reports on February, 1870 that Mexicans had been prospecting where placer mining had been reported near Boise City. Mexicano miners brought with them much of the mining technology being used in California and other southwest states. Suffice is to say that Mexicanos like many other gold seekers, came to find their niche in Idaho's gold fields.

The Mexican/Chicano Presence in the Northwest Between 1900 and 1930

The year between 1900 and 1930 marks the years of our third *"Viaje al Norte"*. Several historical events precipitated this subsequent northward journey. These events included the economic development taking place in the U.S., particularly agriculture in the West; WWI, which generated an increase need for agricultural goods and workers; and the Mexican Revolution which initiated a significant movement of Mexicans to the U.S. and corresponded to the upsurge in U.S. labor needs. Collectively these and other related events contributed to Mexicanos/Chicanos journeying northward.

One of the major areas reflecting the economic development taking place in the U.S. at the turn of the century and which directly affected Mexicanos/Chicanos was southwestern United States. The stage for this growth had been set decades earlier by the extension of the rail road throughout the Southwest. The established railroad system gave impetus to economic activities such as mining, ranching and agricultural efforts. In the agriculture area the total farm acreage in the West had tripled between 1870 and 1900, and lands under irrigation had increased dramatically from 60,000 to 1,446,000 acres.[6] Reclamation and Irrigation efforts associated with the Reclamation Act of 1902 continued to spur agricultural related economic activity in the Southwest. This legislation was specifically targeting the development of irritable lands in the West. By 1915 about twenty five reclamation projects costing upward of $ 80 million were being promoted by the Act.[7]

World War I also contributed to the increased need of agricultural production. The outbreak of WWI forced American industrial and agricultural production to shift into overdrive. Every agricultural sector experienced the wartime pressures of expansion. The enhancement of farm prices and production levels bode well for farmers. Farmers strove to meet the heighten agricultural production levels critical to meet war time consumption and trade. The Southwest contributed to meeting the agricultural production pressures. Texas, California, and Arizona produced cotton and other agricultural goods needed for the war efforts.

The expansion of agricultural activity taking place nationally and in the southwest between 1900 and 1920 and the labor needs created by WWI required an increasing labor force. Mexicanos were seen as an answer to this labor need. Successful efforts by organized agricultural interest secured a clause in the Immigration Act of 1917 easing the entry of Mexicanos to the U.S. during this period. Additionally, the 1910 outbreak of the Mexican revolution which ran until 1921 created economic and political distablization in Mexico. The Mexican revolution generated a windfall for U.S. agriculture and other economic sectors. Mexicanos leaving to escape the turmoil of war immigrated to the U.S. It is generally estimated that about one million Mexicanos came to the U.S. as a result of the revolution.[8] The bulk of these immigrants became part of the Mexicano/Chicano communities in the Southwest, particularly border communities. Many leaving Mexico soon became employed in agriculture, rail road work, and mining operations in the Southwest and beyond. Mexicanos leaving their war torn country continued to come to the U.S. throughout the decade of 1910 to 1920.

Abel Maravilla is one of thousands of Mexicanos that journeyed north to the United States during the 1920's. His personal story is one of several included in the publication titled "Nampa's People: Discovering Our Heritage" (1986) which highlights some of Nampa, Idaho long time residents. In early 1920 Abel had heard that railroad companies in the U.S. were hiring Mexicanos to work on the railroad. He and his young wife secured a work visa and headed to Ft. Worth, Texas where the rail road company was hiring.

Soon he was on his way to Banks, Idaho as a rail road worker where he worked on a section gang laying new track, replacing old ties and other railroading work. In 1928 he requested and obtained a transfer to Nampa. He worked with the rail road company for sixteen years. While many Mexicanos remained in the southwest others like Abel Maravilla began a northward journey beyond the southwest and to areas including the Mid West, Rocky Mountain states, and the Northwest. Santiago Jaramillo who traveled to eastern Oregon also came as a rail road worker. He came to eastern Oregon in 1917. Today, the Jaramillo family has deep roots in Ontario, Oregon. Several of his children have established some of the earliest Mexicano businesses in the area.[9]

Migration routes to the Mid West, Rocky Mountain states and the Northwest soon became clearly established by the 1920's. Agricultural and particularly sugar beet production which had begun decades earlier in these areas, served as an impetus for this northward journey.

In Idaho, the Utah Sugar Company had established an initial sugar factory in 1903. By 1912, sugar factories were operating in Idaho Falls, Sugar City, Burley, Buhl, Nampa, and Twin Falls.[10] In 1918 a letter from the Consulate General of the Republic of México at San Francisco is routed from Idaho Governor M. Alexander to Mr. W. J. A. McVety, Labor commissioner focusing on some labor complaints raised by Mexicanos working in the sugar factories in Twin Falls, Idaho.[11] There were about 1500 Mexican laborers including 500 females in the Idaho Falls, Shelley and Blackfoot area. The complaints being raise by the Mexican workers involved wages, housing, labor practices and other worker issues. Mr. McVety charged by the Governor to investigate these issues visits the sugar factories in Twin Falls, Paul, Blackfoot and Idaho Falls. Some of the complaints were substantiated while others resulted from poor communication between the sugar company and the Mexicano workers.[12] By the 1920's, Mexicans were clearly present in the agricultural scene in Idaho. In Washington and Oregon Mexicanos were also present during these early years. Manuel Gamio's research on Mexican Immigration cites information indicating the number of money orders sent from the U.S. to Mexico during the mid 1920's. The states of Oregon, Washington, and Idaho are clearly recorded as points of origin of some of the money orders.[13]

Some Mexicanos/Chicanos coming to the Northwest during the 1920's would travel to more than one state in the Northwest region. Erasmo Gamboa who has written a number of references on Mexicans in the Northwest offers examples of such inter state movement including the case of Geraldo Cardenas who left Twin Falls, Idaho and moved to Northwest Washington during the 1920's.[14] It is safe to say that Mexicans and Chicanos coming to the Northwest in the 1920's were pulled or made a logical extension of their travel from Colorado and other Mountain Rocky states into Idaho, Washington and Oregon.

The small Mexicano/Chicano population in the Northwest between 1900 and 1930 was slowly growing. The 1930 U.S. Census reflected this growth. In 1930 Mexicanos/Chicanos numbered 562 in Washington, 1,568 in Oregon, and 1,278 in Idaho. Most likely some Mexicanos/Chicanos were not counted as has been the historical pattern in the U.S. Census.

Whereas the decades between 1900-1930 represent the early years when Mexicanos/Chicanos intermittently came to the Northwest, Mexicano/Chicano migration into the Northwest during the proceeding decades represented a substantial increase in the number of Mexicanos/Chicanos making the *"Viaje al Norte"*.

The Mexicano/Chicano Presence in the Northwest During the 1940's, 50's, and Early 60's.

The *"Viaje al Norte"* between the 1940's and early 1960's is dominated by active recruitment of Mexicano/Chicano labor, significant influx of Mexicanos/Chicanos into specific areas of the Northwest, and the settling of a growing number of those making the *"Viaje al Norte"*. Todays Mexicano/Chicano community established its roots during these critical years.

WWII proved to be a significant watershed of historical developments and events which affected the U.S. abroad and the home front. Similar to the years of WWI, industry and agriculture were once again called upon to heighten production to meet the needs of war time consumption and trade. This heighten levels of production, as was the case during WWI, was compounded by a drain of labor being redirected to military and military related needs. Regions throughout the U.S. including the Northwest were impacted by the war. WWII played a significant role in Mexicanos/Chicanos coming to the Northwest.

Mexicanos/Chicanos coming to the Northwest during this period represented various groups. First, were the countless Mexicanos/Chicanos coming to the Northwest as military personnel. In the case of Washington, Mexicano/Chicano GIs from the southwest came as military personnel to train and work in the various military installations in the state. Some were station at Fort Lewis in Tacoma; Fort Larsen in Moses Lake (which no longer exists); Ephrata Air Terminal in Ephrata; Fairchild Air Force Base in Spokane, Washington.

Among these included Manuel Melendrez, whose family originated from northern New Mexico and Colorado, but migrated to Montana. In 1941 Manuel enlisted and was stationed at McCord Air Field for training. He later went into action in the pacific. He returned to Spokane, Washington after his tour. He married, raised his family and operated his own hair salon business.[15]

Joe Treviño, who was stationed at Ft. Lewis in Tacoma came from south Texas. During week end passes he would travel to visit the Yakima Valley. While visiting there he met and married Dominga Ybarra, whose family had come to Washington as agricultural workers. The Treviños lived in Yakima Valley for a time and later moved to Spokane, Washington.[16] Other Mexicanos/Chicanos who came to Washington as military personnel and subsequently remained rather than returning to their home states in the Southwest also include Fred Valdez, Carlos Landa and others.

In Idaho, the Mountain Home Air Base, the Farragut Naval Base and the Gowen Field Army Air Base (Farragut and Gowen installations were deactivated after the war) also attracted Mexicanos/Chicanos during the war years. The *Farragut News* a base newspaper at the U.S. Naval Training Station at Farragut, Idaho reports the names of numerous Mexicanos/Chicanos at the base. It is interesting to read Spanish names including Basta, Duarte, Luna, López and Muñoz. Many appeared in stories about boxing competitions on and off base.

Anastacio "Don" Gonzáles, originally from Los Angeles, California first came to the Northwest in 1943. He came to train at Mountain Home Air Force Base located in Idaho. While at Mountain Home Air Force Base, he met Mary Jaramillo who worked as a secretary for the base's payroll master. They married before being shipped to England where he spent 20 months during the war. After being discharged he returned to the Northwest and established residency in Oregon. Anastacio and his wife Mary went on to establish one of the earliest Mexican businesses in eastern Oregon.[17]

These are some specific examples of those Mexicanos/Chicanos who came to the Northwest during the war years. Some subsequently decided to remain in the area and became part of the Mexicano/Chicano community in the Northwest.

The second group of Mexicanos coming to the Northwest during the war years included the thousands of Mexicano "Bracero" workers who came to the Northwest and worked in fields and orchards. Some also worked in rail road work.

The *Bracero* Program originated from an agreement between the U.S. and México in 1942. Initially, the *Bracero* Program was set up where Mexico provided a much needed labor force while the U.S. employers provided jobs. The *Bracero* Program underwent several extensions until it was terminated in 1964. The 1942-47 phase of the *Bracero* Program brought most of the Mexicano *braceros* to the Northwest. Community newspaper stories throughout the Northwest announced the arrival or departure of *bracero* workers.

The Oregonian a Portland based newspaper carried numerous news stories about the Mexican *bracero* workers. One such story tells a about a *bracero* contingent arriving in Hillsboro, Oregon in 1943. The news story states that the workers had arrived from México after traveling for six days. The *braceros* were housed and fed in the basement of the Hillsboro High School during their brief stay. The Mexican *braceros* were being use as emergency crews for the frozen food cannery, which send a large share of its pack to the lease-lend initiative and to the armed forces.[18]

Other newspapers stories note *bracero* workers being transported to other sites including; The Dalles, Dayton, Hood River, Oregon; Toppenish, Yakima, Wapato, Washington; and other sites in Idaho. A lengthy newspaper article appearing in the *Oregonian* gives a detail description of the bracero workers and everyday life including the warm and cold reception extended by local people. The article includes a series of excellent photos.[19]

A letter from E.L. Peterson, Director of Agriculture in the Oregon Department of Agriculture to Governor Earl Snell dated August 2, 1945 discusses labor problems Mexicanos were experiencing. Six hundred Mexicanos were working as section rail workers in the Eugene area. Another 100 plus were working in the agriculture harvest.[20]

An effort by some local people to organize a recreational club for the Mexicanos ends when a site at the local labor house is found, rented and later forced to be given up because local unions with offices at the labor house vowed to leave if the Mexicanos came in. Suffice to say that some local people welcomed the Mexicano workers while others view them as intruders.[21]

The third group of Mexicanos coming to the Northwest were families who were recruited or came to the Northwest on their own account. Among these included families from Texas, Colorado, California, and other southwestern states. Some families merely extended their travel beyond the Rocky Mountain states where agriculture, particularly sugar beets, had attracted them in earlier years. Families traveled to various areas of the Northwest including Oregon's Willamette Valley; Washington's Yakima Valley; and Idaho's southwestern agricultural counties. By in large, this third group proved to be the most significant not only in numbers but also in settling out in numerous Northwest communities.

Today migrant Mexicano/Chicano communities including Woodburn, Oregon; Sunnyside, Washington; and Caldwell, Idaho are only a few of the numerous rural agricultural driven communities in Oregon, Washington and Idaho where this third group of Mexicanos/Chicanos established new roots as a community.

◆ *"Nuestro Hogar del Norte"*

The influx of Mexicanos/Chicanos into the Northwest continued after WWII and into the 1950's and early 1960's. A significant historical transition for Mexicanos/Chicanos was gradually taking place during the decades of the 1950's and early 1960's. Even though the notion of the *"Viaje al Norte"* was and would continue in subsequent decades, a parallel notion was emerging. The notion of *"Nuestro Hogar del Norte"* (Our Northern Home) was becoming a reality for an increasing number of Mexicano/Chicano families. This notion of *"Nuestro Hogar del Norte"* began to be reflected in various ways. Some families decided to stay and make their new home in the Northwest. The number of births and enrollments in local school districts became more visible during the non harvest season. Community organizations began to emerge; and Mexicano/Chicano community cultural celebrations began to be staged. These early community developments gradually emerged in the various rural agricultural communities in the Northwest where Mexicano/Chicano families settled.

Among the increasing number of families who decided to make their new home in the Northwest included the Domingo García family from Edingburg, Texas. Domingo and his family would travel yearly to Oregon's Willamette Valley and then return to Texas after the harvest during the 1950's. Work and extended family members who had remained in Oregon in earlier years encouraged Domingo to stay. They decided to stay and settled in Independence, Oregon. The family subsequently moved to Woodburn. Today Domingo's grand children and great grandchildren are native Oregonian living in Woodburn.[22] Woodburn, Oregon is representative of the various rural agricultural communities in Oregon, Washington and Idaho which attracted Mexicanos/Chicanos during the 1940's, 50's and early 60's.

The families who settled in the Northwest during these years began to establish the foundation of many Mexicano/Chicano communities of today. Early signs of this community evolution increased the presence of Mexicano/Chicanos in the Northwest. Jerry García, in his masters thesis, alludes to this presence by highlighting an annual Mexican *fiesta* staged in Quincy, Washington begun in 1957. The *Quincy Post Register*, a local newspaper describes this yearly *fiesta* as being organized by the local Mexicano community and attracting a large crowd.

In Woodburn, Oregon community people established the *"Pro Fiestas Mexicanas"* organizing group to plan and stage an annual Mexican fiesta. The first fiesta was staged in 1964. Local merchants gave strong support in staging the first *fiesta*.[23] Woodburn's *"Fiesta Mexicana"* is one of the largest and longest running cultural celebration in Oregon's Willamette Valley. In 1994 the local Mexicano community commemorated the 30th anniversary of this enduring annual *fiesta*.

In Idaho cultural Mexican fiestas can be traced back to the 1940's and 1950's when labor camps would stage celebrations. *The Wilder Herald* a local newspaper in Wilder, Idaho highlighted one of these camp celebrations in 1944.[24] Tony Rodrigues of Nampa, related his experience coordinating various labor camps groups participating in a large Mexican fiesta held in Nampa in the late mid 1950's.[25]

This evolving presence was also reflected in upstart cultural based Mexicano/Chicano businesses. A few Mexicano/Chicano owned businesses, particularly restaurants began to appear gradually during these early years..

In Washington one of these early Mexicano businesses included Espinoza's, a restaurant begun by the the Espinoza family in 1954 in Seattle.[26] Today the Espinoza family owns restaurants in Yakima and in Lacey, Washington. Hipolito and Herminia Mendez, from Sunnyside opened Casa Mendez, a Mexican restaurant in 1955.[27] *La Mexicana*, a distributorship of Mexican specialty foods was begun by Rudy Martínez in Seattle, Washington in 1955. He sold the business a decade later to a non-Mexicano. *La Mexicana* still operates today as a distributorship of Mexican foods.[28] In Spokane, Washington *"La Copa de Oro"* and "El Comal" were opened in 1960-61.[29] "El Comal" was unique in that it also doubled as a *"tortillería"* producing *tortillas* for the area market. Additionally, *El Comal* was unique because its Spokane location fell beyond the geographical area where the bulk of the Mexicano/Chicano community was settling. In Othello, Washington the Benavides and Zavala families began their respective restaurants in 1964-65. Both restaurants will soon mark their 30th year doing business.

In Oregon, Mexicano businesses include the *tortillería* of Anastacio "Don" Gonzáles established outside of Ontario in early 1952. González Tortillería was initially begun by Mary González and her mother, Rita Jaramillo. Don joined in soon after. The *tortillería* expanded quickly. *Tortillería* González soon had a distribution territory including the Treasure Valley, the numerous communities between Ontario and Portland, Oregon. Tortillería González operated until 1987.[30] In 1965 Francisco and Carmen Rodríguez established *Panadería* Rodríguez in Nyssa. The same year the Medina family establish *"El México Lindo"* in Woodburn, a small store selling Mexican imports, music records, religious items and other specialty items. Today, *"El México Lindo"* is one of the oldest Mexican stores in the Willamette Valley marketing groceries, a fast food menu, music and a host of other Mexican specialty items.[31] These early culture base businesses give witness to an established Mexicano/Chicano community growing to a level adequate enough to support these businesses.

In Idaho, Tony Rodríguez who came to Nampa in 1941 started a barber shop business in 1949. Later, in 1954 Rodríguez established *El Charro*, Nampa's first Mexican restaurant. Rodriguez operated both barbershop and restaurant concurrently. Later, the restaurant became his main business. Today, *El Charro* still continues the Mexican restaurant tradition begun in the early 1950's.[32]

The early existence of Spanish radio broadcasting was also reflective of the growing presence of Mexicanos/Chicanos in the Northwest. Spanish radio programming offered cultural, entertainment, and informational benefits to the growing Mexicano/Chicano community in the Northwest.

In Washington the KREW radio station located in Sunnyside began Spanish radio programming in 1951. Herminiā Méndez directed the first Spanish programming broadcast in the Yakima Valley on KREW's radio waves. The Mendez family first came to Sunnyside, Washington from Eagle Pass, Texas in 1943. The family returned to Texas each year after the harvest. In 1948 they decided to stay. Herminia Méndez having had no pior experience in radio yet moved by the need for Spanish radio programming approached the KREW station owner in 1951 to highlight this need. He accepted Herminia's proposal to integrate Spanish programming and Herminia soon begins broadcasting Mexican music in the area. Due to the lack of a Mexican record collection to use, Herminia initially invited musicians to play live over the radio. Initially the Spanish radio broadcast ran only 1/2 hour every Tuesday and Thursday. Later the format and length of the broadcast were enhanced.[33]

KREW was the sole radio station that broadcasted Spanish programming in the Yakima Valley for many years. It also has the distinction to have been the first station to broadcast Spanish programming in the Northwest.

In Oregon, KWRC based in Woodburn began its Spanish radio programming in 1965. KWRC was Oregon's first station to broadcast Spanish programming. A couple from Texas by the name of Alfredo (Fred) Herrera and Nelly Jiménez approached the station owner about giving them an opportunity to broadcast Mexican Music. In contrast to Herminia in Sunnyside, Alfredo had DJ experience. The owner agreed and the couple began Spanish radio programming in Oregon's Willamette Valley with about two dozen Mexican records.[34] Similar to Idaho and Washington, Spanish broadcasting was limited to a part time format. The station's call letters were changed to KWBY in 1987 and subsequently sold. The new station has continued Spanish programming in the area. Today, it serves as the second radio station in Oregon which offers 24 hours of Spanish programming.

In Idaho, Caldwell's KCID initiated its Spanish programming on September, 1956. Gregorio Hernandez served as the station's first announcer. The standard broadcast format included music request, news, sports, information, and weather.[35] According to Dale Peterson, station owner and general manager, KCID has been broadcasting Spanish programming in the area long before other stations joined in. KCID, like numerous other stations in the Northwest broadcasted Spanish programming only on week ends or evenings.

Other signs which reflected the growing presence in the Northwest included local movie theaters which screened Mexican movies. In Woodburn,

Oregon Lafe Potter owner of the Pix theater began screening Mexican movies in 1964-65. Dan Stitt took over the theater in 1966 and continued the screening of Mexican movies. Mr. Stitt relates that the theater was more than a just a theater for the Mexicanos. For instance "when some well known Mexicano in the community died, family or family friends would announce the individual's death and funeral during intermission. The lack of a communication avenue precipitated these announcements. I would also permit people to set up voter registration booths outside the theater to sign up Mexicano voters". Mr. Stitt recalls that other theaters in Washington later begun screening Mexican movies as well.[36] In Toppenish, the Pix Theater (not associated with the Pix in Oregon) also screened Mexican movies during the mid 1960's. Ray and Ellen Young, theater managers, recall that once the INS raided the theater. The raid negatively impacted business.

Collectively the growing visibility of the Mexicanos/Chicanos as reflected by school enrollments, upstart Mexican owned and cultural based businesses; emerging Spanish radio broadcasting and other initiatives premised the evolving and growing presence of the Mexicano/Chicano community in the Northwest during the 1940's, 50's and early 1960's.

The Mexicano/Chicano Community During the Years of Activism in the Northwest: Late 1960's -1970's

The 1960's were watershed years for significant social and political activism in America. Activism challenging established practices of discrimination and inequality based on race, class, and gender permeated throughout America. Grassroot activism among ethnic groups including blacks, native Americans, and Chicanos contributed to a widening of activism and resistance which historically existed in these communities. The activism taking place in the Chicano community was being projected by diverse individuals and groups with varying issues and strategies leading to addressing and resolving issues. Among these included Rodolfo "Corky" Gonzáles and the Crusade for Justice in Colorado; Jose Angel Gutierrez and La Raza Unida Party in south Texas; Reis López Tejerína and the Alianza Federal de Mercedes in New Mexico; Cesar Chávez and the United Farm Workers Union in California; and Chicano student groups throughout the Southwest which gave much energy to the Chicano Movement.

Chicano political activism although centered in the southwest extended its impact into other regions beyond the Southwest, including the Northwest. This activism was transmitted through the media, by individuals and groups that moved constantly between the Southwest and the Northwest; state and local organizations which were affiliated formally and/or informally with national organizations; self initiated activism in the Northwest and other avenues. This Mexicano/Chicano Northwest activism spearheaded grassroot efforts to advocate and enhance the circumstance of *"nuestro hogar del norte"*. This grassroot activism culminated in diverse organizations throughout the Northwest. The following are examples of this activism and organizations emerging in Oregon, Washington and Idaho during the late 1960's and 1970's.

In Oregon, the Willamette Valley by far served as the primary seed bed that nurtured the germination of Mexicano/Chicano organizational development taking place during this period. Some argue that the Valley Migrant League (VML), sponsored by the Oregon Council of Churches' department of Migrant Ministries and later funded by the federal Office of Economic Opportunity, contributed to pushing forward the Chicano movement in Oregon. An article in the *Capitol Journal* in 1970, quoted John Little VML director as stating that the "VML can claim much of the credit in providing the seed bed for the [Chicano] movement [in the Willamette Valley]. Lets say there were no VML, unless something unusual had happened, I don't think the (Chicano) movement would have existed [in the Willamette Valley]. Well it might have existed, but only among a few people".[37] The VML did in part contributed to creating the climate for the Chicano movement to flourish in Oregon's Willamette Valley. The VML contributed to voicing the rhetoric of activism, provided opportunity for some community members to participate in cultural based leadership and empowering seminars sponsored or supported by the VML, placed community people on decision making position within VML, and promoted the notion of community development. Nonetheless the energy of activism in the Chicano movement and community development efforts rather linked or not to the movement would have had its impact regardless of the VML as evident with the various Mexicano/Chicano organization which emerged independent of the VML.

Additionally, an active communication link connecting individuals and groups between the Northwest and the Southwest, where the Chicano movement was most active, played a significant role in promoting activism in Oregon and the Northwest. Furthermore, the fundamental fact that the Chicano Movement was part of a much larger social political movement of the late 1960's which transcended geographical regions would have impacted Oregon regardless of any efforts tied to any specific organization.

Mexicanos/Chicanos in Oregon captured the spirit of self determination and founded organizations including: VIVA (Volunteers in Vanguard Action)— Established in 1966 in Washington county. The organizers of VIVA, including Emilio Hernández who headed the organization were former VLM participants who splintered off from the programs conducted by the VML. Organized in 1966, VIVA holds the distinction of being one of the first activist community groups in the Northwest.

Campesinos Forum—established in 1967 in Hillsboro, Oregon also resulted from dissatisfaction with the VML. The Forum also served as an advocacy group for farm workers.

The Latin American Club was established in 1968 in Woodburn, Oregon to promote social and cultural initiatives for the Mexicano community. The Latin American Club has sponsored the Mexican Fiesta in Woodburn for almost thirty years.

The United Farm Workers of Oregon—established in 1968 and headed by Ventura Rios was also moving forward the notion of unionization for Oregon agricultural workers (Oregonian 28, 1969).

Centro Chicano Cultural—established in 1969 on a site located between Woodburn and Gervais, Oregon served as a cultural center for the community. Community organizing meetings were frequently held at the Centro. David Aguilar served as director of the Centro. The Centro later played a central role in the continued operation of Colegio Cesar Chávez.

The Chicano United Farm workers of Oregon was quasi organized in 1970 in Independence, Oregon. Tito Aguirre headed this initiative. During the hop harvest the group staged a successful strike against the Has Farms in Independence. The group did not fully develop.

El Centro Cultural—established in 1972 in Cornelius, Oregon serves as a multi-service center for farm workers and the community. El Centro Cultural still continues today as a key player in community development.

CISCO was established in 1972 at Camp Adair, an inactive Air Force installation located on highway 99W between Independence and Corvalis, Oregon. CISCO operated vocational, educational and cultural programming.

Salud de la Familia, which later became the Salud Medical Center was established in 1972 in Woodburn, Oregon to provide primary health services to low income and migrant families.

Colegio Cesar Chávez—established in 1973 in Mt. Angel, Oregon to provide higher educational opportunity to the Chicano/Mexicano community.

The Chicano State Concilio—established in 1974 to facilitate communication and networking among Chicano advocates and organizations.

ORO Oregon Rural Opportunities—emerged in the mid 1970's and assumed the role of being major provider of services to farm workers. By the late 1970's ORO loses its funding base and the California Human Development Corporation (CHDC) takes over the main role as a multi service agency serving farm workers. Soon after (CHDC) establishing itself, the Oregon Human Development Corporation emerges as the area entity. The Oregon Human

Development still continues today as a major player in providing services to agricultural workers in Oregon.

COSSPO (Commission on the Spanish Speaking People of Oregon) was established in 1977 in Portland, Oregon. COSSPO sponsored a variety of initiatives including, programs on nutrition for the elderly, employment assistance, ESL classes and disseminated information about the community through its newspaper *"Informa"* and a monthly television program highlighting community issues.

This is only a sampling of the diverse organizations which emerged in Oregon, particularly in the Willamette Valley in the late 1960's and 1970's. These organizations' political orientations varied and in no fashion formed a homogenous collective as is the case in any community. The existence of these organizations gives credence that the Mexicano/Chicano community in Oregon was active in enhancing its circumstance in *"nuestro hogar del norte"*. Today, some of these organizations no longer exist, nonetheless it is important to cite their one time presence to reaffirm the activism founding these organizations. Some of the cited organizations continued to mature in subsequent years. These organizations continue to provide leadership and reflect the spirit of self determination which premised their founding.

In the state of Washington, Mexicanos/Chicanos were also active striving to enhance their own circumstance. Whereas Oregon's Willamette Valley gave birth to many of the Mexicano/Chicano organizations during these years, Washington's Yakima Valley served as the seed bed for early activism in the state. Similar to Oregon, Washington's Mexicanos/Chicanos established diverse organizations during this period as well. The following is a sampling of organizations which emerged in Washington.

Similar to Oregon, efforts to secure federal funding from the Office of Economic Opportunity to extend the War on Poverty to the Yakima Valley to serve the low income and migrant community were successful. Community centers were organized in the valley to assist those needing support. Whereas in Oregon the OEO funded VML had in some sense contributed in developing the Mexicano/Chicano community, Jesús Lemos in his study focusing on the Yakima Valley, argues that in Washington, the Yakima Valley Community Action Committee, the entity funded by the OEO did not have the same impact. He argues that this absence of impact culminating in community organizing among the Mexicano/Chicano resulted in the emergence of alternative organization based in the community. Jesús Lemos' M. A. thesis entitled "A History of the Chicano Political Involvement and Organizational Effects of the United Farm Workers Union in the Yakima Valley", was extremely useful in identifying Chicano organizations in Washington.

The community in Washington formed the United Farm Workers Co-op in Toppenish in 1967. The UFW Co-op operated a store where farm workers could purchase food at a reduce retail cost. The UFW Co-op was also involved in promoting activism and community development among Mexicanos/Chicanos. The UFW Co-op can be seen as the precursor to the farm workers union established years later. The UFW Co-op also has the distinction as being the first activist group in the state of Washington.

The Mexican American Federation—established also in 1967 involved itself in community development work by running voter registration drives and supporting local political candidates.

"La Sociedad Mutualista"—established in 1968 in Granger, Washington served as a mutual support organization to its membership. Its membership were involved in organizing social events such dances and other events. The notion of *"mutualistas"* or mutual aid societies have been organized throughout history by Mexicans in Mexico and Mexicanos/Chicanos in the U.S. Many have been related to labor efforts. "La Sociedad Mutualista" served more as a support and social group rather than an activist or labor entity.

UMAS (United Mexican American Students)—formed by students at the University of Washington, Seattle established a local chapter of UMAS in 1968. UMAS was a national Chicano student organization which emerged in 1967 in California and spread to other states.

UMAS at the UW staged a statewide Chicano student conference in Toppenish the same year. UMAS, MASA and other similar organizations provided an avenue for students to become active in the political development of the Mexicano/Chicano community.

Young activists established a local chapter of the Brown Berets at the UW in 1968. The Brown Berets was an organization established in 1967 as Young Chicanos for Community Action in Los Angeles. It later became known as the Brown Berets. Members often wore para military dress including a brown beret and voiced a nationalistic stance. A second Brown Beret group also got founded in the Yakima Valley in 1969.

Students at Yakima Valley Community College established a local chapter of MASA (Mexican American Student Association) in 1969, another student organization begun in California which spread to other states as well.

La Escuelita was an initiative begun in 1969 in Granger, Washington and served as a cultural center in the area La Escuelita became the host of the Calmecac project in the summer of 1970. This project promoted and staged classes in Chicano history, culture and theater.

Active Mexicano—established in 1969 in Seattle, Washington worked towards providing individuals social services including job placement and legal assistance.

El Año del Mexicano—A community organizing initiative begun in Granger, Washington. The initiative was directed by students interested in promoting community political involvement. It concentrated on voter registration efforts in the community.

El Teatro del Piojo (Theater of the Lice)—established at the UW in Seattle, Washington in 1970 was the Northwest's reflection of activist theater groups such as the national and international performing *El Teatro Campesino*. *El Teatro del Piojo* performed throughout Idaho, Oregon and Washington highlighting issues affecting the Mexicano/Chicano community. The group participated in several theater festivals held in California and México City.

Whatcom Chicano Consilio, established in 1970 and headed by Jorge Chacon in Lynden, Washington also served as a Chicano advocacy group in Western Washington.

Centro de La Raza was established in 1972 in Seattle, Washington by a group of activists who occupied a vacant school building and refused to leave until the school district leased the building to the group. El Centro is a multi-service community organization which provides services regardless of ethnicity. It operates a preschool, serves hot meals to the needy and elderly, offers ESL classes, stages cultural events, and a host of other progressive community initiatives.

Mujeres Unidas—established in the mid 1970's at Washington State University, Pullman, Washington not only reflected the activism of Chicanas but also extended the notion that women issues as they relate to Chicanas were important organizing causes.

RADIO KNDA—established in 1979 as a Spanish language public radio station in Granger, Washington. The station provides music, information and other radio base initiatives to the community. It identifies itself as *"La Voz del Campesino"*—The Voice of the Farm worker. KNDA has been recognized nationally as a progressive public radio station.

Even though the following initiatives were not community base it is worthwhile to cite that Chicano Studies components at the University of Washington, Seattle; Washington State University, Pullman, Washington; and Eastern Washington University were established in the 1970's

These organizations represent a sampling of organizations that Mexicanos/Chicanos were establishing in the state of Washington, particularly in the Yakima Valley where much activism was centered during the late 1960's and 1970's. Similar to Oregon, organizations in Washington were diverse. Some of these organization have ceased to exist, while others continue to contribute to the development of the Mexicano/Chicano community in Washington. The documenting of these organizations is critical in highlighting the activism reflected in the founding of these organizations. These organizations are also testimony to the communication link between southwest and Washington activists.

In the state of Idaho, Mexicanos/Chicanos had also been active in community development during the late 1960's and 1970's. The reality of a smaller Mexicano/Chicano community in Idaho contributed to fewer community organization emerging in the state. None the less Idaho holds the distinction of having the first community base organization in the Northwest. Tony Rodríguez a Nampa resident WWII veteran, established a local chapter of the American G.I. Forum in 1955. The G.I. Forum emerged soon after WWII in Texas to fight discrimination against Mexicanos. The thrust behind the formation of the Forum came after the refusal of a local anglo community in Texas to allow the burial of a Mexicano G.I., who had been killed in action. Tony Rodríguez served as president of the Nampa chapter of the G.I. Forum from 1955 to 1965.[38] This community base organization was the precursor to subsequent Mexicano/Chicano organizations in Idaho.

The War on Poverty campaign of the 1960's had funded initiatives through the Office Of Economic Opportunity to assist the low income. In Oregon. OEO funded the VML and the Treasure Valley Migrant Education Program in Ontario. In Washington the agency funded the Yakima Council for Community. Oregon and Washington OEO funded projects established a number of centers in their areas.

In Idaho an OEO funded project was not evident. Mexicanos/Chicanos in southwestern Idaho made efforts to linked themselves to the Treasure Valley Migrant Education Program (TVMEP) administered by the Treasure Valley Community College (TVCC) in Ontario. In the late 1960's some Mexicano/Chicano activists felt that those being targeted by the program should have more direct input and control over the program. The activists initiated a legal suit to determine this argument legally. The activists were successful in the legal battle. Subsequently the college decided it no longer wanted anything to do with the OEO funded Migrant project and withdrew its sponsorship. The leadership mobilized and took advantage of the emerging opportunity and submitted their own proposal to the OEO office. Meanwhile the IMC leadership secured support from the Colorado Migrant Council. Thereafter, the IMC efforts to get government funding proved successful.

The Idaho Migrant Council (IMC)—incorporated in 1971 is one of the longest running organization in Idaho advocating for the Mexicano/Chicano community in general and the migrant farm worker in particular. Today, it is one of the key Mexicano/Chicano grass root organizations in Idaho. IMC has staged information workshops, runs emergency supports services, operates educational initiatives for migrant families and children, sponsors conferences, distributes scholarship funds and a host of other initiatives benefiting the Mexicano/Chicano community including migrant workers. The IMC is a membership organization which secures government funding. The IMC is consistently and productively pushing community issues to the forefront.

In 1971 a quasi farm worker organization called *Campesinos Unidos* emerged in the Caldwell area. This effort aimed to organize farmworkers in Idaho.

In 1972 the United Farm Workers Union Organizing Committee was active in Idaho promoting the Union's grape and lettuce boycotts started in California.

FAMA (Familias Mexico Americanas-Mexican American Families)—founded in 1972 in Caldwell. FAMA served as a mutual aid society and offered emergency aid to families in need including food, lodging, etc.

Mexican American Association—established in 1976 in Boise to stress the perpetuation of Mexicano culture and values. The group is also involved in promoting education among its youth and has raised monies for scholarships. The association viewed its self as a social club as well, and staged picnics and dances.

Comite de Habla Español (Committee for the Spanish Speaking)—established in 1977 as a statewide voter education group. The members were also involved in getting the vote out in the Spanish speaking community.

AYUDA (HELP)—established in 1979 in eastern Idaho to help Latinos and migrant workers. The group provided information and referral services, and promoted self help and advocacy for the community. It was based out of Idaho Falls and it published the *"Vida Nueva"* newsletter.

In late 1979, community people rallying against issues of discrimination and non response from local government soon form the Chicano Committee for Justice in Nampa. In January of 1980 the group held a mass demonstration at city hall. The group pushed for a citywide race relations entity to deal with community issues.

These organizations represent only a sampling of the numerous organizations established in Idaho during the late 1960's and 1970's. They provide a sense as to the activism and issues Mexicanos/Chicanos deemed significant in Idaho. Comparatively, organizational initiatives were fewer in Idaho than in the other Northwest states.

Beyond these state bound organizations their exist evidence that Northwest states were interacting as a region or an extended community in discussing issues facing the larger Mexicano/Chicano Northwest community. Organizations such as the Northwest Chicano *Concilio* set up in the mid 1970's, served as a network and a forum for communication among Northwest *Raza* activists.

Collectively, the organizations which emerged in Oregon, Washington, and Idaho during the late 1960's and 1970's are important to document because they reflect Mexicano/Chicano activism, highlight critical issues the community was discussing, and affirm the presence of *"La Raza"* in *"nuestro hogar del norte"*.

It will be important for scholars in political science, sociology and Chicano Studies to do analysis which may illuminate why some of these organizations ceased to exist while others went on to mature and flourish. How did the political climate, leadership or organizational mission contribute to their success or demise. This analysis may provide information as to the real or perceived impact these organizations had on the development of the Mexicano/Chicano community in the Northwest. Perhaps a comparative analysis between Northwest states and/or other regions including the southwest or the midwest might prove illuminating as to the development of the Mexicano/Chicano on a national context. This analysis might also be helpful in determining what lessons or strategies have we as a community learned in regards to our development. And finally, perhaps this analysis might answer questions as why some of the same issues we as a community have faced historically are still pervasive today.

The Presence of the Mexicano/Chicano Community in the Northwest in the 1980's and 1990's

The presence of the Mexicano/Chicano community in the Northwest continues to grow in the 1980's and 1990's in varying ways. The notion of *"nuestro hogar del norte"*, which culminated from a historical northward journey, is much more pronounced today. Some in our community however, have only recently made their initial *"viaje al norte"*. The last fifteen years or so has generated some change in our community. Additionally, issues which have historically undermined our community's development have only become heighten. The proceeding discussion will highlight some significant developments in the Mexicano/Chicano community during the 1980's and 1990's.

One of the most significant changes which has impacted our community nationally and in the Northwest concerns the significant demographic growth of the Mexicano/Chicano community in the past fourteen years. This demographic growth will impact every sector of the community including educational institutions, job market, public policy, politics and a host of others.

In Idaho, the total Hispanic population numbered 52,927 in 1990. Hispanics are the largest ethnic group in Idaho representing 67.8% of the state's ethnic community. The Hispanic community grew 44.5% between 1980-1990. The Mexican descent community constitute the largest Hispanic sub group numbering 43,213 or 81.6% of the total Hispanic population in Idaho.[39]

In Oregon, the total Hispanic population numbered 112,707 in 1990. Hispanics are the largest ethnic group in Oregon representing 42.9% of the state's ethnic community. The Hispanic community grew 70.3% between 1980-1990. The Mexican descent community constitute the largest Hispanic subgroup in the state.[40]

In Washington, the total Hispanic population numbered 214,570 in 1990. Hispanics are the largest ethnic group in Washington. The Hispanic community grew 78.8% between 1980-1990.[41] The Mexican descent community constitute the largest Hispanic subgroup in Washington. These significant changes in Mexicano/Chicano demographics and the implications these demographics entail are far reaching for the Northwest. The future projected demographic growth will also compound the issues and complexities the Mexicano/Chicano community is presently and will confront in the near future.

A second area of development in the Mexicano/Chicano community in the Northwest is its heighten visibility. This is evident in the communication network which has developed. Each of the Northwest states has newspapers, radio broadcasting initiatives, and some television efforts that promotes communication among the Mexicano/Chicano community. Spanish radio broadcasting by KNDA-Granger, Washington; KZHR-Walla Walla, Washington; KWIP-Dalles, Oregon; and other stations have 24 hour or extended Spanish radio programming. Newspaper by community efforts and by mainstream publishers have contributed to the communication print media targeting the Spanish language community. Some of these initiatives include the *Hispanic News*, Seattle, WA; *La Voz*, Seattle, WA; *El Mundo*, Wenatchee, WA; *VIVA*, Toppenish, WA; *El Sol*, Tri-Cities, WA; *El Sol de Idaho*, Idaho Falls, ID; *Latino Goal, El Hispanic News*, in Salem and Portland, OR. Spanish television on various cable companies offer Telemundo and/or Univision. These media initiatives contribute to affirming the notion of *"nuestro hogar del norte"*. These media initiatives also contribute to the Mexicano/Chicano community communicate statewide.

A third development in the Mexicano/Chicano community in the Northwest has been the continuing growth of Mexicano/Chicano owned businesses. Even though, Mexicano/Chicano businesses still continue to show strength in the restaurant industry, Mexicano/Chicano business people have extended their domain to include non-cultural related businesses. Construction, manufacturing, consulting services and a host of other business areas have attracted Mexicanos/Chicanos. This growing business presence had resulted in the emergence of business and professional organizations which Mexicanos/Chicanos contribute to, such as the Washington State Hispanic Chamber of Commerce, the Idaho Hispanic Business and Professional

Association and the Portland Metropolitan Hispanic Chamber of commerce. These organizations promote Latino business in the Northwest. These organizations compile and publish business directories which reinforce the diversity of business initiatives existing in the Northwest.

A fourth area of development in the Mexicano/Chicano community relates to the political sphere. Several individuals presently hold political state offices in Washington and Oregon. Margarita López-Prentiss (Demo) and Ricardo Cantú (GOP) hold legislative offices in Washington State. Jessie Berain holds a legislative office in Idaho. Rocky Barilla, held a legislative office in Oregon in the mid 1980's. Additionally, each of the Northwest states have State level commissions on Hispanic affairs. Mexicanos/Chicanos also hold local political positions in city councils. The contributions these individuals make in their service benefit the whole community. Mexicano/Chicano political participation and presence is a major issue of focus in the future.

A fifth development in the Mexicano/Chicano community has been the establishment of Chicano Studies initiatives in higher education. The state of Washington hosts three Chicano Studies initiatives at the University of Washington, Seattle; Washington State University, Pullman, and Eastern Washington University in Cheney. Additionally, Eastern Washington University's Chicano Education Program houses the national office of the National Association For Chicano Studies. A Northwest chapter of this association is spearheaded by Chicano Studies faculty in Washington. The 1995 National Association for Chicano Studies annual conference will be staged in Spokane, Washington. Oregon and Idaho colleges and universities have yet to establish Chicano Studies initiatives

A sixth development in the Mexicano/Chicano community in the Northwest is the existence of a diverse infrastructure of groups and organizations that address and/or provide services to the Mexicano/Chicano community. These groups and organizations are involved in initiatives targeting farm workers, (*Pineros y Campesinos de Noroeste*-Woodburn, Or); Latino elderly, (Othello Latin Seniors, Othello, WA); professionals,(Idaho Hispanic Professional and Business Association, Idaho); political activists; (La Raza Coalition for Political Action, Spokane, WA); college students, (MECHA); culture (Los Bailadores del Sol, Yakima, WA.); religion (La comunidad Guadalupana de Spokane, (Spokane, WA.); women(Mujeres Unidas, Pullman-WSU); athletics, (Les Compadres Golf Association, Lacey, Washington) and a host of other special interest areas. The number and diversity of Mexicano/Chicano organizations in the Northwest is significant. These organizations exist in urban sites including Boise, Seattle and Portland. They also exist in small rural communities throughout the Northwest. These community based organizations reflect the level of activism and development of the Mexicano/Chicano community in the Northwest

A seventh development in the Mexicano/Chicano community in the Northwest is the influx of recent Mexican immigrants to the Northwest in the past ten to fifteen years. Historically, the majority that came to the Northwest were Chicanos from the southwest or Mexicans who initially settled in the southwest and than made a subsequent journey north. Today, the more recent Mexican immigrant is the overwhelming new comer to the Northwest. This reality is reflected by the phenomenal growth of Mexican specialty stores in the Northwest. A simple drive through Washington's Yakima Valley, Oregon's Willamette Valley and Idaho's Canyon county area will aquaint the individual with *panaderías* (Mexican bakeries), *Taquerías* (taco fast food venders), and Mexican grocery stores which carry Mexican brand name products. Banda music (a particular style of music from west central Mexico) gives heavy competition to the Tex-Mex or *Tejano* music tradition that once dominated the radio air waves and Mexican music shops. The convergence of the recent Mexican immigrants and Chicanos creates an interesting scenario in community intra-action in relation to identity, politics, and historical orientation.

These developments which have emerged in the Northwest reaffirm that the Mexicano/Chicano is not a transitory population traveling through the Northwest. These developments clearly reaffirm the notion that the Northwest has become *"nuestro hogar del norte"*. The feeling of community disorientation that initial Mexicano/Chicano sojourners experienced in the Northwest has and continues to be replaced by a feeling of home and belonging in the Northwest. Many Mexicanos/Chicanos may travel to the Southwest or México but as one of my informants stated, "I visit the Río Grande Valley often, but when I go, Washington tugs within me. Upon returning, something tells me that I'm home."

◆ Issues Facing the Mexicano/Chicano Community

These developments in the Mexicano/Chicano community have generated positive affects upon the community. Nonetheless some of these developments have heighten some fundamental issues which currently confront the Mexicano/Chicano community throughout the Northwest.

One significant issue confronting the Mexicano/Chicano community concerns education. Mexicano/Chicano students are dropping out or being pushed out of our schools at an overwhelming rate.

A number of reports focusing on the poor educational status of Mexicanos/Chicanos reflect this issue. In Idaho, a report entitled "Public Education in Idaho—Does It Meet the Needs of All Students," produced by the Idaho Advisory Committee to the U.S. Commission on Civil Rights, November 1992, quoted the Superintendent of Public Instruction acknowledging that nationally "somewhere between 40 and 60%" of Latino students are dropouts compared to the statewide average of about 20%". Some believe that the state drop out rate for Latinos is higher. The lack of state statistics tracking drop out information has contributed to a growing concern by Mexicanos/Chicanos regarding its youth. Reports by the Idaho Migrant Council (1978) and the Task Force On The Participation Of Hispanic Students In Vocational Education Programs (1990) which focused on Hispanic youth dropouts have raised the dropout concern in the Idaho. The Idaho Human Rights Commission in its report titled Hispanic in Idaho: Concerns and Challenges (1990) states that Hispanic drop out "rates in Idaho are probably 30-50%". A news story appearing in *El Sol de Idaho* on February, 1994 shares some obstacles that some students face which at times leads to not doing well academically and becoming disillusion. Some of these include languages issues, teachers who are not prepare or make the special effort to assist a failing students, and that the resources needed for tutors and other supportive staff is not available.

The educational status of Mexicanos/Chicanos in Idaho can easily serve as a template for Oregon and Washington. In Portland, Oregon two separate groups raised the condition of Latino education as a significant issue. A news article appearing in *El Hispanic* on February 9, 1994 reported that Hispanic Parents for Portland Portland Schools filed a formal complaint with the U.S. Department of Education Region 10 Office of Civil Rights on the issue of educational discrimination resulting from a Hispanic student drop out twice higher than the statewide average. Subsequent to this MECHA college students and community organizations including the Hispanic Parents for Portland Schools staged a public demonstration involving over 300 protesters in downtown Portland to bring attention to the educational inequalities faced by Latinos in education in Oregon. When we address the issue of higher education, Mexicano/Chicano college participation rate is not proportional to the states' population levels. University initiatives promoting Chicano Studies is only found in one of the three Northwest states.

Mexicano/Chicanos have historically been underrepresented throughout the educational system as faculty, administrators, board members and other settings where debate and decision making about effective education is carried out. Considering the significant demographic growth in the Mexicano/Chicano community, education will play a significant role in the future leadership, economic and political development of Northwest Mexicanos/Chicanos.

A second significant issue confronting Mexicanos/Chicanos in the Northwest is the issue of political empowerment. It has only been since the mid 1980's that Mexicanos/Chicanos have been elected to state legislative office. Presently there are only three Mexicano/Chicano state legislators in the entire Northwest. Although voter registration and getting the vote would prove useful, the reality that some in the Mexicano/Chicano community are not yet voting age or not eligible to vote due to non citizenship status are significant community issues. A related issue is the need to continue to upgrade the presence of Mexicanos/Chicanos in the elective political structures that aid in recommending and/or drafting directions in public policy issues. The issue of political empowerment is an area that requires attention considering the significant demographic growth taking place in the Mexicano/Chicano community in the Northwest.

A third issue impacting the Mexicano/Chicano community in the Northwest, which is somewhat related to the preceding issue, is that generally speaking the Mexicano/Chicano community has not been fully included nor has it had the opportunity to participate in the affairs of the general community. The need to include the Mexicano/Chicano voice in local city councils, school boards, and other elected or appointed local community positions is badly needed. Some communities have already moved to include Mexicano/Chicano representation. Yet many times the Mexicano/Chicano representative is often times the first and only one serving in such positions at the time. This type of efforts have theoretically afforded inclusion but have not promoted substantive inclusion. The burden for one individual to carry the voice of a diverse Mexicano/Chicano community is a tremendous load that usually leads to frustration. The need for substantive inclusion rather than theoretical inclusion is needed to fully integrate the Mexicano/Chicano community in the affairs of the general community.

A fourth significant issue facing the Mexicano/Chicano community in the Northwest is the persistent forms of racism and discrimination that continue to be present at various levels of society. One form of discrimination in Oregon which gained much public exposure was the actions of the Oregon State Police's (OSP) efforts of drugs interdiction. The OSP armed with a "drug courier profile", intended to aid OSP officers identify possible drug traffickers was disproportionally stopping Latinos. Where as Latinos represent about 4% of the states population, a 1991 OSP sample data indicated that 54% of those being stopped and searched were Latinos. Additionally the data also indicated that the overwhelming number of Latinos stopped and searched were innocent of any suspected drug involvement. Many Mexicanos/Chicanos have voiced a complaint about the apparent harassment and disproportionate impact of the OSP drug interdiction program.[42]

The relationship between the local police and the Mexicano/Chicano community is also a related problem area. In Idaho a 1993 report Entitled "Finding and Recommendations Following Community Forums Held to Assess Inter-Group Tension in Canyon County" indicated that the Mexicano/Chicano community expressed frustration in working with law enforcement. The report also stated that some Latinos have given up trying to work with the police, indicating that when they bring their concerns to officials they are only met with a defensive attitude. Racial tension at times exists beyond state and local community structures.

Racism at times permeates from the general community rather than from public agencies as illustrated in Washington. In the Yakima Valley community advocates organized and staged a march and rally in mid March of 1994 to bring attention to the anti Mexican immigrant bashing taking place in the valley. Perceptions of Mexicano immigrants over taxing public agencies including schools, are involved in drugs, and other stereotypical images have served to rationalize the anti-Mexican Immigrant sentiment in the Northwest. This anti-immigrant sentiment is reflective of what is taking place nationally and particularly in states which border Mexico. The issue of racism and discrimination also emerges in other settings. Forms of racism and discrimination arise in business, education, government, employment, housing and other settings in the Northwest. Inter-racial tension is easily evident in communities where Mexicano/Chicanos constitute a considerable percentage of the total community.

A fifth issue which affects the Mexicano/Chicano community in the Northwest is the status of agricultural workers. Agriculture in the Northwest is a major economy sector. The labor that is required to maintain agriculture is significant. Agricultural workers in the Northwest occupy numerous high risk jobs including exposure to potentially harmful pesticides used in farming. Agricultural workers earn low wages, at times live in crowded and inadequate housing, struggle to obtain fundamental health services, and lack basic legislation critical for organizing and self empowerment. Thousands of agricultural workers and their families lead difficult lives. Job security, quality health and education, adequate wages are only a few basic needs that continue to elude agricultural workers and their families. It is critical that agricultural workers issues occupy a center place in the development of the Mexicano/Chicano Community in the Northwest.

The selected issues raised in the preceding segment represent only a few of numerous issues confronting the Mexicano/Chicano community in the Northwest. Being that the Northwest has become "nuestro hogar del norte" it is important that this and other similar issues serve as the foundation of an agenda critical in the future development of the Mexicano/Chicano community in the Northwest.

Summary

The Mexicano/Chicano presence in the Northwest dates back to the age of Spanish exploration of the late 1700's. In subsequent years Mexicanos traveled and settled throughout the Northwest. Mexicanos came to the Northwest as miners and mule pack drivers in the mid 1800's. Mexicanos/Chicanos coming to the Northwest contributed to the agricultural development and production throughout the decades of WW I and WW II. The Mexicano/Chicano northward journey of the 1940's and 1950's began the early foundations of communities present throughout the Northwest. The initial notion of the northward journey has clearly been replaced by the notion of *"nuestro hogar del norte"*. Although family ties to the Southwest and Mexico may continue to be strong, the feeling of home in the Northwest is just as equally or stronger for many. The Mexicano/Chicano community faces significant community issues as it looks towards the 21st century. These issues will require attention by Mexicano/Chicano community leaders in efforts to enhance their *"hogar del norte"*.

Endnotes

1. Donald C. Cutter, "The Other Explorers: Alcadá Galiano and Valdez." Columbia Summer 1991 p. 17.
2. Iris H. W. Engstrand "Jose Mariano Moziño: Pioneer Mexican Naturalist." Columbia Spring 1991 p. 19.
3. Giles French, *Cattle Country of Peter French* (Portland, Oregon: Binfords and Mort Publishers, 1965), p. 49.
4. No title, "Gliden/Soto" *Boise* (Idaho,) *Idaho Territorial Statesman*, 6 October 1870, p. 3.
5. James W. Watt *Journal of Mule Train Packing in Eastern Washington in the 1860's* (Fairfield, Wa.: Ye Galleon Press, 1978) pp. 39,40.
6. Matt S. Meier and Feliciano Rivera, *The Chicanos: A History of Mexican Americans* (New York: Hill and Wang, 1972), p. 124.
7. Murray R. Benedict, *Farm Policies of the United States, 1970-1950* (New York: The Twentieth Century Fund, 1953), p. 127.
8. Lawrence A. Cardoso, *Mexican Emigration to the United States: 1897-1931* (Tucson, Arizona: University of Arizona Press, 1980), p. 38.
9. Interview with Juan Jaramillo and Don Gonzales, Ontario, Oregon, 11 July 1994.
10. Patricia K. Ourada, *Migrant Workers in Idaho* (Boise State University, 1980), p. 9.
11. Correspondence from the Consulate General of Mexico (San Francisco) to Idaho Governor Moses Alexander, Complaints of Mexican Laborers in Idaho, Oct. 1, 1918.
12. Correspondence from W. J. A. McVety, Idaho Labor Commissioner to Idaho Governor Moses Alexander, report about visits to sugar factories in southern Idaho. October 24, 1918.
13. Manuel Gamio *Mexican Immigration to the United States* (New York: Dover Publications, Inc., 1971), p. 32.
14. Erasmo Gamboa *Mexican Labor and World War II: Braceros in the Pacific Northwest, 1942-1947* (Austin: University of Texas Press, 1990), p. 8.
15. Interview with Manuel Melendrez, Spokane, Washington 12 February 1991.
16. Interview with Joe Treviño, Spokane, Washington 27 March 1991.
17. Interview with Anastacio "Don" Gonzales, Ontario, Oregon 15 July 1994.
18. "150 Mexican Farm Workers Take to Hillsboro Fields," Portland (Ore.) *The Oregonian*, 15 June 19453, p. 5.
19. "Crop Savers From South of the Line," Portland (Ore.) *The Oregonian*, 3 October 1943, p. 4.
20. Correspondence from E. L. Peterson, Director of Agriculture Salem, Oregon to Oregon Governor Earl Snell, Mexican Workers in Eugene, preliminary investigation, August 2, 1945.
21. Correspondence from Paul Van de Velde, Oregon Settlement Association, Eugene, Oregon to Mr.Williams, Mexican Worker Situation in Eugene, Oregon May 31, 1945.
22. Interview with Santos Garcia, Woodburn, Oregon 8 August 1994.

23. Interview with Sra. Villatrigo, Woodburn, Oregon 14 July 1994.
24. "Camp Celebrates Mexican Holiday," Wilder (Idaho) *Wilder Herald*, 22 September, 1994, pg. 5.
25. Interview with Tony Rodriguez, Nampa, Idaho 11 July 1994.
26. Interview with Chester Espinoza, Lacey, WA. 5 August 1994.
27. Interview with Paul Mendez, Sunnyside, WA. 9 August 1994.
28. Interview with Keith Bloxham, Seattle, WA. 15 July 1994.
29. Interview with Ida Soto and David Hummer, Spokane, WA. 15 March 1991.
30. Interview with Anastacio "Don" Gonzales, Ontario, Oregon 15 July 1994.
31. Interview with Ermindina Medina, Woodburn, Oregon 22 July 1994.
32. Interview with Tony Rodriguez, Nampa, Idaho 11 July 1994.
33. Interview with Paul Mendez, Sunnyside, WA. 9 August 1994.
34. Interview with Nelly Jimenez and Don Cost, Woodburn, Oregon 22 July 1994.
35. Interview with Dale Peterson, Caldwell, Idaho 7 July 1994.
36. Interview with Don Stitt, Woodburn, Oregon 22 July 1994.
37. "Valley Chicano Movement Laid to VML," Salem (Ore.) *Capital Journal*, 23 April 1970 p. 21.
38. Interview with Tony Rodriguez, Nampa, Idaho 11 July 1994.
39. Profile of the Hispanic Population of Idaho; 1990 IdahoDepartment Commerce Boise, Idaho n.p.
40. Biennial Report 1991-1993 State of Oregon Commission on Hispanic Affairs Salem, Oregon n.p.
41. "Minority Population up 24.8 percent, but Spokane remains mostly white." *Spokane* (WA) *Spokesmen-Review*, 13 March 991 p. A2.
42. "Highway to Harassment: State Police Target Hispanics in Highway Searches." Oregon ACLU News Vol XXIV No. 4 Winter 1992 p. 6.

Bibliography

◆ Books

Acuña, Rodolfo. *Occupied America: A History of Chicanos*. New York: Harper and Row 1981.

Benedict, Murray R. *Farm Policies of the United States*, 1719-1950. New York: The Twentieth Century Fund. 1953.

Brimlow, George Francis. *Harney County, Oregon, and Its Range Land*. Portland: Binfords and Mort Publishers, 1951.

Cardoso, Lawrence A. *Mexican Emigration to the United States: 1897-1931*. Tucson: University of Arizona Press 1980.

Cutter, Donald C. Malaspina and Galiano: Spanish Voyages to the Northwest Coast, 1791-1792 Seattle; University of Washington press. 1991.

French, Giles. *Cattle Country of Peter French*. Portland: Binfords and Mort Publishers, 1965.

Galarza, Ernesto: *Merchants of Labor: The Mexican Bracero Story*. Santa Barbara: McNally and Loftin Publishers, 1964.

Gamboa, Erasmo. *Mexican Labor and World War II: Braceros in the Pacific Northwest, 1942-1947*. Austin: University of Texas Press, 1990.

Gambio, Manuel. *The Life Story of the Mexican Immigrant*. New York: Dover Publications, Inc. 1971.

Grebler, Leo; Moore, Joan W.; Guzman Ralph C. *The Mexican American People: The Nation's Second Largest Minority*. New York: The Free Press.

Meir, Matt S.; Rivera, Feliciano. T*he Chicanos: A History of Mexican Americans*. New York: Hill and ..... 1972.

Ourada, Patricia K. *Migrant Workers in Idaho*. Boise: Boise State University 1980.

Watt, James W. *Journal of Mule Train Packing in Eastern Washington in the 1860's*. Fairfield: Ye Galleon Press 1978

Winter, Oscar Osburn. *The Great Northwest: A History*. New York: Alfred A. Knopf, 1948.

Winter, Oscar Osburn. *The Old Oregon Country: A History of Frontier Trade, Transportation, and Travel*. Stanford: Stanford University. Press, 1950.

◆ Journals

Cutter, Donald C. "The Other Explorers: Alcadá Galiano and Valdez." *Columbia* (Summer 1991), p. 17.
Engstrand, Iris H.W. "Jose Mariano Moziño; Pioneer Mexican naturalist." *Columbia* (Spring 1991), p. 19.
Maldonado, Carlos S. "Mexicanos in Spokane"; 1930-1992. *Revista Apple* (Spring 1992), p. 118.
Slatta, Richard W. "Chicanos in the Pacific Northwest: A Historical Overview of Oregon's Chicanos." *Aztlan* (Fall 1975), p. 327.

◆ Newspaper

No title,"Gliden/Soto." *Boise Idaho Territorial Stateman.* 6 October 1870, p. 3.
"150 Mexican Farm Workers Take to Hillsboro Fields." *Portland* (Ore.) *Oregonian.* 15 June 1943, p. 5.
"Crop Savers From South of the Line." *Portland* (Ore.) *Oregonian.* 3 October 1943, p. 4.
"Camp Celebrates Mexican Holiday." Wilder (Idaho) *Wilder Herald* 22 September. 1944, p. 5.
"Farms to Get 500 Mexicans." *Portland* (Ore.) *Oregonian.* 9 April 1943, p. 1.
"Valley Chicano Movement Laid to VML." *Salem* (Ore.) *Capital Journal* 23 April 1970 p. 21.
"Minority Population up 24.8 percent, but Spokane Remains Mostly White." Spokane (WA) *Spokane Review* 13 March 1991 p. A2.

◆ Theses, Dissertations and Unpublished Materials

Lemos, Jesus. "A History of the Chicano Political Involvement and the Organizational Effects of the United Farm Workers Union in the Yakima Valley, Washington." M.A. Thesis, Portland State University 1974.
Loprinzi, Collen Marie. "Hispanic Migrant Labor in Oregon, 1940-1990 M.A. Thesis, Portland State University, 1991.Slatta, Richard W. "Chicanos in Oregon: A Historical Overview. Masters Thesis, Portland State University 1974.
Correspondence from Consulate General of México (San Francisco) to Idaho Governor Moses Alexander, Complaints of Mexican laborer in Idaho. October 1, 1918.
Correspondance from W.J.A. McVety, Idaho Labor Commissioner to Idaho Governor Mosses Alexander, report about visits to sugar factories in Southern Idaho. October 24, 1918.

Correspondence from E.L. Peterson, Director of Agriculture, Salem, Oregon to Oregon Governor Earl Snell, Mexican Workers in Eugene, preliminary investigation. August 2, 1945.

Correspondence from E. L. Peterson, Director of Agriculture, Salem, Oregon to Oregon Governor Earl Snell, Mexican workers in Eugene, Oregon. May 31, 1945.

Profile of the Hispanic Population of Idaho; 1990, Idaho Department of Commerce. Boise, idaho.

Biennial Report 1991-1993: State of Oregon Commission on Hispanic Affairs, Salem, Oregon.

◆ Interviews

Bloxham, Keith. Seattle, WA., Interview 15 July 1994.
Espinoza, Chester. Lacey, WA. Interview, 5 August 1994.
Garcia, Santos. Woodburn, Ore. Interview, 8 August 1994.
Gonzales, Don. Ontario Oregon, Interview, 15 July 1994.
Hummer, Lucas. Spokane, WA., Interview, 15 March 1991.
Jaramillo, Juan. Ontario, Oregon, Interview, 11 July 1994.
Jimenez, Nelly. Woodburn, Ore.,2 Interview, 22 July 1994.
Medina, Ermendina. Woodburn, Ore., Interview, 22 July 1994.
Melendrez, Manuel. Spokane, WA., Interview, 12 February 1991.
Mendez, Paul. Sunnyside, WA., Interview, 9 August 1994.
Peterson, Dale. Caldwell, Idaho, Interview, 7 July 1994.
Rodriguez, Tony, Nampa, Idaho, Interview, 11 July 1994.
Stitt, Dan. Woodburn, Ore., Interview, 22 July 1994.
Treviño, Joe. Spokane, WA., Interview, 27 March 1991.
Villatrigo, Sra. Woodburn, Ore. Interview, 14 July 1994.

A Demographic Profile of Chicanos in the Pacific Northwest

Guadalupe Friaz

Introduction

In 1990, Hispanics were 8.8 percent of the nation's total population, making them the second largest ethnic minority group in the United States. Growth rates indicate Hispanics will be the largest ethnic minority group by the turn of the century. They are the largest ethnic minority group in the Pacific Northwest. Yet public perception about Hispanics is clouded by lack of accurate information.

Inaccurate information about Hispanics in the Northwest is pervasive, not only among EuroAmericans but among Hispanics as well. Two examples illustrate the degree of this misinformation. Students in an introductory Chicano/a Studies class were asked why almost half of all Hispanics did not complete a high school degree. One EuroAmerican student surmised that it was related to Hispanic families' lack of concern for education and the need to have their children work in the fields. The assumption that all Hispanics are migrant farm workers and that they do not value education is firmly rooted in the minds of most EuroAmericans. In 1994 Chicano/a students from Washington state traveled to Arizona to attend a national Chicano/a student conference only to be told by conference participants that they were not "Chicanos" since they were not from "Aztlan."[1] The assumption that the definition of a Chicano/a lies solely in geography stems from a regional approach to Chicano Studies versus a national approach in which no region is at the center.

Accurate information is necessary in order to understand ourselves better as a nation composed of ethnic and racial groups. The study of Hispanics in different regions is important and essential to a comparative inter-regional and intra-regional analysis. In this chapter I provide a brief overview of the size, growth, and residential distribution of the Hispanic[2] population between 1980 and 1990 in the Pacific Northwestern region of the United States. I focus primarily on Mexican Americans or Chicanos, the largest of the Hispanic origin groups. A broad historical overview of Hispanics in the Pacific Northwest is followed by a demographic, social, and economic profile of this group. Education, employment status, and household characteristics are also presented.

The Pacific Northwest is defined in this chapter as the region encompassing the states of Idaho, Washington, and Oregon. The two largest populated areas in the region are Seattle, Washington and Portland, Oregon. These two cities are home to the greatest concentrations of Hispanics. Hispanics have also grown rapidly in several of the region's smaller cities including Yakima and Spokane, Washington and Boise, Idaho.

Census Data

Census data is the primary source for this chapter. Although census data is the most comprehensive and clearest data available for enumerating and describing the Hispanic population, the census historically has reflected a "constant confusion" around the adequate definition and thus identification of Hispanics.[3] Hispanics do not have a singular characteristic that ties them together or identifies them as Hispanic. They do not share one language, nationality, religion, or ascriptive trait. Latinos have been counted on the basis of Spanish surname, Spanish Heritage, and Spanish language, to name a few identifiers. The number of Hispanics varies with the specific identifier.[4] This inconsistency in identifiers makes comparisons with previous census figures difficult. Not until the 1980 census was there a single definition of Hispanic used nationwide for the entire population. Respondents were asked "is this person of Spanish/Hispanic origin or descent?" In the 1990 census, respondents were asked to self-identify in a similar way.[5]

Accurate and reliable demographic data on Hispanics is crucial on both theoretical and practical grounds. Empirical data can serve to bolster, verify, or call into question a theoretical or policy analysis of Hispanics. Political representation and funding for education and other social services is based on this data. Yet, the census has repeatedly undercounted the number of Hispanics in the country. This fact has received much attention from policy makers, representatives of Latino organizations, and analysts.[6] The data reported on here are thus a conservative approximation of different dimensions of the Hispanic population in the Pacific Northwest.

Census figures point to rapid growth in the Hispanic population and to an increasing dispersion of this population outside the Southwest towards the Midwest and the Pacific Northwest. While studies of Hispanics in the Midwest have increased markedly in the 1980's[7], very little research has focussed on the Northwest.

◆ Geographic Distribution and Growth of Hispanic Population

In 1990, 398,374 Hispanics resided in the Pacific Northwest region.[8] The following analysis will focus on Washington, Oregon, and Idaho. As Table 2.1 illustrates, Hispanics are the largest ethnic minority in Oregon and Idaho, but in Washington Hispanics lost the statistical distinction to Asian and Pacific Islanders in 1990. Nevertheless, Hispanics remain the largest ethnic minority group in the three state region. Asian and Pacific Islanders, African Americans, and American Indians represent the second, third and fourth largest ethnic minority groups in those states.[9]

Table 2.1. ◆ Race and Hispanic Origin by State, 1990

State	Hispanic	Black	Asian & Pacific Islander	Amer. Ind Eskimo or Aleut	Other Races
Washington	206,018	147,364	211,292	83,212	111,223
	4.2	**3.0**	**4.3**	**1.7**	**2.3**
Oregon	110,606	45,423	67,641	41,626	49,901
	3.9	**1.6**	**2.4**	**1.4**	**1.8**
Idaho	51,679	3,653	9,096	14,677	28,521
	5.1	**.4**	**.9**	**1.5**	**2.8**
% in Region	**4.6**	**1.7**	**2.5**	**1.5**	**2.3**

Source: 1990 U.S. Census of Population, Social and Economic Characteristics. Table 135, pp. 158-159. 1980 U.S. Census of Population, Table 99.

In the 1990's Hispanics continue to grow at rapid rates as illustrated by Table 2.2. Between 1980 and 1990 Hispanics grew by 70 percent in Washington, by 67 percent in Oregon, and by 41 percent in Idaho. By comparison the White not Hispanic[10] population grew at a much slower pace of 15.7 percent, 7.2 percent, and 7.1 percent respectively. Hispanics in Oregon and Washington grew at a much faster rate than Hispanics nation-wide (53 percent) in the same time period.[11] In 1990 Washington state ranked 10th in the states with the largest increases in Hispanic population.[12]

Table 2.2. ◆ 1980-1990 Hispanic and White not Hispanic Population Growth

	Hispanic			White not Hispanic		
	1980	1990	% chg	1980	1990	% chg
WA	121,286	206,018	70%	3,725,878	4,313,601	15.7
ORE	66,164	110,606	67%	2,459,399	2,637,730	7.2
ID	36,560	51,679	41%	887,691	950,802	7.1

Source: 1990: U.S. Census of Population, Social and Economic Characteristics. Table 135, pp. 158-159.

The growth of the Hispanic population largely reflects the rapid growth of Mexican Americans, the largest component of this group. Figure 2.1 illustrates the percentage of each Hispanic group in the region.[13] In every state, Mexican Americans are by far the largest Hispanic group.

Figure 2.1. ◆ Percentage of Hispanics Northwest Region by State: 1990

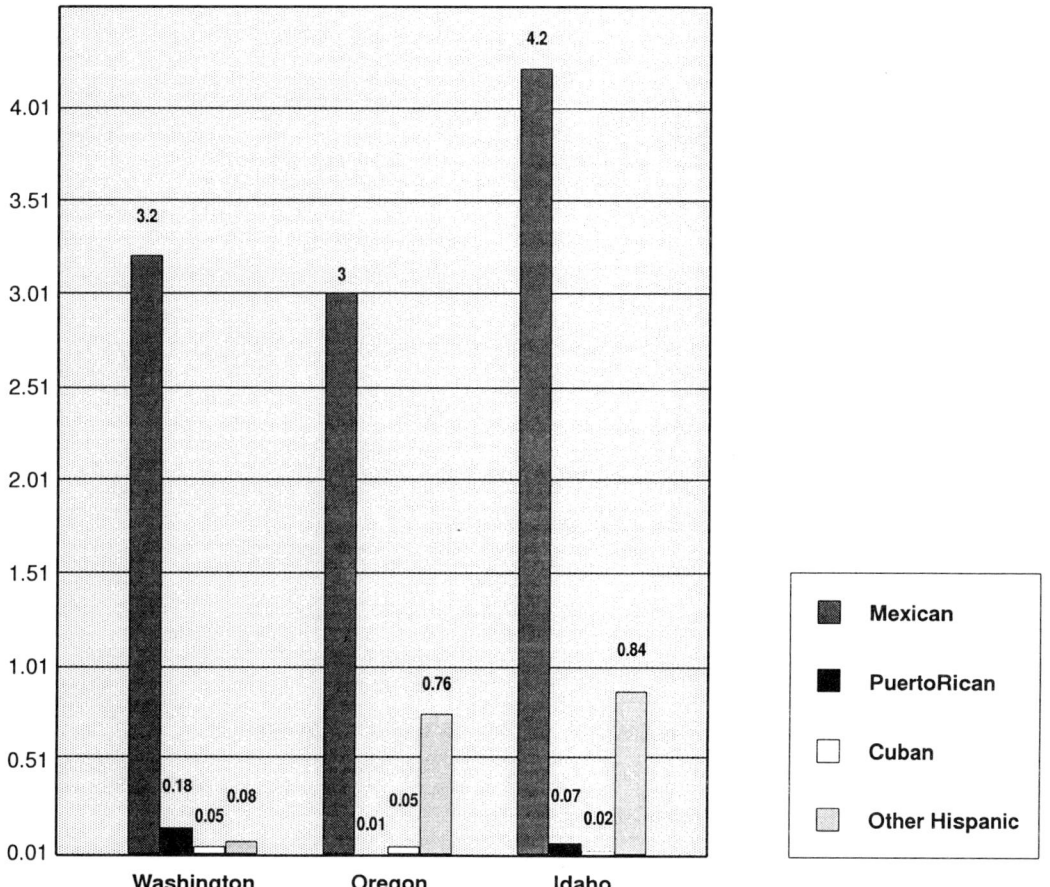

Table 2.3 compares 1980 and 1990 census figures for Hispanics in Washington, Oregon, and Idaho. It illustrates the proportionate size, geographic distribution, and growth of the various Hispanic subgroups between 1980 and 1990. For example, in 1980, Mexicans comprised an average of 69 percent of all Hispanics in the region. Puerto Ricans comprised an average of 2.6 percent of all Hispanics in the region. Between 1980 and 1990, the Mexican American component of this population in Washington state grew from 66 percent of all Hispanics to 74.4 percent. During these ten years, Mexican Americans grew from a regional average of 69 percent of all Hispanics to about 78 percent. The Puerto Rican proportion of the Hispanic population in all three states increased slightly in 1980, (from 2.6 to 2.7 percent), while the Cuban proportion of the Hispanic population remained constant in Washington, decreased in Oregon, and increased in Idaho. Other Hispanics includes Central or South Americans; the proportion of this group declined considerably in every state from an average of 26.9 percent in 1980 to 18.7 percent in 1990. Thus, although almost every group in every state increased numerically, the proportions of Hispanic subgroups varied in the region. By 1990, Hispanics became less diverse as Mexican Americans increased their percentage of the Hispanic population.

Table 2.3. ◆ Hispanic Subgroup by State: 1980-1990

	Washington	Oregon	Idaho	Region
1990	N=206,018	N=110,606	N=51,679	Aver %
Mexican	74.4	76.7	82.0	78.0%
P. Rican	4.3	2.6	1.3	2.7
Cuban	1.1	1.3	.3	.9
Other Hsp.	20.2	19.6	16.3	18.7
1980	N=121,286	N=66,164	N=36,560	
Mexican	66.0	66.5	76.4	69.0%
P. Rican	4.2	2.6	1.0	2.6
Cuban	1.1	1.5	.1	.9
Other Hsp	29.0	29.3	22.4	26.9

Source: U.S. Census, Table 99 1980; U.S. Census, Table 135 1990.

Table 2.3 indicates steady growth among all Hispanic subgroups except for the decline exhibited by Other Hispanics. An explanation of this decline can most likely be found in the unique history of this group in the United States. Not until the late 1960's and early 1970's did Central and South Americans[14] arrive in large numbers in the United States, and in the Northwest. Reasons for this are briefly explored in the next section.

The Northwest is similar to the Southwest in the high proportion of Mexicans in relation to every other Hispanic group. In the Northwest, Mexicans comprise 78 percent of all Hispanics compared to 77 percent in the Southwest compared to about 65 percent in the Midwest.[15]

◆ Historical Overview

A historical overview of Hispanics in the Pacific Northwest is essential to an understanding of the present situation of Hispanics. Mexicans were the earliest and largest number of Hispanics to migrate and settle in the Pacific Northwest. The United States Census figures on country of birth of the foreign born population between 1860 and 1950 yield a low estimate of the Mexican population in Washington, Oregon, and Idaho.[16] Between 1860 and 1910 these figures are very small but increase dramatically between 1910 and 1920. For example, the number of Washington residents born in Mexico jumped from 133 in 1910 to 434 in 1920; these numbers were even more dramatic for Idaho where this figure jumped from 129 in 1910 to 1,125 in 1920. Like immigration figures today, these early figures reflect socio-economic and political conditions in both Mexico and the U.S. These increases no doubt reflect the tumultuous upheaval of the population in Mexico caused by the Mexican Revolution of 1910. At the same time, they reflect the labor shortages in the U.S. arising from World War I.

Table 2.4. ◆ Foreign-Born White in Mexico in 1860-1950			
Year	Washington	Oregon	Idaho
1950	1,546	618	326
1940	406	361	307
1930	514	1,291	914
1920	434	569	1,125
1910	133	194	129
1900	73	53	28
1890	81	49	30
1880	19	40	50
1870	13	51	46
1860	16	26	—

Source: U.S. Census, General Characteristics, T-24, 1950, for Washington, Oregon, and Idaho.

In Washington by 1930, there were a total of 562 Mexicans (91.5% foreign-born). The sex ratio (males per 100 females) was 244.5 or 900 males to 371 females. This ratio is lower than that for European immigrant workers at the turn of the century. It could be that many Mexicans were in the Northwest for only brief stays or that they planned to send for their wives and families. Pierce County had the highest number of Mexicans (128) followed by King County (109), and the City of Seattle (91).[17] A much smaller number of Mexicans were recorded in Klickitat (38), Yakima (37), and Spokane (33). These figures indicate the majority of workers were in the urban areas. Gamboa indicates some workers were lured to Washington state by jobs in Alaska's salmon canneries; construction and railroad jobs also pulled Mexicans north.[18]

In Oregon by 1930 there were 1,568 Mexicans (82.3% foreign-born). The sex ratio of 388.5 was even higher than Washington's for this same year and likely reflects a much larger Mexican population in Oregon. The largest concentration (510) resided in Klamath County. The second highest (189) concentration of Mexicans in Oregon resided in Multnomah county and the third highest (158) resided in the City of Portland.[19] Gamboa notes many Mexicans were employed by the Gunn Supply Company in Portland as well as by railroad companies such as the Union Pacific, the Northern Pacific, the Oregon Railroad and others.[20] Even less is known about the history or presence of Mexican women during this period.

Beyond the census data, little is known about Mexicans in any of these states between 1860 and 1900. Gamboa writes, ". . . Mexican migration to the Northwest, in contrast to that of other groups, was characterized by erratic transiency and therefore no discernible pockets of population can be identified for that period."[21] (my emphasis). In the absence of intermarriage, with the Native or the Anglo population, the high sex ratios in every state in the region would impede settlement. The historical studies of Mexicans in the Southwest and Midwest document very high levels of discrimination against people of color including Mexicans, and no doubt existed in the Northwest as well and perhaps also forestalled stable settlements.

In Washington state, Gamboa's informants date the first Mexican families in the Yakima Valley to the late 1920's.[22] The data above indicates Mexican residence as early as 1860 in both rural and urban areas in the Northwest. Mexicans worked in agriculture harvesting potatoes, sugar beets, and hops. They also worked on the railroads, sugar beet factories, and on construction crews. Gamboa indicates two main routes into the Northwest: one from New Mexico across the Rockies and then to Eastern Washington and a second along the Pacific Coast from California up to Oregon and Washington.

As can be seen in Table 2.4, the relatively small number of Mexicans increased steadily after 1860 and peaked in 1930. Restrictive legislation and oppressive social conditions during the Great Depression undoubtedly explain the dramatic decrease of Mexicans in all three states by 1940, though this decrease was much smaller in Washington state. According to Gamboa, the agricultural industry recovered sooner than other industries, and labor was needed. Research utilizing local sources such as newspapers and public assistance records should shed light on this period. Did nativist groups in the Northwest organize repatriation drives similar to those in the Southwest? Were Mexicans targeted as scapegoats or were more subtle measures utilized? How did Mexicans finance their trip to and from the Northwest?

Various factors account for a reversal in the number of Mexicans in the Northwest in 1950. First and foremost was the colossal demand for labor resulting from the onset of World War II. Erasmo Gamboa's *Braceros in the Northwest* documents the Emergency Farm Labor Program, (better known as the Bracero Program) a bilateral agreement between the United States and Mexico, to provide emergency farm labor to agriculture. Table 2.5 lists the number of contract workers in the Northwest. Gamboa documents the systematic recruitment of Mexican labor from Mexico but also of Mexican Americans from the Southwestern states of this country. English speaking Mexican Americans were hired as contractors by agricultural interests to actively recruit Mexican labor. Methods used by Southwestern agricultural and industrial employers such as Spanish language radio advertisements and the printing of handbills with exaggerated claims were also distributed in Mexico.[23]

Table 2.5. ◆ Mexican Contract Workers Employed in the Pacific Northwest

	Washington	Oregon	Idaho
1943	1,220	3,138	985
1944	4,351	3,631	2,539
1945	5,393	3,730	3,401
1946	2,788	1,625	1,959
1947	1,277	883	2,204

Source: Rasmussen, Wayne D. 1951. A History of the Emergency Farm Labor Supply Program: 1943-47. Agriculture Monograph No. 13. (Table 8). USDA. Washington D.C. p. 226.

Larger historical forces such as the Great Depression, WWI and WW II, demand for labor in agriculture and industry, the guest worker programs, and immigration laws, radically shaped and influenced the development of Mexican American communities in the Pacific Northwest. Mexican American communities in the Northwest are similar to those in the Southwest and Midwest in many ways. Barrioization[24] or the multi-faceted process of segregation—residential, cultural and political is one experienced in the Northwest by Mexican American communities. The people of these communities brought with them a particular culture and organized and responded to their environment, uniquely shaping and molding their surroundings, slowly evolving into Mexican Northwesterners.

On-going oral histories collections and Maestas' and Johansen's Gallegos' family history tell of the cold climate of this region, of the distance from their home communities, and of discriminatory practices,—all of which impeded the pace of settlement of Mexicans in this region until the Second World War. Thus, in addition to geography and climate, the timing of migration and subsequent settlement distinguish Mexican American communities in the Northwest from those in the Southwest.

What we know of Mexican Americans in the Northwest is based on a few studies. Among the most widely disseminated works are those of Gamboa on the history of Mexican Americans in the Pacific Northwest, Maestas and Johansen's family history of migration and settlement in the Northwest (1983) and Richard Slatta's (1976, 1979, 1984) socio-demographic and historical analyses. These works supplemented by government and agency reports, and a few masters' and doctoral theses provide a better sketch of the Mexican American community than of the Central and South Americans. More published works on Hispanics in selected areas of the Northwest are slowly being disseminated.[25] Oral history projects in Idaho and Oregon begin to fill the dearth of information.

The relative newness, extreme diversity, and small size of Puerto Ricans, Cubans, Colombians, Salvadorans, Guatemalans, Nicaraguans, Chileans, Peruvians, and others in the Pacific Northwest has generated even less research than on Mexican Americans.[26] Historical and sociological literature on Puerto Ricans, Cubans and Central and South Americans in the United States is largely limited to the large communities outside of the Northwest.[27] Most Central and South Americans came to the United States in the late 1960's, throughout the 1970's and 1980's. Many came as political refugees from war torn countries such as El Salvador, Chile, and Guatemala, others came in search of economic opportunities. Carlos Gil identifies a pre 1960 and a post 1960 phase of "non-Mexican Hispanics" in Washington state (White and Solberg, 1989).

Research on Central and South Americans is needed to understand questions such as: how does the host society's reception of these immigrant groups impact the formation and growth of Hispanic communities in the Pacific Northwest? How important are kin and friendship networks in the migration process? Do Hispanics move into the state and then find they are not willing or able or to adjust to the climate and/or to the absence of family? Does the absence of a visible Hispanic presence, especially in large urban areas also imply the absence of basic amenities such as ready availability of Hispanic foodstuffs or organized social functions? To what extent do Hispanics intermarry and become fully integrated into EuroAmerican communities?

For all Hispanics we may ask, do communities go through stages of becoming established, waning, and disappearing or growing until they reach a stable number or threshold level. What role do women and families play in creating stability and growth in these communities? Once these communities reach a certain size, perhaps they generate Hispanic owned businesses, an increase in support services, community organizations, entertainment spots, in short into a viable Hispanic community. These and other questions constitute an important research agenda for interested scholars.

Surely Puerto Rican, Cuban and Central and South American communities are similar in many ways to communities in New York, Miami, or Chicago. In the same way, Mexican American communities in the Northwest share much in common with those in the Southwest and Midwest.

According to the 1990 Census there are thirteen Urban Areas (UA) encompassed by the three state region. UA's are regions where there is a central place and where a combination of cities creates a population center of over 50,000 people. The majority of Hispanics live in urban areas. In 1990, 74 percent of Washington state Hispanics resided in urban areas compared to 75 percent of whites. In Oregon, 73 percent of Hispanics were urban compared to 70 percent of whites and in Idaho, 58 percent of Hispanics were urban compared to 57 percent of whites in that state. There has been little change in the distribution of Hispanics between rural and urban areas in the last ten years. The rural urban distribution of Hispanics varied by state and in each state mirrored the white not-Hispanic population.

As illustrated in Table 2.6, in the Yakima and the Richland-Kennewick-Pasco UA's, the percentage of Hispanics exceeds 10 percent. In Washington's Puget Sound region comprised of the combined Seattle-Tacoma-Olympia UA's, Hispanics make up 9.1 percent.

Table 2.6. ◆ Urbanized Area, Race and Hispanic Origin

Urbanized Area	White, not Hispanic	Hispanic
Yakima, Wa	81.8	13.6
Spokane, Wa	93.8	1.5
Richland-Kenn-Pasco	83.1	12.1
Seattle, Wa	84.2	2.8
Tacoma, Wa	81.5	3.6
Olympia, Wa	88.4	2.7
Bremerton, Wa	85.5	4.0
Bellingham, Wa	92.3	2.3
Salem, Ore	89.3	5.6
Medford, Ore	93.0	4.5
Portlnd-Vncver, Ore	88.5	3.1
Eugene-Springfield	92.7	2.8
Boise, Id	94.9	2.5

Source: U.S. Census, 1990, Table 165.

The percentages of Hispanics in Oregon's urban areas are lower: Salem has 5.6 percent, Medford 4.5 percent. Thus, although Hispanics are only 4.6 percent of the three state region, in Washington state, two urban areas represent two to three times that amount. Hispanics in urban areas exceed the percentage of their state's Hispanic population in every state in the region.

Table 2.7 shows that in 1990, about half of all white non Hispanic people were born in their state of residence. An average of 33 percent of Hispanics in this region were born in their state of residence. About 34 percent of Hispanics were born in a different state with most of these coming from the southern and western states. On average, 30 percent of Hispanics in the region were foreign-born in 1990 compared to just three percent of white not Hispanic individuals. Nationwide, 26 percent of Hispanics are foreign-born.

Table 2.7. ◆ Geographic Mobility by Race and Hispanic Origin

	Washington		Oregon		Idaho	
	White	Hispanic	White	Hispanic	White	Hispanic
all person	4,229,131	206,018	2,580,591	110,606	929,109	51,679
Native	97%	70%	98%	68%	99%	73%
Brn in St.	50%	33%	48%	30%	52%	37%
Brn in Diff. St.	45%	34%	49%	35%	47%	34%
South	6%	10%	6%	8%	5%	12%
West	20%	20%	25%	24%	27%	19%
Foreign brn	3%	30%	2%	32%	1%	27%

Source: U.S. Census 1990, T-48 Washington, Oregon and Idaho.

◆ Social and Economic Characteristics

Like Hispanics in the nation, Hispanics in the Pacific Northwest are younger than the non Hispanic white population. For example, Washington Hispanics had a median age of 23 years compared to 33.8 years for whites.[28] This younger median age means a higher proportion of Hispanics are of child-bearing age than the general population and greater proportions of Hispanics are school age.

Nationally, the average number of persons per family was 3.83 for Hispanics and 3.11 for whites.[29] In Washington, Hispanic urban families had an average of 3.59 persons per family and 4.09 average for rural families.[30] Thus, Northwest Hispanics are not much different that Hispanics nation-wide.

Table 2.8 illustrates fertility rates for Hispanic and White not Hispanic women for Washington state in 1990.

Table 2.8. ◆ Total and Marital Fertility: 1990

	WA urban Hispanic women	WA rural Hispanic women	Urban white women not Hispanic
Tot. women, aged 15-24	14,039	4,534	216,266
% ever married	28%	36%	23%
Marital fertility[31]	1,115	1,775	838
Total fertility	498	731	264
Tot. women, aged 25-34	14,30	14,400	288,864
% ever married	80%	87%	77%
Marital fertility	2,002	2,415	1,472
Total fertility	1,781	2,122	1,191
Tot. women, aged 35-44	9,345	2,897	263,133
% ever married	92%	94%	91%
Marital fertility	2,610	3,169	1,919
Tot. fertility	2,467	3,079	1,766

Source: U.S. Bureau of the Census, Social and Economic Characteristics, Washington, 1990, T-60 and T-61 p. 100, 101.

Note: Marital fertility is the total number of children ever born per 1,000 women ever married. Total fertility is the total number of children ever born per 1,000 women.

Marital fertility among Hispanic urban women (about 1.1 children for married women) exceeds that for urban white not Hispanic women (.8 children for married women) for ages 25-34 by 38 percent. The total fertility differential between Hispanic urban women aged 35-44 exceeds that for non Hispanic white women by 40 percent. Traditional explanations of high fertility rates among Hispanic women emphasized the importance of familism and the church. A number of subsequent studies emphasize structural aspects such as poverty and education. Fertility rates for all groups tend to decrease with education.[32] Structural factors such as lack of access to health care have also been used to explain higher fertility rates especially for rural women.[33] A full analysis of statistics on family size must be done in the context of additional factors such as education, income, and socialization processes which are in turn nuanced by cultural factors.

Labor Market Status

The youthfulness and larger family size among Hispanics influences this group's labor force participation.[34] Table 2.9 illustrates the labor market status of the region's civilian, non institutional population aged 25-34. The labor force participation rate, or the proportion of each population group that is employed (full-time or part-time) or unemployed and actively seeking employment, is shown in Table 2.9. Hispanic men in the region have labor force participation rates of about 89 percent, lower than the 92 percent for White not Hispanic men.

The percentages in Table 2.9 are highly aggregated thus they hide differences across age groups. Hispanic men's lower labor force participation rate may reflect the higher proportion of foreign born among Hispanics which will lower labor force participation depending on length of stay. As length of stay increases, labor force participation rates of the foreign born resemble those of native born men. Based on an analysis of census data one study indicates it takes roughly three years for immigrants to make labor market contacts and gain needed skills.[35] Hispanics' lower labor force participation may also reflect higher numbers of discouraged workers or those who stop looking for work after an extended period of time.

Table 2.9 also illustrates womens' labor force participation. Women's labor force participation rates historically have been lower than mens' labor force participation, reflecting womens' child bearing abilities. Women's participation in the workforce falls during their child bearing years and rises as their children enter school. Hispanic women's labor force participation rates are historically lower than that for white non Hispanic women. This may reflect a host of factors such as for example, Hispanic women's work in the informal sector, women's larger family size, and the role of familism.

Table 2.9. ◆ Labor Force Characteristics by Race and Hispanic Origin, 1990

	Men White/Not Hisp.	Hispanic	Women White/Not Hisp.
Washington	N=955,643	N=44,386	N=944,696
Employed	87%	79%	71%
Unemployed	4%	8%	3%
Not in Labor Force	7%	9%	25%
Oregon	N=557,276	N=24,690	N=562,405
Employed	87%	83%	72%
Unemployed	5%	7%	4%
Not in Labor Force	8%	10%	25%
Idaho	N=186,342	N=10,889	N=186,028
Employed	88%	85%	70%
Unemployed	4%	5%	3%
Not in Labor Force	6%	9%	27%

Source: U.S. Bureau of the Census. 1990. T-49 Oregon, Washington, Idaho. Social and Economic Characteristics.

Unemployment rates illustrated in Table 2.9, indicate that Hispanic men suffer higher unemployment rates than their white counterparts in every state in the region. The disparity between these two groups was greatest in Washington where Hispanic men's rates were twice as high as those of white non Hispanic men (8 and 4 percent respectively.) Hispanics in the Northwest had slightly higher rates than Hispanics nation wide (7.8 percent).[36]

The incidence of unemployment was more severe for Hispanic women than for white non Hispanic men or women. The unemployment rate for Hispanic women in the region was a stark 8 percent compared to about 3.5 percent for white non Hispanic women. Surprisingly, Hispanic men and women had similar unemployment rates (about 8 percent) except in Idaho where Hispanic women have significantly higher unemployment rates than Hispanic men. Nation wide, all women experienced higher unemployment rates than men. In summary, Hispanics' labor market status is negatively affected by their relatively younger age, English language fluency, lower education, and race discrimination. Hispanic women's labor market status is further affected by sex discrimination and the presence of young children.

Education

Education is perhaps the single most important factor influencing the socio-economic position of Hispanics everywhere. Yet it is in the area of education that Hispanics are most severely disadvantaged. A focus on individuals 25 years and older allows us to exclude from this analysis 16-24 year olds who have not yet concluded their formal education.

Table 2.10 shows that only 51 percent of Hispanics in the Northwest complete at least a high school diploma compared to 83 percent of whites.[37] Hispanics in the Northwest are slightly better off than Hispanics (25 years or older) nation wide, 49.8 of whom attained at least a high school education in 1990.

Table 2.10. ◆ Educational Attainment in Region: 1990

less than 5th grade	Hispanic	White not Hisp.
Washington	15.3	.6
Oregon	15.7	.6
Idaho	17.2	.6
Aver for region	48.2	.6
H.S. Grad or more		
Washington	56.7	85.3
Oregon	53.0	82.6
Idaho	43.4	81.3
Aver for region	51.0	83.0
men	46.9	83.0
women	56.2	83.0

Source: U.S. Census of Population, Social and Economic Characteristics, 1990, T-47, Washington, Oregon, Idaho.

Significant gender differences in education are evident among Hispanics but are absent for pre-college white non Hispanics. A higher proportion of Hispanic women in this region, attain at least a high school degree compared to Hispanic men (56.2 versus 46.9 percent). This is also true for Hispanic women in the nation. This may reflect the less educated male dominated foreign born population. Slatta, writing about Hispanics in the 1970's finds that males exhibit slightly higher levels of education than females and that men are a slightly higher percent than Hispanic women. Twenty years later among Hispanics aged 25 years and older, men outnumber women by 8 percent in Washington State (46% women and 54% men). Men are an even greater percentage of the Hispanic population in Idaho, 44 percent Hispanic women and 56 percent men. Idaho is also the state in which fewer Hispanics have at least a high school education.

Table 2.11. ◆ School Enrollment by Race and Hispanic Origin: 1990 Persons three years and over

	Washington		Oregon		Idaho	
	White	Hisp.	White	Hisp.	White	Hisp.
	N=10377226	N=.69346	N=634128	N=355932	N=269128	N=174469
3 - 4 yr	28.3	19.2	24.8	16.1	18.9	14.1
5-14 yr	91.8	90.2	91.6	89.2	93.4	91.3
15-17 yr	93.4	82.9	91.8	84	93.8	81.1
18-19 yr	65.3	47.7	63.6	45.3	66	50.2
20-24 yr	30.5	20.5	32.4	22.9	32.9	16.8
25-34 yr	10.5	12.2	11.1	12.5	10.8	9.5
35 yrs & over	4.1	7.7	4.3	6.9	4	5
Persons 18-24 years Percent Enrolled in College						
	N=39698	N=30239	N=225656	N=16716	N=86933	N=70663
Male	31.0	15.6	32.9	15.6	34	13.8
Female	31.9	21.3	34.3	23.0	35.3	18.0

Source: 1990 U.S. Census

In every state shown there is a dramatic drop off of all Hispanics enrolled in school between the ages of 15-19. An average of 35 percent of all Northwestern Hispanics are no longer enrolled in school by age 19. For white non Hispanics, the average is 28 percent. Yet studies indicate that a relatively high percentage of high school graduates go on to complete some college. Policy intervention is required at or before age 15 in order to curb this trend. The implications of Hispanics leaving schools are further illustrated in Table 2.11. White non Hispanics are enrolled in college at twice the rate of Hispanics. On average fifteen percent of Hispanic men in the region are enrolled in college compared with 33 percent of white non Hispanic men. The percentage of Northwest Hispanic women (21 percent) enrolled in college is also much lower than the 34 percent for white non-Hispanic women. These statistics illustrate a serious problem for the state and for the Hispanic communities in particular.

Industry and Occupational Employment

Education has strong implications for employment. Table 2.12 illustrates the percentage distribution of employed persons by Hispanic origin. On average, 24.3 percent of all Northwestern agricultural jobs are held by Hispanics in the region compared to 5.4 percent held by white non Hispanics. Nationwide 14.2 percent of all agricultural jobs are held by Hispanics.[38] Thus, although the majority of Hispanics work in retail trade, services and manufacturing jobs, the image of Hispanics as farmworkers prevails. Fueling this stereotype is the high percentage of Hispanics in rural towns. The relatively small size of such towns makes Hispanics much more visible, especially during the harvest season. The perception then, is that most Hispanics are migrants and will return to their homes after the harvest. Such a perception reinforces EuroAmericans' view of Hispanics as "the Other" and works against Hispanics insofar as communities fail to assume responsibility for providing adequate housing and other services for this segment of the community.

Hispanics and whites hold a similar percentage of jobs in retail trade (general merchandise stores, eating and drinking places etc) about fifteen percent except in Idaho where only 7.5 percent of retail jobs are held by Hispanics. Services represent the largest number of jobs in all three states, and Hispanics hold about 3 percent of these jobs in the region.

Table 2.12. ◆ Percentage of Employed Persons by Industry and Hispanic Origin. Employed Persons 16 years and over

	Washington		Idaho		Oregon	
	White	Hispanic	White	Hispanic	White	Hispanic
Agriculture	3.3	20.7	8.2	29.1	4.7	23.2
Mining	0.18	0.1	0.84	0.3	0.2	0.13
Construction	6.6	4.1	6.6	3.3	5.8	4.1
Manufac/non-	4.5	8.1	6	15	4.5	7.5
Manufac/dur.	12.9	8.9	8.3	6.3	13	12.6
Transport	6	4.8	5.3	3.7	5.5	3.2
Commun	1.3	1.9	0.94	1.2	1.1	0.77
Whsl. Trade	4.8	4.7	4.8	6.5	4.7	5.2
Retail Trade	17	15.2	17.5	7.5	18	15.3
Finance/Ins.	6.5	3.7	5.2	2.3	6	3
Business Serv.	3.3	3.6	2.3	2.3	3	2.5
Per Services	1.9	2.7	3	2.3	3	3.3
Entertainment	0.66	1	1.3	0.5	1.3	1
Health Services	3.4	5.8	3.5	4.3	1.2	2.7
Educational	5.3	5.6	9.4	4	8.5	5.2
Other Prof/rel.	1.8	4.7	1.5	3.2	3.2	1.4
Public Adm.	2	4.3	2.3	2.9	4.1	2.8
	N=2069158	N=80629	N=421295	N=20886	N=1233373	N=47079

Source: U.S. Census 1990 Social and Economic Characteristics Tables 51.

If we examine the occupational distribution of Northwesterners we find that men and women are concentrated in different occupations. For example, figures 2.2 and 2.3 show roughly 36 percent of Hispanic women in Oregon and Washington employed in the white collar occupations of service and administrative support. Less than 8 percent of Hispanic women worked as farm workers. Hispanic men were largely employed in blue collar occupations of farm workers and precision production, craft and repair workers. Less than ten percent of all Hispanics were employed in the top paying occupations as managers, professionals and technicians. Hispanics in the Northwest reflect a similar occupational distribution as their counterparts in the nation.

A Demographic Profile ◆ 55

Figure 2.2. ◆ Occupational Distribution by Sex and Hispanic Origin: Washington.

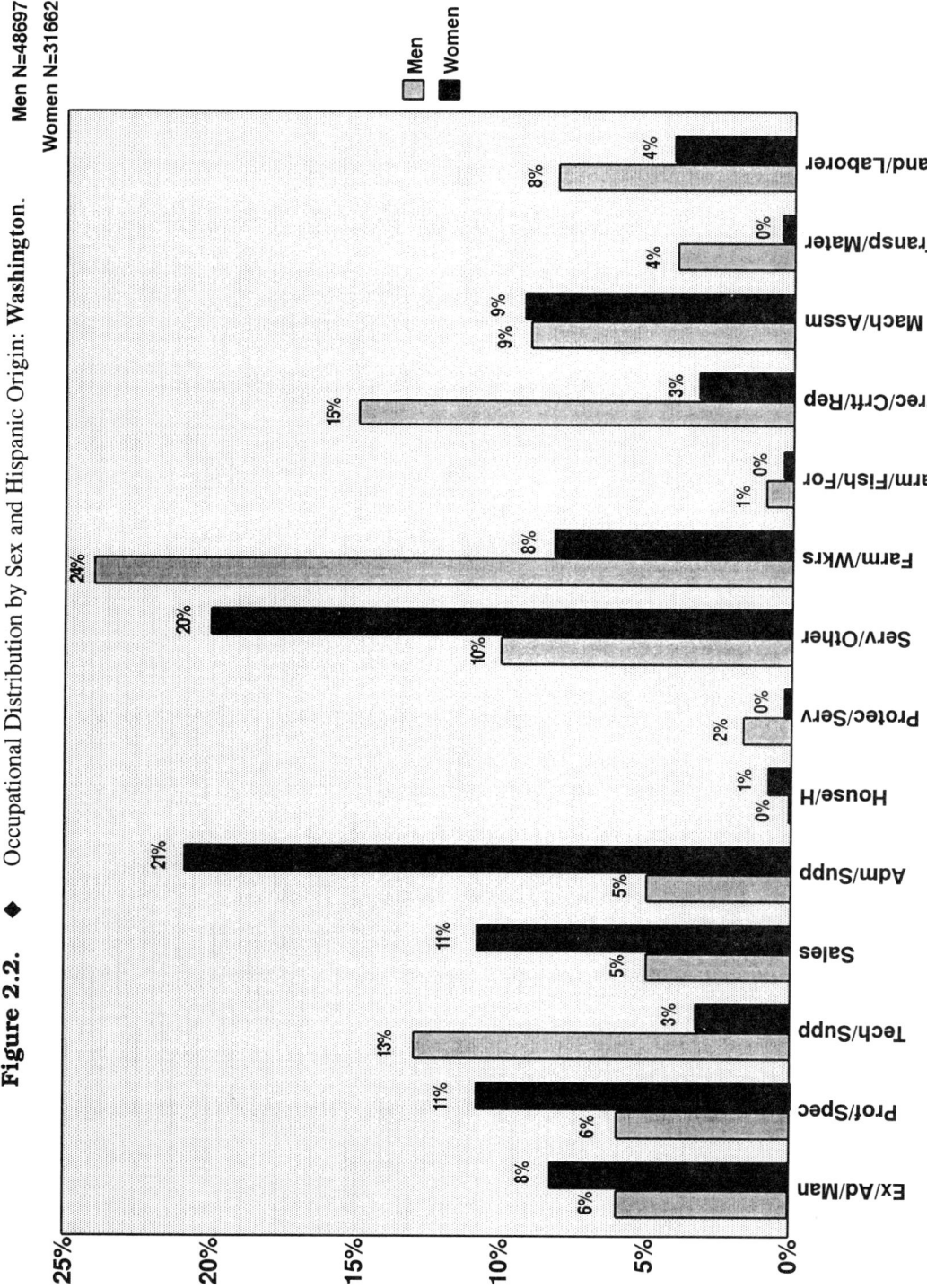

Source: U.S. Census 1990, Table 50, Washington Social and Economic Characteristics

Figure 2.3. ◆ Occupational Distribution by Sex and Hispanic Origin: Oregon.

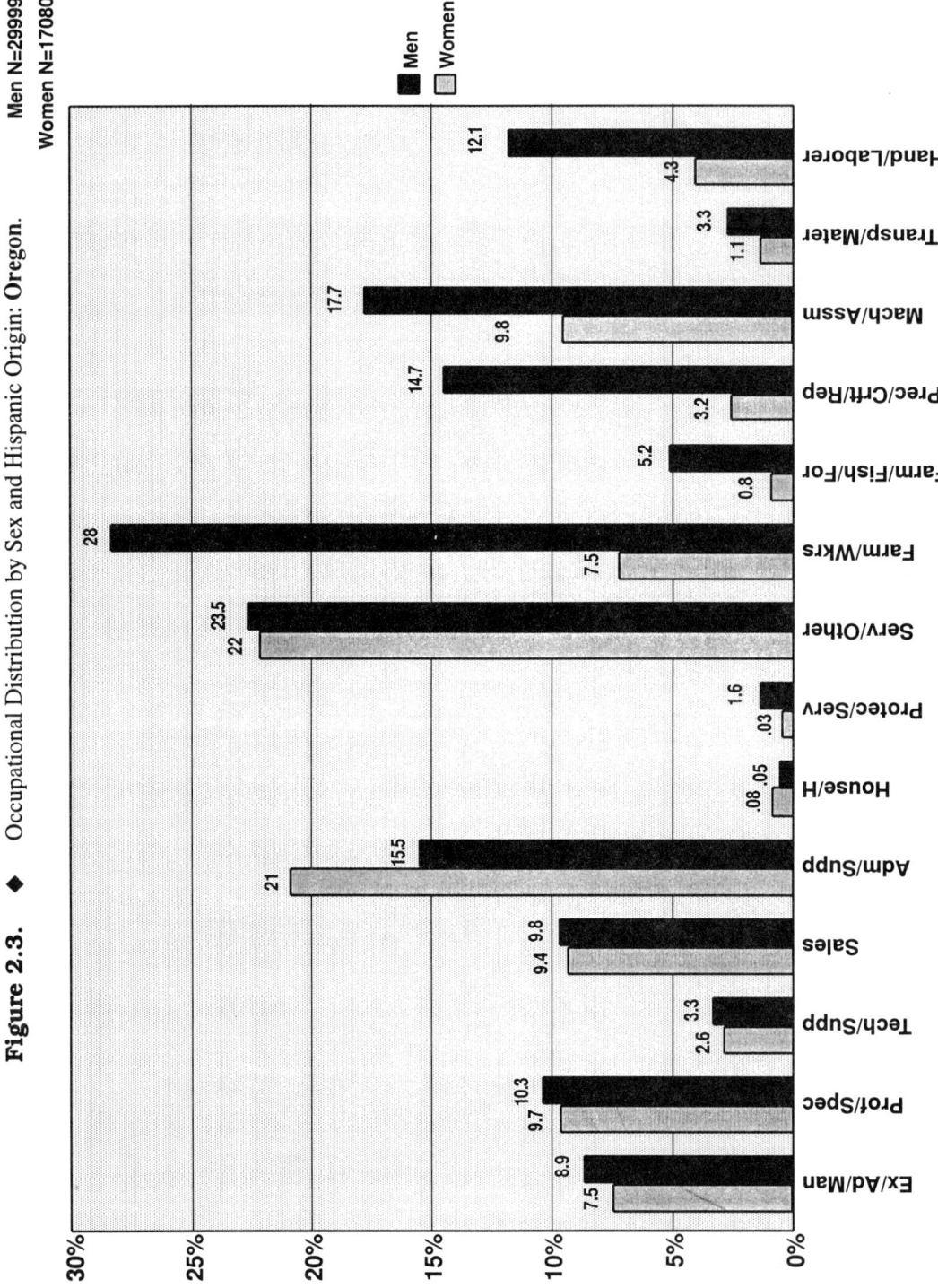

Source: U.S. Census 1990, Table 50, Oregon Social and Economic Characteristics

A Demographic Profile ◆ 57

Figure 2.4. ◆ Occupational Distribution between Whites and Hispanics: **Idaho**.

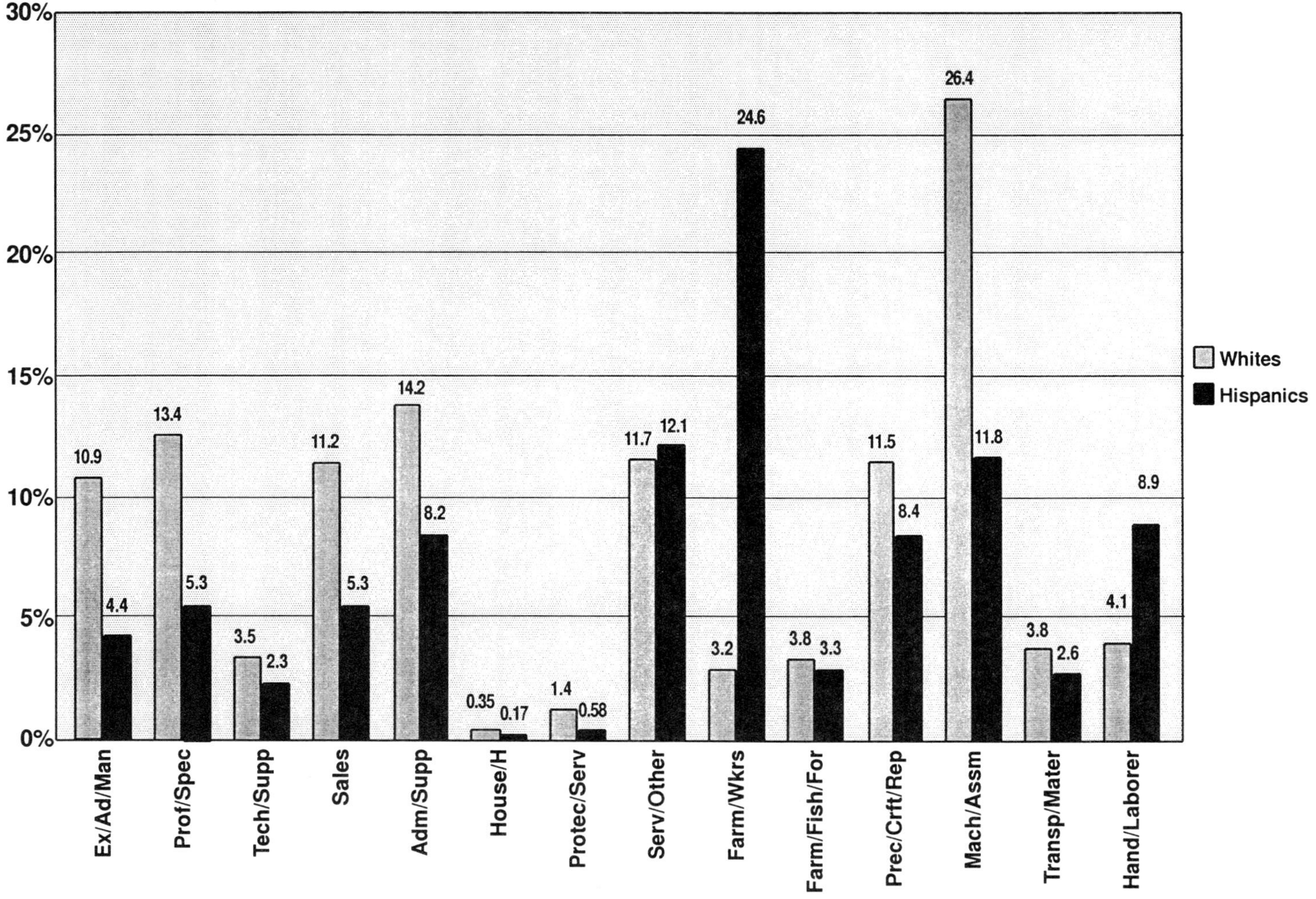

Source: U.S. Census 1990, Table 50, Idaho Social and Economic Characteristics

The relatively low educational levels coupled with the concentration of Northwestern Hispanics in the lower paying less prestigious occupations leads to lower earnings and lower income levels in general. Table 2.13 shows Hispanics' median income in three Northwestern states.

Table 2.13. ◆ Median Family Income Percentage Change by Race

Median Income: 1979 to 1989

	1979	1989	Difference	% Change
Washington				
White	$22,028	$37,610	$15,582	71%
Black	$15,881	$27,229	$11,348	71%
Hispanic	$14,993	$23,478	$8,485	57%
Idaho				
White	$17,729	$29,988	$12,259	69%
Black	$12,961	$28,203	$15,242	118%
Hispanic	$12,294	$20,353	$8,059	66%
Oregon				
White	$20,246	$32,790	$12,544	62%
Black	$13,246	$21,923	$8,677	66%
Hispanic	$15,917	$21,871	$5,954	37%

Source: U.S. Census 1980 Table 103 General Social and Economic Characteristics
U.S. Census 1990 Table 53 Social and Economic Characteristics

In 1989, Hispanics' income was lower in every state than the income of white not Hispanic families. Hispanics earn on average between 50 and 60 percent of the income of white families in the region.

Between 1979 and 1989, incomes rose for both Hispanics and non Hispanics, but the percent change for Hispanics was much smaller.

Table 2.14 shows the percent of families below poverty level by Hispanic origin. In Washington, 6.6 percent of 115,697 families white families were below the poverty level. About 24 percent of Hispanic families were below the poverty level in 1989. But 30-50 percent of mother centered households with children under age 18, were below the poverty level. Data on income reveals the grave disparities that are due to a host of related factors such as low educational levels, occupational concentration in lower paying jobs, a higher percentage of immigrants (which tend to have low rates of education), as well as to race, and sex discrimination in labor markets.

Table 2.14. ◆ Percent of Families Below Poverty Level by Race

	Families Below Poverty Level (1989)		Female H/H with child<18		child<5
Washington					
White	N=115697	6.6	N=75967	47.5	24.4
Black	N=33805	19.4	N=6549	67.5	37.7
Hispanic	N=42017	23.8	N=9986	36	21.4
Oregon					
White	N=715021	7.9	N=56820	40.9	21.7
Black	N=9694	25.6	N=2478	63.7	36.5
Hispanic	N=20834	23.3	N=4852	33.5	21.3
Idaho					
White	N=253304	8.9	N=22480	33.6	15.8
Black	N=789	13.1	N=103	28.1	23.3
Hispanic	N=10638	26	N=2770	28.4	16.3

Source: 1990 U.S. Census Table 54 Social and Economic Characteristics

In addition to lower incomes Hispanics tend to have fewer assets (autos, homes, savings accounts, etc.) than their white not Hispanic counterparts. Hispanics' median net worth (the sum of the market assets owned by every member of the household, minus liabilities owed by household members) in 1988 was $5,524 compared to a median net worth of $43,279 for white householders.[39] This means that whites are able to fall back on their assets in the event of job loss. They are also able to draw on their equity for investments. Since a higher percentage of Hispanics are foreign born, they are less likely to inherit assets from their parents.

Conclusion

Mexican Americans, the largest and earliest Hispanic group to settle in the Pacific Northwest, came to the Pacific Northwest as early as the 1860's. Mexican Americans came in larger numbers in the 1940's during World War II when they were recruited by industry and agricultural interests. As a result of the systematic use of Mexicans as contract workers in agriculture, Hispanics have become permanently molded in the psyche of the American public as migrant agricultural workers. Yet only 1/5 of Hispanics work in agriculture. The majority of Hispanics work in retail trade, services, and manufacturing. The majority of Hispanics are born in this country and speak English fluently. The majority of Hispanics live in urban areas. The majority of Hispanics in this region are Mexican, but many are Central and South American.

Research examining Hispanics in the geographic regions in which they reside is important in order to understand Hispanics as a national ethnic minority group. The region they reside in is simply one dimension of their identity. With the advent of the North American Free Trade Agreement (NAFTA) and General Agreement on Trade and Tariffs (GATT) it is important that scholars of Latinos and Latinas adopt an approach that places the heterogeneity and complexity of the experience of the various Hispanic subgroups at the center. Such an approach has the advantage of leading towards much needed comparative regional studies as well as inter and intra ethnic studies.

This historical overview and socio-demographic profile shows the diversity of Hispanics in the Northwest and points to important policy issues that must be addressed if Hispanics are to become integrated at all levels of the Pacific Northwest's society.

Endnotes

1. Aztlan was said to be the mythical homeland of the Aztec indians of MesoAmerica. In the 1960's during the Chicano movement, Chicanos reclaimed Aztlan as their homeland.
2. Hispanic and Latino will be used interchangeably and both refer to Mexican Americans, Puerto Ricans, Cuban Americans, Central and South Americans and Other Hispanics. When explaining statistics I will use the Census term, Hispanics.
3. See Hayes-Bautista, David and Jorje Chapa, 1987. They argue effectively that the Census has confused race for nationality.
4. See Bean, Frank D. and Marta Tienda, 1987; for an excellent discussion of errors associated with the self identification identifier see Teresa A. Sullivan, "A Demographic Portrait." In *Hispanics in the United States: A New Social Agenda*, edited by Pastora San Juan Cafferty and William C. McCready, (New Brunswick: Transaction Books, 1985), 13.
5. In the 1980 census respondents were asked "is this person of Spanish/Hispanic origin or descent?" In the 1990 census, respondents were asked a similar question. Respondents were then shown a flashcard with 20 choices. Those respondents who selected either Mexican-American, Chicano, Mexican, Puerto Rican, Cuban, Central and South American, and Other Hispanic constitute the Hispanic origin population. [Appendix B. Definition of the "White, Not of Hispanic Origin" Comparison Group].
6. For a discussion of the factors contributing to the undercount see Ruth B. McKay, "Undercoverage of Hispanics in household surveys," *Monthly Labor Review* (September 1993) 38-42.

    For a discussion of the undercount in Washington state, see Dan Guzman, "Yakima County, Washington and the 1990 Census: The Politics of Counting." unpublished paper 1992.

    The Latino/a undercount is a persistent problem due to confusion among the Latino population about the purpose of the census and the distinction between census officials and other government authority figures such as Immigration and Naturalization Service (INS) officials. Poor training of non Spanish speaking census takers and the lack of affordable housing which leads Latinos, especially rural migrant farm workers to live in orchards and other out of the way places exacerbates this problem.
7. See for example the work of Dennis Nodin Valdes, 1994, Santos, 1989; Santiago, 1994.
8. Ethnic Minorities as a Percent of U.S. Population 1990

Black	12.0
Hispanic	8.8
Asian or Pac. Islander	2.9
White not Hispanic	75.8

    Source: United States: U.S. Bureau of the Census, Social and Economic Characteristics 1980, 1990. Race and Hispanic Origin: 1990. T-5 p. 5.

9. If we include Montana and Alaska, American Indians, Eskimos, or Aleut are the largest ethnic minority group in the five state region. Hispanics comprise 18 percent of the total population in the five state region. In 1990, Washington state ranked 12th in the number of Hispanics in the country (up from 14th in 1980).
   In Washington state Asians and Pacific Islanders surpassed Hispanics as the largest minority group in 1990.
10. This is the terminology used by the census and refers to persons who reported "White" on the race question and "Not Spanish/Hispanic" on the Hispanic origin question.
11. U.S. Department of Commerce, Bureau of the Census. *Race and Hispanic Origin* #2 June 1991 Figure 1.
12. *Race and Hispanic Origin*, 1991 Figure 13.
13. Previous researchers noted a growing dispersion of the Hispanic population between 1970 and 1980. For example, Annabel K. Cooke, 1986, notes that the Mexican origin population in the Southwest declined from 87 percent in 1970 to 83 percent in 1980. However according to the 1990 Census this percentage seems to have stabilized at about 84 percent between 1980 and 1990.
14. Central Americans are 12 percent of "Other Hispanics" in Washington. South Americans are 14 percent of "Other Hispanics"
    1990 Census T-135 p 159.
15. Figures for the Midwest derived from Santiago, 1990 p.14. (Ohio has about 43% Mexicans).
16. This estimate does not include the number of Mexicans born in the U.S. residing in these states. A note on definitions found in the 1950 Census, p. XVI may be helpful here:
    "Persons of Mexican birth or ancestry who were not definitely Indian or of other nonwhite race were classified as white in 1950 and 1940. In the 1930 publications, Mexicans were included in the group "Other races," but the 1930 data published in this report have been revised to include Mexicans in the white population."
17. By comparison, 8,448 Japanese Americans resided in Seattle in 1930.
18. Gamboa, 1990: 7.
19. Source: U.S. Census, 1950, T-17 and T-2, Washington, Oregon, and Idaho.
20. Gamboa, 1990, p. 9.
21. Erasmo Gamboa, "Mexican Migration into Washington State," *Pacific Northwest Quarterly*, 72 (July 1981): 121.
22. Erasmo Gamboa, "Chicanos in the Northwest," *El Grito* VI (Summer 1973): 59.
23. Gamboa, 1981. p. 127
24. Camarillo, 1979.
25. See for example Carlos S. Maldonado in *Revista Apple*, Spring 1992, V. 3, Numbers 1-2, and Gilberto Garcia (1992).
26. for an abbreviated overview see Gabriel E. Gallardo, "The Composition of Oregon's Hispanic Population," in *Oregon Humanities* Summer 1992 .
27. Rodriguez, Clara. *Born in the U.S.A.* _____ blue green paperback on Immigration of Central and South Americans.

28. U.S. Census, Social and Economic Characteristics, Washington, 1990, Tables 60 and 61.
29. Alfred N. Garwood (ed). *Hispanic Americans: A Statistical Sourcebook.* (Boulder: Numbers and Concepts: 1992). T-3.08
30. U.S. Bureau of Census, Washington, T-60 and T-61.
31. This terminology was used by Slatta, 1979.
32. See Maxine Baca Zinn (ed) *Diversity in American Families*, 2nd Ed. 1990.
33. Andrade, Sally in Margarita Melville *Twice a Minority* and Edward Murguia, *Chicano Intermarriage.*
34. Labor force participation, employment and unemployment rates, are all different types of labor force status. These terms have a very specific meaning within the census: they refer to the United States population over 16 years of age not in institutions (armed forces, detention centers, hospitals etc).
35. See Joseph R. Meisenheimer II. "How do immigrants fare in the U.S. labor market?" in *Monthly Labor Review.* December 1992, p. 4-5.
36. Alfred N. Garwood (ed, Table 7-11 p. 146. White men in Northwest had lower unemployment rates than white men nationally (4.8 percent).
37. *We the American . . . Hispanics*, U.S. Department of Commerce, Bureau of the Census, September 1993. Figure 7 p. 5.
38. Garwood, Table 7.08.
39. Current Population Reports, Consumer Income Series P-60, No. 179, p. 26.

Bibliography

Acuna, Rodolfo. *Occupied America: A History of Chicanos*. 3rd ed. New York: Harper & Row, 1988.

Barger, W.K. and Ernesto M. Reza. *The Farm Labor Movement in the Midwest: Social Change and Adaptation among Migrant Farmworkers*. Austin: University of Texas Press, 1994.

Bean, Frank D. and Marta Tienda, 1987. *The Hispanic Population of the United States*. New York: Russell Sage, 1987.

Camarillo, Albert. *Chicanos in Changing a Society: From Mexican Pueblos to American Barrios in Santa Barbara and Southern California, 1848-1930*. Cambridge: Harvard University Press, 1979.

Cardenas, Gilbert. "Who are the Midwestern Chicanos: Implications for Chicano Studies." in *Aztlan International Journal of Chicano Studies Research*. Thematic Issue Chicanos in the Midwest. edited by Gilbert Cardenas. 7 (1976): 141-152.

Cattan, Peter. "The diversity of Hispanics in the U.S. workforce." *Monthly Labor Review*. (August 1993): 3-15.

Eitzen, Stanley and Maxine Baca Zinn. *Diversity in American Families*. New York: Harper & Collin, 1990.

Galarza, Ernesto. *Merchants of Labor*. Santa Barbara: McNally and Loftin, 1964.

Gamboa, Erasmo. "Chicanos in the Northwest: An Historical Perspective." *El Grito: A Journal of Contemporary Mexican-American Thought*. VI (Summer 1973): 57-70.

——————. "Mexican Labor in the Pacific Northwest, 1943-1947: A Photographic Essay." *Pacific Northwest Quarterly*. 73 (October 1982): 175-181.

——————. "Mexican Migration into Washington State: A History, 1940-1950." *Pacific Northwest Quarterly*. 72 (July 1981): 121-131.

——————. *Mexican Labor and World War II: Braceros in the Pacific Northwest, 1942-1947*. Austin: University of Texas, 1990.

——————. "Oregon's Hispanic Heritage." *Oregon Humanities* Special Issue. (Summer 1992): 1-6.

——————, ed. "Voces Hispanas: Hispanic Voices of Idaho: Excerpts from the Idaho Hispanic Oral History Project." Idaho Commission of Hispanic Affairs and Idaho Humanities Council. 1992.

Gallegos, Joseph. "Portraits: Four Hispanic Widows of the Portland Area." *Oregon Humanities* Special Issue. (Summer 1992): 27-29.

Garcia, Gilbert. "Chicano Elders in Othello, Washington," presentation at the Northwest National Asso. for Chicano Studies, University of Washington, Seattle, WA, October 1992.

Garwood Alfred N., ed. *Hispanic Americans: A Statistical Sourcebook*. (Boulder: Numbers and Concepts: 1992). Table 3.08.

Gil, Carlos. "Washington's Hispano American Communities." In *Peoples of Washington: Perspectives on Cultural Diversity*. edited by Sid White and S.E. Solberg, 157-193. Pullman: Washington State University Press, 1989.

Guzman, Dan G. "Yakima County, Washington and the 1990 Census: The Politics of Counting." unpublished paper, 1992.

Hayes-Bautista, David and Jorge Chapa. "Latino Terminology: Conceptual Bases for Standardized Terminology." *American Journal of Public Health* 77 (January 1987): 61-68.

Leek, Mark et. al. "A Community Analysis of the Hispanic Population in Yakima County." Fred Hutchinson Center, Seattle Washington, (1991).

Maestas, Roberto and Bruce Johansen. *El Pueblo: The Gallegos Family's American Journey: 1503-1980.* New York: Monthly Review Press, 1983.

McKay, Ruth B. "Undercoverage of Hispanics in Household Surveys." *Monthly Labor Review* (Summer 1993): 38-42.

Maldonado, Carlos. "Mexicanos in Spokane: 1930-1992," in *Revista Apple* 3 (Spring 1992): 118-125.

Martin, Philip L. *Harvest of Confusion: Migrant Workers in U.S. Agriculture.* Westview Special Studies in Agriculture Science and Policy. Boulder: Westview Press, 1988.

Meisenheimer II, Joseph R. "How do immigrants fare in the U.S. labor market?" in *Monthly Labor Review* (December 1992): 3-19.

Melville, Margarita, ed. *Twice a Minority.* St. Louis: Mosby Press, 1980.

Mitchell, John and Paul Sommers, *Northwest Portrait,* Northwest Policy Center, University of Washington. 1993.

Murguia, Edward. "On Latino/Hispanic Ethnic Identity," *Latino Studies Journal* 2 (September 1991): 8-17.

Santiago, Anne. "Life in the Industrial Heartland: A Profile of Latinos in the Midwest." Julian Samora Research Institute Research Report No. 2, (May 1990).

Slatta, Richard. "The "Spanish Origin" Population of Oregon and Washington." *Pacific Northwest Quarterly* 75 (July 1984): 108-116.

_____. "Chicanos in the Pacific Northwest," *Pacific Northwest Quarterly.* 70 (October 1979): 155-162.

_____. "Chicanos in the Pacific Northwest: An Historical Overview of Oregon's Chicanos." *Aztlan* 6 (Fall 1975): 327-340.

Sullivan, Teresa A. "A Demographic Portrait." In *Hispanics in the United States: A New Social Agenda,* edited by Pastora San Juan Cafferty and William C. McCready, (New Brunswick: Transaction Books, 1985): pp. 7-32.

Valdes, Dennis Nodin. *Al Norte: Agricultural Workers in the Great Lakes Region, 1917-1970.* Austin: University of Texas Press, 1991.

3

Organizational Activity and Political Empowerment: Chicano Politics in the Pacific Northwest

Gilberto Garcia

The Chicano political experience in the Pacific Northwest is an area neglected in Chicano Studies Scholarship. A study on the political life of one of the fastest growing minorities in the region and the largest in the Pacific Northwest requires attention from scholars. Studies on the region consist of historical and demographic interpretations of the Mexican origin community. Historical studies document the presence of Latinos in the states of Idaho, Oregon and Washington, with the Mexican origin population playing an important role in the character and direction of the community. Due to the scarcity of political studies of the communities in the region, the principal objective of the study is to document the various organizational strategies utilized in the Pacific Northwest. A focus on the organizational history of the region provides some insights on the struggle for political empowerment of Chicanos in the Pacific Northwest. First, it examines the early political activism of Mexicans in the states of Oregon, Idaho and Washington. Second, the study documents the impact of the Chicano Movement in the Pacific Northwest and the establishment of protest political organizations. Third, the investigation analyzes the rise of "Hispanic" politics and its impact on the new generation. Finally, the study concludes with an analysis of the demographic growth and its significance in the Chicano community search for political power.

Early Organizational Activity of Chicanos in the Pacific Northwest

An examination of the available information on the organizational history of Chicanos in the Pacific Northwest reveals a similar pattern from that established in the Southwest and the Midwest. However, the difference between those regions and the Pacific Northwest is the time of appearance in the communities beyond the Southwest. Perhaps, this is the result of the later emergence of permanent communities in the region. While, Mexicans entered the region in the early 1900's with the expansion of agriculture permanent communities did not develop until later decades. Even though, there is no documentation, it is possible that the early immigrants to the area formed patriotic organizations or "sociedades honorificas" to celebrate Mexican holidays. More than likely, such organizations appeared when a relatively large group of Mexicanos concentrated in those areas located in the Yakima Valley, Willamette Valley, the Eastern Oregon and Idaho communities connected by the agricultural economy of the Snake River. As early as 1940, Mexicans in labor camps organized such activities with the support of camp councils and recreational clubs.[1] Mexican holidays were celebrated in Idaho towns and the locals organized fiestas that attracted many people.[2]

In Oregon, the Catholic Church advocated on behalf of Chicano migrant workers when it began a statewide campaign through the Oregon Council of Churches in 1955. Several years later, the campaign conducted by the Church impacted legislation on various issues critical to migrant workers.[3] Besides the above early attempts, there are very few sources citing other types of organizations advocating for the Mexican origin population.

There are more sources and information on organizations for the 1960's, however, the studies primarily cover communities in the state of Washington. In the Yakima Valley, three organizations stand out in the 1960's: the Sociedad Mutualista of Granger, the Mexican American Federation and the United Farm Workers Cooperative. Where as the Sociedad Mutualista of Granger represents the more traditional organization, the other two represent a transition to the groups of the Chicano Movement period. The Sociedad Mutualista of Granger resemble the early form of organizations created by 1st generation Mexican Americans in the Southwest and the Midwest. The name implies mutual aid or support for the membership in times of need, though, it is perceived as a social club. According to Lemos, the political orientation of the organization tends to be conservative and opposed many of the issues promoted in Chicano Movement organizations. The membership prefers to be left out of political controversy and emphasizes social activities for the community such as dances.[4] In 1967, the United Farm Workers

Cooperative was formed out of dissatisfaction with ineffectual poverty programs weakened by the intrusion of the funding sources. Members of the cooperative confronted government neglect in the areas of health regulations for labor camps and farm worker coverage in the Washington industrial insurance law. Other activities of the cooperative included advocacy and support for the establishment of the American Civil Liberties Union(1968) in the Yakima Valley and the Farm Workers Family Health Center(1970).[5] The Mexican American Federation emerged in the state of Washington during the 1960's focusing on the political aspects of the Chicano community. Several Chicanos from the Yakima Valley founded the organization in 1967 with an ambitious and unprecedented set of goals and structure in the valley. The group divided the state into regions including the Puget Sound, Moses Lake-Spokane, Tri-Cities, Bellingham-Lynden, and Yakima Valley. During the second year of existence, the organization boasted a membership of 155 individuals from all over the state. Though, the largest number of supporters came from the Yakima Valley and the Puget Sound. Organizers in the Puget Sound focused on employment and placement issues affecting Mexican Americans moving into the urban areas of the western part of the state. On the other hand, the Yakima chapter was involved in political activities such as voter registration and civic education.[6] In 1968, the organization financed the unsuccessful campaign of a Chicano candidate for County Commissioner. More significant, the Mexican American Federation initiated a law suit to remove the English literacy requirement in Washington and pressured the Yakima County Auditor to increase the number of Spanish-speaking registrars.[7] The organization emphasized the need to involve the community at all levels of government including precincts, school boards, city councils and other forms of political influence.[8]

In the Columbia Basin, the Mexican population concentrated in several cities such as Othello, Quincy, Moses Lake, Warden and Connell. Studies of communities beyond the Yakima Valley record the existence of other forms of Mexican American organizations. A recent study of Othello, Washington reported the early organizational efforts of the Chicano community in the Columbia Basin. In the 1960's, organizational activities in the Mexican community of Othello began with the work of the Spanish American Club. Originally established in 1964 and reactivated in 1968, the leadership proposed several areas of community involvement. It planned to organize a Mexican fiesta for the large migrant population in the spring and summer and sponsor dances with Mexican music. Also, it planned to cooperate with other Othello mainstream organizations and start a voter registration drive for the elections in the fall of 1968. The Spanish American Club cooperated with the Washington State Migrant Education by establishing a community center in the Othello Labor Camp. One of the units in the labor camp was schedule to provide adult education classes and other camp gatherings. The club was responsible for scheduling the activities in the center.[9] A second community study of the Columbia Basin discovered similar type of organizations in the city of Quincy, Washington. As early as 1964, discrimination and prejudice motivated Chicanos in Quincy to organize and establish an organization in the community. The Latin American Association sought to promote the economic, social, and religious betterment of the Spanish speaking people. Activities recorded in the local newspaper included fund raising campaigns for the participation of youth in camps, the promotion of Mexican Fiesta activities, and health educational series for the Quincy community.[10] By 1967, some Chicanos of Quincy recognized the need for a more active organization who could advocate for the needs of the community. Thus, several concerned leaders formed the Progressive League of Mexican Americans and organized around the issue of assess to government service agencies. Some of the agencies targeted by the group were the Department of Licensing and the Department of Social and Health Services. Evidently, the organization spread throughout the Columbia Basin with groups operating in Moses Lake, Quincy, Othello, and Warden.[11] Other forms of organizing activity involved the Grant County Community Action Council concerned over the issues of economic development, political and social concerns. During the same year, the organization conducted a survey on the availability of services for the Chicano community. The group promoted the active participation of low income individuals in civic affairs, community organizations and to challenge institutions in public meetings.[12]

The Chicano community in the period of the early 1960's and late 1960's created organizational forms that included aspects of older and traditional Chicano organizations and the seeds of the radical organizations of the Chicano Movement. Affected by events occurring in communities located in the Southwest, Chicanos in the Pacific Northwest replicated and adapted organizational forms to the realities of Chicanos in the region. The following sections discusses the impact of the Chicano Movement in the Pacific Northwest with special attention on the states of Washington and Oregon.

◆ The Politics of the Chicano Movement, 1968-1977

While Chicanos in the Yakima Valley and the Columbia Basin in the state of Washington, the Snake River valleys in Idaho and Oregon, and the Willamette Valley in Oregon were far away from the centers of Chicano political activism, the Chicano Movement reached the isolated and distant Chicano communities of the Northwest.

In the state of Washington, the Chicano movement stirred the minds of young students attending colleges and universities. As in many parts of the Southwest students began to question the status quo, specially, the nature of inequality in the United States and the contradictions of the Vietnam War. Many of the students attending the universities were sons and daughters of farm workers who had migrated to the Pacific Northwest. They did not have to read about the conditions of their communities and the unequal treatment faced day to day in the rural communities of the state of Washington. The first signs of the Chicano Movement occurred with the establishment of the United Mexican American Students organization in 1968. Originally based in California, the concept of UMAS reached the University of Washington influencing students all over the state. One of their early forages began in the Yakima Valley organizing a Chicano student conference in Toppenish. The ultimate goal of the thrust into the heart of the Chicano communities in the Pacific Northwest was to establish student organizations in the high schools. By 1969 students utilized the United Farm Workers boycott of grapes to politicize the growing supporters of the embryonic movement. Eventually, the group forced the University of Washington not to buy grapes in support of the boycott.[13]

During the same year, the early organizing of UMAS made an impact on Chicanos in the Yakima Valley Community College and Washington State University. In those institutions, students formed the Mexican American Student Association(MASA) following similar goals and objectives of the UMAS organizations. On February 1969, the foundation of MASA in the Yakima Valley Community College almost went unnoticed when the college newspaper announced the meeting of a new organization.[14] During 1969, the college engages in discussions on defining the role of the institution and the presence of ethnic minorities. The first ethnic studies courses are approved by the social sciences division. Students and college administrators discuss issues dealing with faculty and student recruitment, scholarships and curriculum.[15] In January 1970, Chicano students organize their first successful "Awareness" symposium focusing on cultural and political themes. Activists such as Roberto Maestas and Tomas Ybarra from Seattle and three representatives of the Brown Berets participated in the conference.[16] In 1971, the organization changes name from MASA to MECHA to link up with the national student organization.[17] Chicano students organize the first state wide MECHA conference in 1972 and it is attended by a group of 165 students from throughout the state. Participants discuss the philosophy of "Chicanismo", the status of public education, and constitutional rights. The outcome of the conference resulted in the creation of a statewide board authorized to inform all MECHAS in the state of Washington and to coordinate statewide activities. The first officers included students from the Evergreen State College and Washington State University.[18]

The conferences instilled confidence in the students, thus, between 1970 to 1972, students pressure the college for the establishment of relevant curriculum and educational resources for the library.[19] On November 1971, the community college approves the first Chicano Studies courses in the history of that institution.[20] However, at the end of 1972 and the beginning of 1973, Chicano students, Chicano Studies faculty and the white administration clash over issues of discrimination and institutional neglect. Based on a complaint from a Chicano Studies instructor, HEW initiates a probe into charges of discrimination.[21] Imitating students in the southwest, on January 23, 1973 Afro American students and Chicanos students occupy a building and present a list of demands to the college. The protesters demanded from the administration the establishment of an Ethnic Studies Program and the hiring of two counselors(one Black and one Chicano). When protesters refuse to vacate the building, the college administrators called in the local police and arrested nine of the student protesters.[22] On April 1973, the student protesters who became known as the "Yakima Nine" received suspended sentences and fines. The judge charged them with "petty treason" and "juvenile evasion". Pickets are formed outside the college while negotiations between the two groups follow for several months.[23]

In the southeastern part of Washington Chicanos and Chicanas entered Washington State University through a special program: the High School Equivalency Program. Eventually, a handful of students were admitted to the university in 1969 beginning the first stage of the Chicano Movement in Pullman, Washington. Following the example of students in Seattle and in Yakima Valley, Chicano students formed the Mexican American Student Association launching the first attacks on the white institution. Between January and November of 1969, the university supports the establishment of Chicano Studies courses and begins the discussion of minority programs.[24] However, in 1970 the university faces a major crisis fueled by American policy in Cambodia. Students demanded a letter to the President of the US expressing their opposition to involvement in Cambodia and the university's endorsement of teach ins on the war. Later in the month, students staged a protest demanding Chicano Studies programs. Washington State University officials announce plans for workshops on racism and the establishment of a Chicano Studies Program.[25] Just like in the University of Washington and Yakima Valley Community College students changed the name of the organization from MASA to MECHA. Student activism in Pullman, Washington continued into the late 70's by organizing Chicano conferences on various social, cultural and political themes.[26] Chicano leaders such as Reies Lopez Tijerina and Jose Angel Gutierrez visited the region infusing students with the philosophy of the movement. Just as important, women have played an important role in the political life of students in MECHA. In the early 1970's, women established Chicanas de Aztlan to address the issue of gender equality in the university.

The Chicano movement impacted Eastern Washington University at a much later date. In 1977, Chicano and Chicana students formed the Chicano Student Organization which later changed to MECHA(1978). Initially, the organization reflected the ideals of the Chicano movement through activities such as Chicano Awareness Week, Art Shows, films, and guest speakers on contemporary issues. Students met with school administrators to establish a Chicano Studies Program to recruit Chicano students into the university. By 1977, the students succeeded in the establishment of the Chicano Education Program. MECHA-WSU and the Chicano Studies Program cooperate and support the activities of the Chicano students and faculty at Eastern Washington University. In 1978 students were involved in the development of MECHA Central(meetings at the state of level).[27]

The Brown Berets, originally, from the state of California appeared in the Pacific Northwest. In the media, the organization was portrayed as the most militant Chicano movement group. As early as 1968 and 1969, the Brown Berets established three chapters in the state of Washington: two in Seattle and one in Yakima. According to one source, by 1970 the Brown Berets attracted around 200 members on both sides of the Cascades. The Seattle chapter included both university students and youth from the surrounding communities. Actually, the militant perception of the group was fictionalized in the media since the activities were far from being radical. The chapter in Seattle mobilized its members to garner support throughout the state of Washington for a project called "Food for Peace". The goal of the project included a food, clothing, and money drive for Christmas baskets to be distributed to the most needy Chicano families in the Yakima Valley. Other activities of the Brown Berets were directed towards the development of legal defense funds on behalf of Chicano activists. In the Yakima Valley, the members and leadership of the Brown Berets originated from the community. Two of the early founders were widely known for their work with the youth in the Yakima Chicano community. Besides their participation in support of the La Escuelita and El Año del Mexicano, the Brown Berets organized a march to protest the practices of the welfare office in the Yakima Valley. Thus, one of the most militant groups in the Chicano Movement promoted food drives for the poor, legal defense fund drives, peaceful marches and voter registration drives.[28]

Other events and activities highlighted the multi-faceted character of the Chicano movement in the state of Washington. Students and faculty from the University of Washington initiated activities focusing on one of the small communities in the Yakima Valley. In 1969, Chicanos established a project known as La Escuelita, specifically, targeting the community with cultural awareness activities. By 1970, Chicano Studies courses were presented in history, culture, folk theater and communication media information. During the same year, students organize El Año del Mexicano funded through several organizations interested in the political development of the Chicano community. The project became involved in a voter registration drive in Granger, Washington targeting the Chicano population.[29] Similar forms of activism surfaced in Seattle when Chicanos from the urban area confronted school district officials for the use of an old school building. Community people decided to take over the old building in Beacon Hill and occupied the structure until the authorities would accept their demands. Finally, after several months the protesters won the demand to use the building under a reasonable rent ($1 per year). The organizers founded El Centro de la Raza, a community project characterized by a multi facetted set of activities. El Centro de la Raza promoted cultural activities, educational services, training, support and development services. The success of the center is based on the philosophy of coalitions with other groups in the Seattle area. Voter registration drives and coalitions for improved services for the poor communities in Seattle characterized other activities of El Centro de la Raza.[30]

In 1969 and 1974, Cesar Chavez visited the Yakima Valley creating a sensation among the Chicanos and white population. The 1969 visit was filled with controversy when the Granger school board refused to allow the use of a gym for Chavez's presentation. Later, the board was criticized and changed their earlier position and allowed the presentation of Chavez.[31] In 1970, the idea of founding a union for the farm workers in Yakima gradually became a reality in the valley. Hop strikes spread throughout the valley providing the base of support for the establishment of the United Farm Workers Association.[32] The UFW leader returned in 1974 to speak in the Yakima Valley Community College motivating Chicano farm workers to continue struggling for a union in the Yakima Valley. In 1974, Chicano students in the valley showed their support to Chavez by boycotting Safeway stores.[33]

The Chicano community in Oregon adapted the ideas of the Chicano Movement to the realities of their region, thus, the organizational activity for political empowerment focused on the need for social-cultural centers. Organizations were formed but they did not have the impact or influence of the cultural centers. The cultural centers served as focal points for the organizational development of the community. In 1969, the growing population of Mexican descent impacted the predominant white community forcing institutions to respond to the social and economic problems of the Chicano community. Governor Tom McCall realized the need for a communication link to the Chicano population and established an Advisory Committee on

Chicano Affairs. According to reports, the mission of the group was to increase participation of Chicanos in state affairs. The committee included community representatives from Salem, Woodburn, La Grande, Eugene, Nyssa, McMinnville, Forest Grove, and Portland. Such political forum speaks of the growth and significance of the population in the late 1960's.[34] In 1970 newspaper reports cite the presence of organizations from California such as the Mexican American Political Association(MAPA) and the Brown Berets. MAPA representatives set temporary headquarters in Portland and planned visits to communities in the Willamette Valley, Eastern Oregon communities in Ontario and Nyssa. During the same year, members of the Brown Berets attempted the occupation of abandoned Adair Air Force Base to be used for activities for the poor.[35] Nevertheless, the Chicano community in Oregon succeeded in establishing several Chicano centers. One of the most successful centers in the peak of the Chicano movement was the Centro Chicano Cultural located between Woodburn and Gervais. Incorporated in 1969, the center received funds and support from the Catholic Church. It was supported by the Social Action Commission of the Portland Archdiocese of the Catholic Church with the acquisition of land for the actual site of the center. Later, the center was funded by the Council on Human Development. The organizers of the center faced opposition from the surrounding community fearing the influence of the Chicano community. Finally, on December 1971 the building was occupied and began serving the local residents. The center provided many services including arts and crafts, seminars and in service training, inter cultural library and a monthly newspaper. Even though, the building was burned in 1973, it was funded again to continue services to the Chicano community. Thus, it served as a resource and referral center and promoted cultural awareness throughout the use of the media. A second cultural center formed in 1972 following activities similar to the Woodburn experiment. Centro Cultural of Washington County promoted vocational training of farm workers in Oregon as well as cultural activities. The early attempt by the Brown Berets to occupy the Adair Air Force Base finally resulted in the establishment of the Chicano Indian Study Center of Oregon(CISCO) in 1972. The center emphasized involvement in educational and vocational training but it was involved in health care, oral history and library project.[36]

An article in the Oregonian cited 1973 as year of achievement and hope for Oregon's Chicanos. While, the community could boast of the cultural and social impact of the centers, the article reported that the year saw the election of two Chicanos to city councils in Independence and Dayton.[37] In 1974 Chicano candidates failed to win the Democratic and Republican Congressional nomination for their respective districts. But the period recorded a positive contribution towards political empowerment when the Oregon State Consilio Chicano is founded in 1974. The Consilio clearly advocated Chicano concerns through legislation, specially, by providing legislative recommendations and endorsing political candidates. It served as a focal point for other Chicano organizations to join in one voice for the total community.[38]

As elsewhere in the United States, in the late 1970's, the influence of the Chicano Movement declines in the region. At the same time, the economic and political changes taking place in the larger society produces a different type of organization characterized as conservative and status quo oriented. The next section discusses the emergence of groups congruent with the changing character of the dominant society.

◆ The Decline of Chicano Movement Organizations and the Rise of "Broker" organizations in the Pacific Northwest

During the late 1970's and the decade of the 1980's, a conservative and hostile environment hampered the social and economic concerns of Chicano constituencies. The politics of protest characteristic of the late 1960's and mid 1970's was no longer acceptable in a period of conservatism and retrenchment. However, the positive aspect of the new stage of development in the Chicano communities in the Pacific Northwest was the potential for political power through numbers. Due to the conservative nature of the times, Chicano organizations became "Hispanicized" and their methods changed with the times. The organizations were composed primarily of professionals and different types of bureaucrats who gained their position of influence through government appointments and patronage.

In the region, the most common type of organization advocating for the Latino community is the establishment of "Governor's Commissions on Hispanic Affairs." Commissions dealing with the problems of ethnic and racial minority groups in the area are not new in the region. While they reflect the political times of the 1980's and 1990's, the commissions in Oregon and Washington are examples of early attempts to deal with Chicanos in the region.

In December of 1969, Governor McCall established the first Advisory Committee on Chicano Affairs composed of 15 members representing different cities from the Willamette Valley and Eastern Oregon. The committee was charged with the objective of making government more accessible to the Chicano community in Oregon.[39] From the beginning, the commissions were subject to criticisms and friction. A year after the formation of the Oregon Governor's Advisory Committee on Chicano Affairs, the community criticized the ineffectiveness of the organization. The work of the commission was seen as "window dressing" with no real power or influence to bring about change for the Chicano community.[40] One of the first issues to cause enmity between the governor and the committee involved the request of funds for the operation of the committee. Members of the committee requested $25,000 to hire a director and secretary.[41] Friction reached a high point in December of 1970 over several issues, including the demand from the community to use Camp Adair Air Force for a cultural center, the issue over funding for the advisory committee, and disagreements over the political support of the committee to the Council of the Poor.[42] In a meeting held in December of 1970 the committee and the governor appeared to have resolved any differences. However, on March of 1971, Governor McCall abolished the Advisory Committee on Chicano Affairs and established the Committee on Human Rights to include the concerns of all ethnic minorities in the state.[43] The idea to form the commission resurged in house bills in 1977 and 1979 but failed to pass over the issue of operational funds. In 1977, House Bill 3264 proposed the creation of an 11 member Chicano commission for the purpose of studying Chicano problems and to make recommendations to the governor and legislature. The bill recommended that all members be Spanish speaking and of Latino decent; the governor appointed the commission members, chairman and vice chairman; and the commission would have an executive director and other staff necessary for the commissions activities. The Oregon State Concilio, an organization representing several Chicano organizations initiated the idea and it was supported and sponsored by Rep. Gretchen Kifoury and the Committee in Social Services.[44] The same idea was proposed in 1979, however, the idea was rejected in the legislature. Chicano organizations criticized the legislature and charged them with neglecting the problems and concerns of the growing Latino population in the state of Oregon.[45] Finally, Governor Vic Atiyeh issued an executive order forming separate commissions for the Black and Latino communities in Oregon. The recommendation to form the separate commissions originated in a report from the Advisory Committee in Minority Affairs to the governor outlining the problems affecting minorities in Oregon. The report included testimony gathered in town hall meetings where community respondents identified employment as the most critical problem in Oregon for minorities. Other concerns cited in the report included education, job training and placements, racism and discrimination, housing, economic development and minority business, lack of minority leadership and organization, the elderly, and police harassment and crime. But the most important aspect of the new commission was the recommendation for a budget of 131,456 dollars of general fund money for each commission in the 1981-1983 biennial budget.[46] As the commission began to work, it campaigned in 1981 to pass a bill that would provide the funding necessary for its activities. It supported the passage of bills dealing with racial harassment and affirmative action in government. Also, it drafted a letter to the community articulating their concerns over racism and discrimination in employment, education and police relations. In 1983, the House approved the bills recommending the formation of the commissions on Black and Latino constituencies.[47] While the commission did not receive the requested budget, it received $32,000 for its operations in 1983-1985. From its inception, the commission investigated complaints of police harassment and health services for migrants, pushed for affirmative action issues, offered leadership conferences, held regional meetings to hear the concerns of the Latino community, and many other activities.[48] For 1985-1987, the commission acquired $78,000 earmarked for the hiring of staff and operational activities. Problems continued to emerge between the community and the governor's office, in 1987, the chairwoman of the Oregon Commission on Hispanic Affairs criticized Governor Neil Goldschmidt for his inability to appoint Latinos into positions with authority and policy making power. Latinos had been appointed to the Board of Education and to the Boxing and Wrestling Commission.[49]

In the state of Washington, the Governor's Commission on Mexican American Affairs was established in 1971, but, in 1987 the commission was re-named Commission on Hispanic Affairs. The role of the commission was defined by the legislature as an advisory panel to all branches of government regarding the social, economic and political concerns of the Latino community in the state of Washington. Bi-monthly meetings are held throughout the state and it is made up of representatives from various social backgrounds. The 1987-1989 Biennial Plan listed an ambitious plan of action in the resolution of policy problem areas of the Latino community. The Biennial Plan covered the following areas of concern; the Latino community access to governmental services, primary, secondary, and post secondary education, employment and economic development, farm worker housing, immigration, voter registration, and issues on health and the elderly.[50] The commission succeeded in advocating for farm worker concerns and issues on immigration. More recently, members of the commission confronted the governor over the selection process for the director's position in the commission. Under a new state law, the governor has the authority to appoint the director but with the recommendation of the commission. However, members of the commission argued that the governor was ignoring the input of the commission.[51]

In the state of Idaho, the establishment of a commission emerged in an Interim Legislative Committee proposal. The original proposal recommended the commission include one state senator and one state representative with three lay representatives of the Latino community in Idaho. Members would receive some compensation for attending meetings, mileage and other travel expenses. The commission was to meet four times during the year and it would be housed in a state agency determined by the legislative council. Unless the commission was granted an extension, it would be disbanded in June 30, 1986. Spoke persons of the Latino community voiced some disagreement on aspects of the proposal but supported the need for a commission in the state of Idaho. Community leaders advocated for a commission that would tackle such issues as education, unemployment, voting participation and the treatment of Latinos by the judicial system.[52] Opposition to the commission surfaced in 1985 and 1986[53], however, in 1987 Latino representatives pressured the governor to establish the commission.[54] Eventually, the new bill proposing the commission passed the Senate on March 5, 1987 and the House of Representatives on March 20, 1987. It was signed by Governor Andrus on March 27, 1987. The commission established in 1987 increased the number of representatives to nine members, two appointed by the president pro tempore of the senate and two appointed by the speaker of the house of representatives; and five public members from the Latino community appointed by the governor. The commission was required to meet four times a year, elect the necessary officers, and acquire resources through public and private sources to staff the commission. State departments, agencies, and political subdivisions were to cooperate in gathering information for the commission. The powers of the commission included gathering and disseminating information, conducting hearings, conferences, investigations, and developing studies on problems and programs concerning the Latino community. Other powers and duties of the commission included assisting public and private organizations and advising the governor, legislature, state departments and state agencies. While the commission was given the power to apply and accept funds from government and private sources, the bill did not include a fiscal responsibility. The bill included the termination of the commission on June 30, 1990.[55]

An examination of the commission's minutes revealed the involvement of an organization in the discussion, study and the search of solutions to serious social problems affecting the Latino community in Idaho. Hearings were held in the southwestern, south-central, and eastern regions of the state of Idaho, more specifically, Caldwell, Nampa, Twin Falls, Pocatello, Boise, and Chubbuck.

Issues examined by the commission included education, youth problems, affirmative action, farm worker's rights, immigration, police relations, cultural activities, drug and alcohol prevention, voter education and redistricting.[56] The early meetings of the commission recorded discussion on the topic of education, more specifically, the relations between the schools and the Latino community.[57] However, in December 4, 1993, the commission conducted the most extensive hearing on the educational status of Latinos in Idaho.

Representatives of the State Board of Education discussed the status of Latinos in education from K through Higher Education. References were made to the "Report of the Task Force on Hispanic Education," "The Task Force in the Future of Education in Idaho," and "The Idaho Education Project" which ultimately became the basis for an action plan entitled "Schools for 2000 and Beyond . . . An Action Plan for Idaho." Representatives from the Caldwell School District reported on the school programs targeting the educational problems of the Latino community. Students and parents testified on the problems encountered by students in the schools due to perceived forms of racism. The hearing documented programs and strategies utilized in the schools from K-12 which appear to be working, as well as criticism from community members on the need to do more about the educational status of Latinos in Idaho. The discussion included input from university representatives on the status of Latinos in higher education. Programs in the universities emphasized the importance of Bilingual-ESL education, training in teaching education for diverse populations, and the need for more Latino students and faculty in higher education.[58] Affirmative action was another significant issue tackled in the hearings of the commission. As early as June 10, 1989, the commission began discussion on affirmative action in state government agencies, and continued with expended discussions in subsequent meetings on December 12, 1992 and April 17, 1993. The report contained an analysis and discussion on the reasons for the lack of Latinos employees in state government and recommendations to solve the problem. The second draft of the report was presented and discussed in the commission meeting held on July 17, 1993. A motion was passed to attach recommendations to the affirmative action report with a letter to the Governor requesting a meeting to discuss the affirmative action status of the Latino community in Idaho.[59] Perhaps one of the most difficult issues taken on by the commission concerns farm worker benefits. The issue of farm worker benefits emerged in one of the early meetings of the commission, though, the commission realized the difficult task of collecting data and testimony for any proposed legislation in the future. During the meeting the commission recommended the establishment of an interim committee responsible for organizing and documenting information on farm worker benefits.[60] The importance of the issue is highlighted by the fact that discussion on farm worker benefits was included in the proceedings of at least six commission meetings.[61] Two requests from the Farm Worker Resource were presented to the commission. First, the committee asked the commission to intercede on their behalf with the governor for political support. Second, the committee requested from the commission the sponsoring of legislation on farm worker benefits such as minimum wages, unemployment insurance, and worker's compensation.[62] Further discussion followed on the issue of farm worker benefits documenting the views from various representatives including the Farm Worker Resource Committee, Idaho Legal Aid, Idaho Farm Bureau, State Insurance Fund, Idaho Industries Commission, Idaho Migrant Council, local farmer and farm workers.[63] In hearings held in Eastern Idaho more testimony was gathered in support for worker's compensation. Presentations on the problem of worker's compensation reported on the failure of farm workers to report injuries and the possibility of medical treatment being denied to injured or sick farm workers. In the meeting, announcements were made on the planning of a march down Capital Blvd. to protest the exemption for farm workers under the state's worker's compensation coverage. Other activities announced included the presentation of two panels at the Hispanic Issues Training Conference to address the above issue.[64] The commission focused on strategies to pass the bill concerning worker's compensation and passed a motion in support of a march in favor of worker's compensation for farm workers. Senator Thorne voted against the motion, however, he clarified that he supported worker's compensation not the rally.[65] The date for the rally was set for January 19, 1994 with the participation of the governor in the rally.[66] Besides the above activities of the Idaho Commission on Hispanic Affairs, it examined other issues such as youth problems, police relations, voter education, redistricting, immigration, cultural activities, and drug and alcohol prevention. Several significant programs have contributed in stimulating awareness of the important role of the Latino community in Idaho. The commission actively supports the Annual Hispanic Issues Training Conference which attracts a large number of young participants from the Latino community in Idaho; the Annual Hispanic Women's Conference and Annual Hispanic Women's Writing Seminar which primary focus is on the status of Latina women in Idaho. More recently, the commission established an Hispanic Drug and Alcohol Prevention program funded with federal moneys. In the area of culture, the commission supported the Hispanic Oral History Project and the Bicultural FolkArts Curriculum Development Project. The Hispanic Oral History Project in cooperation with the Idaho Humanities Council produced a small booklet documenting the oral history of Mexicanos in Idaho and a traveling historical exhibit. The Bicultural Folkarts Curriculum Development Project incorporated the idea of using Chicano Theater to promote cultural awareness as part of school curriculum. Both projects succeeded in stressing the importance of preserving the history and culture of the community. In all of the projects undertaken by the commission, it garnered funds from outside sources to support the activities.[67] Despite the short life span of the commission, it has managed to make a strong impact in one of the most conservative states in the Pacific Northwest.

Demographics and the Potential for Political Power

Demographic studies reveal that while the Pacific Northwest is predominantly white, the growth rates of minorities in the region exceeded those of the white population from 1980 to 1990. The Latino population in the region has experienced a growth rate only second to the Asian Pacific population: 118% for the Asian population and 44% for the Latino population.[68] The demographic growth rates recorded by the Latino community in the same decade make it the most numerous minority in the region. According to the Atlas of the Pacific Northwest, Latinos represent the largest non-white population in 36 counties and registered a plurality in eight counties.[69] Politically, the demographic growth of the community raises the question of empowerment. The following section examines the relationship between the population growth of the Latino community and the potential for political power. More specifically, the study analyzes the Mexican origin population in the Pacific Northwest, the Latino sub group with the oldest and longest period of contact to the dominant white culture in the region. Moreover, it is the most numerous as well as the most concentrated in some regions of the Pacific Northwest.

◆ Chicano Political Empowerment in the Pacific Northwest

An analysis of the data supports the following generalizations on the status of the Chicano community's struggle for political power. First, Latinos will gain political power due to the dramatic demographic growth of the population. Second, due to the youthfulness of the population, a large percentage of the population does not meet the voting age requirements Third, the large percentage of the foreign born population which is 18 years or older is not eligible to vote. Finally, many Latinos that meet the voting age requirement do not register to vote.

According to the 1990 Census, four of the selected communities contained a Latino majority of the total population while four recorded a relatively sizable population. At first glance, the significant large population supports the commonly held assumption that with more Latinos this will translate to more political power. The 1990 census data on Wapato (WA), Toppenish (WA), Gervais (OR), and Wilder (ID) report a high percentage of Latinos in the total population.

Table 3.1. ♦ Selected Communities in the Pacific Northwest with Significant Latino Populations

	Total	Latino	Percent
Wapato, Wa	3785	2450	65
Toppenish, Wa	7419	4655	63
Othello, Wa	4638	2093	45
Quincy, Wa	3738	1401	37
Woodburn, Or	13404	4226	32
Gervais, Or	992	523	53
Wilder, Id	1216	798	65
Caldwell, Id	18400	3703	20

Certainly, the demographic growth of the Latino population increases the potential for political representation and political power. However, a closer examination of the data raises questions on the extent of that potential for political power. Lists of registered voters for the selected communities in the study were obtained to complete the analysis of the data. Those communities are the following; Wapato and Toppenish in the Yakima Valley of Washington, Othello and Quincy in the Columbia Basin of Washington, Woodburn and Gervais in the Willamette Valley of Oregon, Caldwell and Wilder in the state of Idaho. Studies on the nature of the Latino electorate emphasize the importance of examining the role of age and foreign born status. When the social characteristics of age and foreign born are correlated to the total population and the number of registered voters, the results reveal several barriers for political power.

Table 3.2. ♦ Number of Registered Voters

	Total	Latinos	Percent
Toppenish, Wa	1682	541	32
Wapato, Wa	781	317	41
Othello, Wa	1487	223	15
Quincy, Wa	1356	172	13
Gervais, Or	347	102	29
Woodburn, Or	6405	480	7

Source: List of Registered Voters, Yakima County, Adams County, Grant County, Marion County, Oregon.

Even though, the communities registered a sizeable Latino population, the power of their numbers is affected by the youthfulness of the population. In comparison with the non-Latino population, the percentage of Latinos meeting the voting age requirement tends to be lower in all communities. The following percentages were reported on the total voting age population in the selected communities: Wapato (55%), Toppenish (51%), Othello (56%), Quincy (56%), Woodburn (57%), Gervais (50%), Wilder (58%), and Caldwell (55%). A second factor that affects the impact of Latinos in the political arena is the presence of a large foreign born population. More significant and revealing is the data on the total foreign born 18 and older population. The percentages vary from community to community due to the specific historical experience of each community and the impact of recent immigrants in the development of those communities. Latino communities located in Washington, Oregon, and Idaho contain large numbers of Mexican American migrants who settled in the region in previous decades. During the 1980's, the population growth of those communities increased due to the entrance of recent immigrants(documented and undocumented). In places such as Woodburn (OR) and Toppenish (WA), the total foreign born 18 and older accounted for 61% and 56% of the total Latino voting age population. Other communities with a growing foreign born voting age population were as follows: Gervais (45%), Wapato (42%), Othello (39%), and Quincy (36%). The communities of Wilder and Caldwell in the state of Idaho recorded the lowest percentage of foreign born voting age population: Wilder (30%) and Caldwell (27%).

Consequently, the weak political power of the Latino community is partially explained by the variables of age and foreign born. For example, the data on registered voters as a percent of the total voting age population reflect lower levels of political participation. If one removes the variable of the foreign born population, the level of political participation is dramatically different in the selected communities. The percentages range from as high as 78% in Toppenish (WA) and 70% in Gervais (OR), Wilder (48%), and Wapato (41%). While some communities reported lower percentages, Othello's (32%) and Quincy's (34%) numbers indicated higher levels of participation. Thus, what emerges from the analysis is that some communities contain many Latinos who qualify to vote but do not register to vote. This is probably the result of an electorate that feels alienated from the political system.[70]

There are other obstacles obstructing the Latino community's struggle to gain political power in the Pacific Northwest. The selected communities for this study recorded lower levels of educational attainment, from as low as 45% to as high as 61% of the persons 25 years and over completed less than a 9th grade education. Political behavior studies affirm that lower educational levels impact political participation. Economic variables affect the level of participation of persons in the political system, in this regard, the selected

Latino communities for the study registered diverse levels of poverty in the population. Caldwell, Idaho registered 29% of the persons 18 years and over lived below poverty levels. Toppenish, Gervais, Othello, Woodburn, and Wapato recorded from as low as 33% who lived below the poverty level to as high as 38% who lived below the poverty level. Quincy, Washington and Wilder, Idaho registered the highest number of persons 18 years and over living below the poverty level (50% and 44% respectively). According to studies, poor people participate at lower levels of political involvement. On the other hand, the non Latino population of those communities recorded lower percentages of persons in the same age category living below the poverty level. A third variable which affects the Latino population is related to the level of English language skills. Persons deficient in the English language do not have access to information necessary in the political process. Of the eighth communities, Toppenish, Gervais, Woodburn, and Wapato had higher percentages of persons 18 years and over who spoke English not well or not all. In Toppenish, 45% of the total number of Spanish speakers did not speak English well or not at all, while in Gervais, Woodburn and Wapato, the percentages were 41%, 40% and 38% of the total number of Spanish speakers were deficient in English.[71]

Once the Latino population resolves the social and economic variables that affect the total application of the power of numbers, the communities must deal with other necessary ingredients for political empowerment. Studies on political representation and empowerment of peoples of color demonstrate that those communities still face institutional barriers in the form of systems of government and elections. Communities in California, Texas, and in many other regions of the United States where Latinos constitute a sizable percentage of the population have taken to court districts excluding them from political participation. A major political issue in those legal battles involves the system of political redistricting and the structure of political systems. Gerrymandering is a practice utilized to weaken the political potential of Latino communities as well as at large election systems of government.[72]

Finally, but just as important, the Latino communities must develop organizations capable of representing the interests of all persons and taking advantage of the demographic changes occurring in the community. The Pacific Northwest experimented with various types of organizational forms, however, there is a need to critically evaluate the nature of contemporary organizations and the types of leadership in those organizations. In this regard, one of the maladies in the Pacific Northwest is the dominant role of top to bottom strategies of organizing Latino communities. Such organizations are restricted due to the character of the leadership and the funding sources. For example, many of the most visible political organizations take on advisory roles and the leadership is a product of appointments. Studies have shown that appointees tend to feel no commitment to the people they are serving but rather to the people that appointed them to positions of influence. In the Pacific Northwest, organizations such as the Governor's Commission on Hispanic Affairs are examples of the above type of organizations. There are Latino organizations composed primarily of professional bureaucrats who become the self prescribed leaders of the communities in the region. A problem associated to those types of organizations is related to the funding sources of their operations. An example of such organizations is the prominent role that Migrant Education Programs play in the Pacific Northwest. While advocating for the needs of the rural population, the funding sources handicap their advocacy role in the political arena. The leadership of those agencies can not take political risks for the community for fear of losing the financial sources of their operations. There is still a third type of organizations present in the Pacific Northwest which play a significant role in the Latino communities. Organizations composed of government employees and professionals of different backgrounds operate in the region. The basic problem of such organizations is the inability of the membership to understand the working class character of the problems affecting the community. Since the majority of the members and leaders are products of middle class families, they will represent the interests of the predominantly working class Latino community as long as their class interests are not endangered. In the Pacific Northwest, though, it is found in other regions of the United States, organizations such as IMAGE fit the above description. On the positive side, all of the above forms of organizations include members and leaders with skills and resources needed to tackle the racial and class barriers imposed on the Latino communities.

Alternative community organizations at the grassroots level emerged in several communities in the state of Washington and Oregon. For example, in the Yakima Valley of Washington and the Willamette Valley of Oregon, organizations connected to the farm workers struggle represent alternative organizational forms to those mentioned above. Even though, they are affected by other problems, those groups have the potential of better representing the interests of Latinos in the Pacific Northwest. Since the majority of Latinos in the region reside in largely rural communities, the organizations address basic issues closer to their social and economic realities. Nevertheless, there is a need to develop other organizational forms that takes into consideration changes taking place in those rural communities. In many of those communities, the population is dealing with problems of settled out migrants no longer working in the fields. This is taking place in cities such as Pasco, Othello, Moses Lake, and most of the important cities in the Yakima Valley of Washington. An example of this type of organizations emerged in Othello, Washington during the late 1980's. In 1988, community leaders from various social backgrounds founded an organization known as Hispanos

Unidos. Initially, the basic thrust of the group was directed in the area of voter registration. Before the local elections, the members of the organization invited candidates running for political office. Subsequent to the voter registration drive, Hispanos Unidos challenged the Othello School District over the issue of affirmative action. Othello's schools were facing a serious crisis due to the changing demographic character of a previously dominant white community. Many of the schools enrolled large number of Latino children who needed qualified bilingual and bicultural teachers. Unable to deal with the challenge, the school district and the larger white community disregarded publicly the issue of affirmative action. Although, the school district was put on notice of the fundamental problem inherent in outdated institutions. Since the last public confrontation, the school district has hired some Latino instructors to tackle the increasing growth of Latino students. Thus, Hispanos Unidos strength came from their grassroots origins and ability to identify the issues affecting the working class population in Othello. It was successful in encouraging the establishment of chapters in cities such as Moses Lake, Pasco and Connell. Their weakness came from the lack of resources needed to address community issues on a continuos basis. After the voter registration drive and the affirmative action issue, Hispanos Unidos ceased to exist.[73]

Conclusion

This essay examined the history of organizational activity in the Pacific Northwest and its relationship to the political empowerment of the growing Latino community in the region. Latinos, primarily composed of Mexicanos, Mexican Americans and Chicanos utilized different types of organizations in their struggle to resolve serious social, economic and political problems. The political life of the Chicano communities in Washington, Oregon, and Idaho demonstrate the evolution of similar types of organizations found in the Southwest and Midwest, but, their emergence in the scene occurred in a different time period. Thus, mutualistas, social action organizations, protest groups, and contemporary "broker" organizations operated in the Pacific Northwest. Finally, the demographic explosion of the Chicano/a population in the Southwest was replicated in the states of Idaho, Oregon, but most significantly, in the state of Washington. The demographic growth of communities with majority or plurality of Latino persons raised the issue of political empowerment. The study examined the impact of various demographic indicators and their relationship to political participation. It raised the question of reassessing our analysis of the complexity of the problems related to political participation and the need for grassroots organizations.

Endnotes

1. Erasmo Gamboa. Mexican Labor and World War II: Braceros in the Pacific Northwest, 1942-1947 (Austin: University of Texas Press, 1990), 106-109.
2. Erasmo Gamboa. Voces Hispanas/Hispanic Voices of Idaho: Excerpts from the Idaho Hispanic Oral History Project. (Idaho Commission on Hispanic Affairs and Idaho Humanities Council. 1992), 13, 25-28.
3. Richarch W. Slatta. "Chicanos in the Pacific Northwest : An Historical Overview of Oregon's Chicanos" Aztlan 6(1975): 329.
4. Jesus Lemos Jr. A History of the Chicano Political Involvement and the Oraganizational Efforts of the United Farm Workers Union in the Yakima Valley, Washington. (Master's thesis, University of Washington, 1974), 50-51. Jerry Garcia. The History of a Chicano/Mexicanao Community in the Pacific Northwest Quincy, Washington, 1948-1993. (Master's thesis, Eastern Washington University, 1993),58-59.
5. Jesus Lemos Jr. A History of the Chicano Political Involvement, 53-55.
6. Mary Hersey. "Mexican American Federation: Its Goals, Structure, Leader" Our Times: A Catholic News Report for Central Washington. 10(Nov 29, 1968): 1-3.
7. Jesus Lemos Jr. A History of the Chicano Political Involvement, 55.
8. Mary Hersey, "Mexican American Federation, 2
9. Gilbert Garcia. "Mexicanos in Othello, Washington: The Excluded Chapter in the History of Adams County" forthcoming. Revista Apple Spring 1994: 8.
10. Jerry Garcia. The History of a Chicano/Mexicano Community, 36-37, 64.
11. Ibid, 73-74.
12. Ibid, 64-65.
13. Jesus Lemos Jr. A History of the Chicano Political Involvement, 56.
14. The Galaxy. Yakima Valley Community College Newspaper, February 7, 1969, February 14, 1969.
15. The Galaxy. Yakima Valley Community College Newspaper, January 17, 1969, May 2, 1969, May 9, 1969.
16. The Galaxy. Yakima Valley Community College Newspaper, January 30, 1970.
17. The Galaxy. Yakima Valley Community College Newspaper, May 21, 1971.
18. The Galaxy. Yakima Valley Community College Newspaper, April 28, 1972, May 5, 1972.
19. The Galaxy. Yakima Valley Community College Newspaper, December 20, 1970, May 21, 1971, April 14, 1972.
20. The Galaxy. Yakima Valley Community College Newspaper, November 19, 1971.
21. The Galaxy. Yakima Valley Community College Newspaper, October 2, 1972, October 13, 1972, January 26, 1973.
22. The Spokesman Review January 25, 1973. The Galaxy. Yakima Valley Community College Newspaper, January 26, 1973.
23. The Galaxy. Yakima Valley Community College Newspaper February 9, 1973, February 16, 1973,March 2, 1973, April 13, 1973.
24. El Mensajero, MECHA-WSU Newspaper December 12, 1968. The Daily Evergreen WSU Newspaper January 6, 1969, November 7, 1969.

25. The Spokesman Review May 6, 1970. The Daily Evergreen May 6, 1970, May 19, 1970, May 21, 1970, May 26, 1970, May 27, 1970, May 29, 1970. The Spokesman Review 29, 1970.
26. El Mensajero MECHA-WSU Newspaper December 12 1978, December 19, 1978, January 23, 1979, March 6, 1979, March 20, 1979
27. El Mensajero December 19, 1978 , January 23, 1979,March 6, 1979, March 20, 1979
28. Jesus Lemos Jr. A History of the Political Involvement, 58-59. Jerry Garcia. The History of a Chicano Mexicano Community, 57-59.
29. Jesus Lemos Jr. A History of the Political Involvement, 58, 60, 62.
30. Bruce Johansen and Roberto Maestas. El Pueblo: The Gallegos Family's American Journey, 1503-1980.(New York: Monthly Review Press, 1983(, 127-132.
31. The Oregonian December 12, 1969. Jesus Lemos Jr, A History of the Political Involvement, 59.
32. Jesus Lemos Jr, A History of the Political Involvement, 65-76..
33. The Galaxy February 8, 1974, May 3, 1974, May 17, 1974.
34. The Oregonian Dec 12, 1969, December 25, 1969, January 14, 1970, February 18, 1970.
35. The Oregonian, February 18, 1970, October 8, 1970,
36. Richard W.. Slatta. Chicanos in Oregon: An Historical Overview (Master's thesis, Portland State University, 1974), 36-47.
37. The Oregonian December 31,1973.
38. Slatta, Chicanos in Oregon, 40-41.
39. Capital Journal Dec 12, 1969, The Oregonian Dec 12,1969, Capital Journal Dec 23, 1969, The Oregonian Dec 25, 1969, The Oregonian Jan. 14, 1970.
40. The Oregonian Feb. 18, 1970, Capital Journal Feb. 18, 1970.
41. Oregon Statesman August 19, 1970.
42. Oregonian Oct. 9, 1970, Oregon Statesman Oct. 9, 1970, Capital Journal Oct. 20, 1970.
43. Statesman Dec 4, 1970, Capital Journal Dec 4, 1970, Statesman March 31, 1971.
44. Statesman Journal May 2, 1977.
45. The Oregonian September 11, 1979.
46. Statesman Journal September5, 1980.
47. Statesman Journal March 29, 1981, Statesman Journal February 26, 1983.
48. Statesman Journal November 2, 1983, The Oregonian August 20,. 1984, Statesman Journal June 10, 1985.
49. The Oregonian August 20, 1987.
50. Washington State Commission on Hispanic Affairs. Hispanics: Washington's Emerging Community. Biennial Plan for 1987-1989.
51. La Voz Seattle, WA, June 1993, February 24, 1994.
52. Idaho Statesman December 26, 1984.
53. Idaho Statesman February 23, 1985.
54. Newspaper articles voicing the position of the community appeared in the Idaho Statesman March 5, 1987, March 8, 1987, March 18, 1987.

55. Legislature of the State of Idaho, Senate Bill No. 1171, Forty-ninth Legislature. First Regular Session, 1987. See articles in the Idaho Statesman on July 9, 1987 and September 17, 1987.
56. The following section is based on materials found in the minutes of the Idaho Commission on Hispanic Affairs held on June 10, 1989, December 20, 1991, April 18, 1992, September 12, 1992, December 12, 1992, April 17, 1993, July 16 & 17, 1993, September 18, 1993, and December 4, 1993.
57. Minutes of the Idaho Commission on Hispanic Affairs, June 10, 1989, December 20, 1991.
58. Minutes of the Idaho Commission on Hispanid Affairs, December 4, 1993.
59. Minutes of the Idaho Commission on Hispanic Affairs, July 17, 1993.
60. Minutes of the Idaho Commission on Hispanic Affairs June 10, 1989.
61. Minutes of the Idaho Commission on Hispanic Affairs June 10, 1989, September 12, 1992, April 17, 1993, July 16, 1993, September 18, 1993, and December 4, 1993.
62. Minutes of the Idaho Commission on Hispanic Affairs, September 12, 1992.
63. Minutes of the Idaho Commission on Hispanic Affairs, April 17, 1993.
64. Minutes of the Idaho Commission on Hispanic Affairs, July 17, 1993.
65. Minutes of the Idaho Commission on Hispanid Affairs, September 18, 1993.
66. Minutes of the Idaho Commission on Hispanic Affairs, December 4, 1993.
67. Idaho Commission on Hispanic Affairs, 1991, 1992, 1993 Annual Reports.
68. Philip L. Jackson and A Jon Kimerling. Atlas of the Pacific Northwest (Corvalllis, Oregon, Oregon State University, 19993), 19-20.
69. Philip L Jackson , Atlas of the Pacific Northwest, 21.
70. List of Registered Voters, Yakima County, Adams County, Grant County, Washington. Marion County, Oregon.
71. 1990 Census of Population and Housing, Toppenish, Wa, Wapato, Wa, Othello, Wa, Quincy, WA, Woodburn and Gervais, Oregon, and Caldwell and Wilder Idaho. Summary Tape 3A.
72. William V. Flores. Chicano Empowerment and the Politics of At Large Elections in California: A Tale of Two Cities" In Community Empowerment and Chicano Scholarship. Edited by Mary Romero and Cordelia Candelaria. (NACS. Proceedings, 1992), 181-200.
73. The Othello Outlook August 17, 1988, September 14, 1988, November 2, 1988, January 21, 1989, May 31, 1989, June 7, 1989, June 14, 1989,June 21, 1989.

Bibliography

◆ Newspapers

The Daily Evergreen. WSU Newspaper, 1969-1974.
The Galaxy. YVCC Newspaper, 1969-1974.
El Mensajero. MECHA-WSU Newspaper, 1978-1979.
The Oregonian, 1969-1987.
The Othello Outlook, 1988-1989.
The Spokane Review, 1969-1973.
La Voz, 1993-1994.

◆ Goverment Documents

1990 Census of Population and Housing, Othello, Washington. Summary Tape File 3A.
1990 Census of Population and Housing, Toppenish, Washington. Summary Tape File 3A.
1990 Census of Population and Housing, Wapato, Washington. Summary Tape File 3A.
1990 Census of Population and Housing, Quincy, Washington. Summary Tape File 3A.
1990 Census of Population and Housing, Wilder., Idaho. Summary Tape File 3A.
1990 Census of Population and Housing, Caldwell, Idaho. Summary Tape File 3A.
1990 Census of Population and Housing, Woodburn, Oregon. Summary Tape File 3A.
1990 Census of Population and Housing, Gervais, Oregon. Summary Tape File 3A.
Adams County, Washington. City of Othello. List of Registered Voters, March 5, 1993.
Marion County, Oregon. City of Woodburn. List of Registered Voters, February 24, 1994.
Marion County, Oregon. Gervais. List of Registered Voters, April 15, 1993.
Yakima County, Washington, City of Toppenish. List of Registered Voters. April 15, 1993
Yakima County, Washington. City of Wapato. List of Registered Voters. April 15, 1993.

◆ Master's Theses

Garcia, Jerry. The History of a Chicano/Mexicano Community in the Pacific Northwest Quincy, Washington, 1948-1993. Master's thesis, Eastern Washington University, 1993.
Lemos Jr, Jesus. A History of the Chicano Political Involvement and the Organizational Efforts of the United Farm Workers Union in the Yakima Valley, Washington. Master thesis, University of Washington, 1974.
Slatta, Richard W. Chicanos in Oregon: An Historical Overview Master's thesis, Portland State University, 1974.

◆ Books and Journal Articles

Gamboa, Erasmo. Mexican Labor and World War II: Braceros in the Pacific Northwest, 1942-1947. Austin: University of Texas Press, 1990.

Gamboa, Erasmo. Voces Hispanas/Hispanic Voices of Idaho: Excerpts from the Idaho Hispanic Oral History Project. Idaho Commission on Hispanic Affairs and Idaho Humanities Council. 1992.

Garcia, Gilbert. "Mexicanos in Othello, Washingto: The Excluded Chapter in the History of Adams County" forthcoming. Revista Apple Spring 1994.

Flores, William V. "Chicano Empowerment and the Politics of At Large Elections in California: A Tale of Two Cities" In Community Empowerent and Chicano Scholarship. Edited by Mary Romero and Cordelia Candelaria. NACS. Proceedings, 1992: 181-200.

Jackson, Philip L and A Jon Kimerling. Atlas of the Pacific Northwest Corvallis, Oregon: Oregon State University, 1993.

Johansen, Bruce and Roberto Maestas. El Pueblo: The Gallegos Family's American Journey, 1503-1980. New York: Monthly Review Press, 1983.

Hersey, Mary. "Mexican American Federation: Its Goals, Structure, Leader" Our Times: A Catholic News Report for Central Washington. 10: Nov 29, 1968.

Slatta, Richard W. "Chicanos in the Pacific Northwest: An Historical Overview of Oregon's Chicanos" Aztlan 6 (1975):

Washington State Commission on Hispanic Affairs. Hispanics: Washington's Emerging Community. Biennial Plan for 1987-1989.

4

Vivemos de la Tierra: Agricultural Workers in the Pacific Northwest

Carlos S. Maldonado

Agriculture is a major industry in the Pacific Northwest. Farming and agriculture-related business ranks as Idaho's number one industry with cash receipts of close to $3 billion in 1990's.[1] Agriculture is Oregon's second largest industry with gross farm sales of over $2.6 billion in 1990.[2] Agriculture in Washington, in terms of employment and value-added ranks as the third largest goods producing industry in the state. The value of Washington's agriculture production totaled $4.29 billion in 1990.[3] The Pacific Northwest leads the nation in numerous crop productions.

The labor needs supporting the agriculture industry in the Pacific Northwest is the focus of this chapter. More specifically, this chapter will discuss the Mexicano/Chicano farm worker experience in the Northwest. This discussion will first outline a brief historical sketch of agricultural workers in the Northwest including Oregon, Washington and Idaho. Second, the discussion will present a profile of agricultural workers in the Northwest including a discussion of selective key issues facing agricultural workers in the three state area and a selective listing and description of organizations which address the needs and issues facing agricultural workers in each state. The author hopes that this chapter will provide some insights about Mexicano/Chicano agricultural workers, a community that has been marginalized in text and society at the national and regional level including the Northwest.

A Brief Historical Sketch of Farm Workers in the Pacific Northwest

The agricultural expansion in southwestern United States in the early 1900's was mirrored to a lesser scale in other regions of the U.S. Mexicanos/Chicanos from Mexico and southwestern U.S. began to respond to the growing labor needs associated with the expansion of agriculture not only in southwestern U.S. but also in the Midwest, Rocky Mountain states and consequently into the Pacific Northwest.

The development of large scale agriculture in Idaho was precipitated by irrigation projects which converted Idaho's southern sagebrush desert into an active farming area. The state's sugar beet cultivation in the early 1900's showed strong economic potential. By the first decade of the 1900's the Idaho Sugar Company, a subsidiary of the Utah Sugar Company had established sugar refineries in Eastern Idaho.

The Amalgamated Sugar Company had plants in at least four sites in Southern Idaho.[4] Irrigation efforts in southern Idaho also enhanced bean, potato and fruit production which required farm labor.

In the state of Washington, the U.S. Reclamation Service began work on the Yakima Project in 1906.[5] This particular initiative significantly increased the amount of irrigated acreage in the Yakima Valley between 1900 and 1910.

In Oregon, the annual rainfall in significant agricultural areas including the Willamette and Hood River Valleys is substantial enough for agricultural purposes. Both valleys receive 30 to 40 inches of rainfall per year. Collectively rain and snow fall maintain abundant water levels in area rivers. During the summer, irrigation is heavily used for agriculture. Water supplies in the numerous and abundant Oregon rivers supply the water needs of agriculture. The Willamette Valley is the state's major agriculture producing area controlling 47% of all agriculture employment in the state.[6]

A combination of historical events collectively contributed to the growing Mexicano/Chicano labor force in the US, including the Northwest. The inception of WWI created the accellerated need for food production in the US. It also cyphoned laborers to serve as military personnel, thus creating a diminished farm labor pool. The development of the refrigerated box car further stimulated the farming industry by enabeling the marketing of perishable foods into distant areas. Concurrently, the Mexican Revolution between 1910 and 1920 spawned a significant migration of Mexicans fleeing the turmoil of the revolution. It is estimated that over a million Mexican nationals migrated to the US during this period. The 1917 Immigration Act exempted Mexicans from the restrictive immigration laws of that era, encouraging the movement of people from México to the US.[7]

By the 1920's the migration routes leading north from Mexico and the southwestern U.S. had clear tributaries culminating in the Midwest, the Rocky Mountain region and into the Pacific Northwest. The 1930 U.S. census recorded that the Mexican descent population was 562 in Washington, 1,568 in Oregon and 1,278 in Idaho. While these figures serve as bench marks documenting the Mexicano presence in the Northwest they most likely do not reflect the actual number of migrating Mexicano/Chicano agricultural workers who journeyed through the northwest states. The level of sophistication in enumerating ethnic groups has historically proven a difficult task for the Census Bureau. The 1930's census was also the first time that the term "Mexican" was used for enumerating purposes. Thus, the possibility for enumerating shortcomings are logically expected during this period.

The 1940's serves as a significant benchmark in the influx of Mexicano/Chicano agriculture workers to the Pacific Northwest. This influx was driven by the continuing agriculture growth in the Northwest and the onset of WWII. The war parralled WWI in the need of agriculture products for the home front and the swelling U.S. military. WWII precipitated the need for agriculture workers to replace those individuals going to war or moving on to war based employment.

During this period, three separate groups of Mexican agricultural workers harvested the crops in the Northwest. The first group consisted of those few Mexicanos/Chicanos who journeyed to the Northwest decades earlier and had settled in the numerous rural communities in Washington, Oregon, and Idaho. The second group of Mexicano/Chicano agricultural workers were those that were making the initial journey to the Northwest. Many of the established Mexicano/Chicano communities in the Northwest can be directly linked to this group. The third group consisted of Mexican nationals recruited as "Braceros" to supply the temporary labor needs caused by W.W.II. The "Bracero" workers was a highly mobil labor force. Documentation of the arrival and departure of Mexican workers can be found in many community newspapers throughout the Northwest.

By the end of W.W.II and the early 1950's, Mexicanos/Chicanos became the major agricultural work force in the Pacific Northwest. A secondary wave of reclamation irrigation projects such as the Columbia Basin Project fed by the Grand Coulee Dam in Eastern Washington continued agricultural growth in the Northwest. The establishment of agricultural processing plants and packing houses throughout the Northwest during the 1950's and 1960's contributed to increased agricultural production. These processing plants also encouraged migrating agricultural workers to settle out of the migrant stream and secure year round employment.

The 1950's and 1960's witnessed continued influx of Mexicano/Chicano agricultural workers into the Northwest. This influx cried out for an infrastructure to respond to the growing Mexicano/Chicano community.

Throughout the Northwest, initiatives linked to the "War on Poverty" and other efforts at the state and local levels resulted in some public and private non profit initiatives responding to the growing Mexicano/Chicano farm worker community. In Oregon, state legislators hearing increasing migrant issues passed legislation responding to migrant issues in housing, health and other areas including a State Migrant Labor Committee.[8] A couple of years later the Department of Migrant Ministry of the Oregon Council of Churches secured a federal grant initiating the Valley Migrant League in 1965 with locations in various Willamette Valley communities. Summer programs targeting migrant children had also been initiated in the early 1960's in Oregon.[9] Several years earlier in 1955, Idaho's Governor Robert Smylie had established The Governor's Migratory Labor Committee.

The committee issued an annual report describing migrant camp housing in Idaho.[10] Efforts to respond to the schooling needs of migrant children in Idaho resulted in some school programs in the labor camps. In Washington, the Washington Citizens for Migrant Affairs emerged in 1965. This organization secured a federal grant to establish modular classrooms for day care programs to serve migrant families and children. These and various other public and private efforts reflected the early initiatives in the Northwest to develop a much needed infrastructure critical in responding to the needs of a growing Mexicano/Chicano agriculture worker community in the 1950's and 1960's.

In the 1970's and 1980's Mexican/Chicano agriculture workers coming to or residing in the Northwest continued to grow and thus expanded the need for services and advocacy. During this period agricultural worker activism became more visible. Much of this activism was undoubtably influenced by the Chicano movement and the efforts of Cesar Chávez and the UFW Union. In Washington farm workers organized in 1967 the United Farm worker Co-op store in the Yakima Valley. This co-op store was the precursor to the United Farm Workers Union of Washington State founded in 1986.[11] In Oregon unionization efforts in the form of the United Farm Workers of Oregon in 1968[12] and the Chicano United Farm Workers of Oregon in 1970 emerged.[13] Although these initiatives did not fully develop, they contributed to heighten the need for organizing farm workers in Oregon's Mid Willamette Valley. This organizing need became a reality in 1985 when *Pineros y Campesinos Unidos del Noroeste* (PCUN) was founded.[14] In Idaho farm worker unionization has trailed other Northwest states. None the less activists in Idaho established the Idaho Farm Workers Association in 1982.[15] This association is yet to develop organizationally but it is hoped that it will mature into a union representing and organizing farm workers in Idaho.

During the 1970's and 1980's we also see the emergence of significant organizations addressing the needs of farm workers. Organizations like the Oregon Rural Opportunity and Washington's Northwest Rural Opportunity existed for about a decade. Other organizations that emerged during this period continue to serve Northwest farm worker in the 1990's. These include the Washington State Migrant Council incorporated in 1983 and highlighted by WSMC literature as being the largest Latino owned and operated non-profit agency in the Northwest serving agricultural workers and their families.

The Idaho Migrant Council incorporated in 1971 still provides a variety of services to farm workers in Idaho in the 1990's. In the late 1970's in Oregon, The Oregon Human Development Corporation emerged and assumed the service role that the Oregon Rural Opportunities held earlier in serving farm workers. The Oregon Human Development Corporation still continues today in providing numerous services to agricultural workers.

Today, agriculture in the Northwest is a major employment and business producing segment. It is important that we become more informed about those individuals and families that are critical in supporting agriculture as an important revenue generating segment in the Northwest. The proceeding section will highlight demographics of agricultural workers in the Northwest.

Agricultural Workers in Washington

The act of counting seems to be a simple straight forward task. The difficulty arises when we pose the following questions. What do we count; who do we count; who does the counting; when do we count; how is this counting accomplished? These simple questions makes the task of counting more complex. This task of counting is compounded when those that are doing the counting act independently of each other. Such is the reality of counting agricultural workers. This segment will provide demographical data of agricultural workers in the Northwest and highlight some of the difficulties involved in developing census data on agricultural workers.

In the State of Washington a 1992 publication produced by the Washington State Employment Security Department marks the total agricultural employment at 78,900 in the state.[16] This figure is generated from two primary data sources including quarterly tax returns filed with the Employment Security Department and monthly In Season Farm Labor Reports. The limitations inherited in these data sources are recognized. For instances the quarterly tax return data does not include students and certain family members. The In Season Farm Labor Report is sample based and does not include regular hired workers. Additionally the report is only conducted when a significant number of seasonal workers are hired, perhaps in peak season. Furthermore, data on some agricultural industries with low number of seasonal workers are not collected.

Alice Larson & Colleagues in their report Estimate of Migrant and Seasonal Farm workers in Washington State cite a figure of 174,922 migrant workers and 156,347 seasonal workers or a total of 331,269 migrant and seasonal workers engaged in Washington agriculture. The Larson report indicates that the bulk of the estimate was calculated using the "Demand for Labor" (DFL) method in which estimates are arrived by calculating the number of workers required to complete a specific agricultural task. Larson recognizes some of the drawbacks in using the DFL methods such as depending on a formula which may not reflect actual circumstances. Nonetheless the incorporation of outside review of the data by individuals and agencies directly providing services to agricultural workers and research experts makes the Larson estimates perhaps more reflected of the number of agricultural workers in the State of Washington. Which set of data does one use to ascertain the "red" numbers of agricultural workers in Washington State? Do we use the Washington State Employment Department's data or the Larson estimate? The enumeration of agricultural workers is plagued with pitfalls difficult to avoid.

Agriculture in the State of Washington is concentrated in Eastern Washington. It is estimated that about 80% of farm related employment is found in Eastern Washington. Major areas of agricultural employment is found in certain Eastern Washington counties including Chelan-Douglas and Yakima counties. Based on County Percentage of 1991 Total Agricultural Employment in Washington State, Yakima County represented 25.4%.

The Yakima Valley also ranks high in its diversity of agricultural products including cherries, hops, grapes, and fruit and vegetable row crops.[17]

Agricultural work is year round in Washington. As the year proceeds from January to December various work is done ranging from pruning trees in January to harvesting the various crops in peak season. Twin peak seasons happens in July and again in October.

The majority of agricultural workers in Washington are from local communities. Interstate workers make up the second largest group. Intrastate movement of agricultural workers is not significant compared to the two former groups. The Washington State Employment Security Department estimates that the average annual earnings for individuals whose sole employment is in agriculture is $4,983.[18]

◆ Issues Facing Agricultural Workers in Washington

There are a number of critical issues facing agricultural workers in the State of Washington in the 1990's. Most significant is that the National Labor Relations Act which exempts agriculture from collective bargaining is still the rule in the State of Washington. The absence of collective bargaining legislation in Washington state has negatively impacted Washington farm workers. The United Farm Workers Union of Washington State has proposed and lobbied for a collective bargaining bill in 1990, 1991, 1992, and 1993.

Many felt that because democrats won control of Washington's State Senate, House of Representatives and the governor's office in 1992 the chances of having enough support to pass a collective bargaining bill was good. By April 1993 House Bill 1287 had been developed. The UFW of Washington State argued that the propose bill would limit farm workers' ability to use the strike as a bargaining leverage. The proposed bill included a provision requiring workers to notify growers 72 hours before striking. Union representatives also argued that the proposed bill gave an appointed state commission only minimal powers in policing labor disputes. This would negatively impact maturing unions such as the UFW of Washington state by burdening them with the heavy cost of investigating labor violations. Additional concerns expressed by union representatives included the composition of workers' bargaining units and the percentage of workers required to be present in order to call an election.[19] The proposed collective bargaining bill did not become a reality. Noting the history of the union pushing forward the call for collective bargaining legislation, the issue will continue to come up in the legislature. A related item to this issue is the ongoing boycott by the VFWWS against Chateau St. Michelle, a major wine producing company in Washington and the Northwest. This boycott began in 1987 as a result of a union representation dispute by some company workers. Union representation had become a significant issue for workers and the union in this boycott.

A second issue facing agricultural workers in Washington state recently was the exclusion of seasonal farm workers from the Washington Health Services Act of 1993. Much furor against the exclusion of seasonal farm workers from the health bill resulted in House Bill 2443 being overwhelmingly passed during the 1994 legislature which extended health care to seasonal farm workers. Much of the details will need to be worked out. Farm worker advocates will surely need to monitor the integration and impact of the state's health plan on farm workers. A key question regarding the issue is how will input from farm workers be heard, gathered and integrated into the details of the health plan.

A third issue affecting farm workers is affordable and adequate housing. The Office of Rural and Farmworker Housing (ORFH) located in Yakima, Washington has conducted a number of surveys assessing the need and demand of agricultural worker housing. This agency's data has proven useful in highlighting the critical issue of affordable and adequate housing for agricultural workers. According to ORFH surveys, completed among farmworkers in ten communities in Eastern and Central Washington, there is indication that significant levels of over crowding exist in farmworker households.[20] In some cases several farmworkers shared the same housing unit. In Sunnyside 94% of those surveyed lived in overcrowded households. In Wenatchee, 55% of those surveyed lived in over crowded households. Sunnyside ranked the highest, while Wenatchee ranked the lowest in over crowding situations. The following provides the complete figures by the survey data.

Table 4.1. ◆ Survey of Overcrowded Households

Community	% of those surveyed living in overcrowded households.
Sunnyside	94%
Basin City	90%
Manson	84%
Chelan	84%
Othello	81%
Brewster	74%
Tieton-Cowiche	74%
Topennish	65%
Wenatchee	55%

In Basin City, 69% of those households surveyed had more than one family living together. Most other communities ranged between 21% to 45% on this variable. The average income level of those surveyed was $8,800 with a median of 5 people per household. This survey information clearly indicates that those farmworker families surveyed in these ten communities are experiencing overcrowding and due to income levels find it difficult to find affordable housing.

A fourth issue facing farm workers in Washington state also include low income earning. The Washington State Employment Security Department reports that the average annual earning for those who worked only in agriculture is $4,983. The department also cites that the majority of farmworkers do not qualify for unemployment benefits due to working less than the 680 hours required to qualify. Due to this low income level many continue to live in poverty, ill health, and remain economically and socially marginalized in our communities.

A fifth issue involves the inherently dangerous working circumstances that farm workers face daily. According to the Washington Department of

Labor and Industries, agricultural workers suffered high rates of injuries including sprains, fractures, dislocations, concussions, and amputations. In addition to these injuries farm workers are exposed to numerous types of toxic materials including pesticides. The workers who apply the pesticides and those who work in the orchards or fields come in contact with chemical residues which remain after spraying. Presently there does not exist an effective mechanism to report or monitor toxic poisoning among farm workers. There exists a number of chemicals used in Washington's agriculture that have yet not been studied for their harmful affects on workers.

Beyond these issues are concerns regarding the schooling of farm workers children and basic empowerment issues. These issues facing agricultural workers in Washington state require us to be better informed about the various organizations existing in Washington state which address and advocate on these issues in the behalf of agricultural workers. The proceeding is a selective inventory and a brief description of these organizations. This list of organizations represents a sampling and not meant to be exhaustive.

Organizations in Washington Serving Agricultural Workers

Radio KDNA, founded in 1979, is a public radio station situated in Granger, Washington. It promotes it self as *"La Voz del Compesino"*-Voice of the Farm Worker. It broadcasts Mexican music throughout the Yakima Valley. It broadcasts information about workers' rights, immigration, health issues such as Aids, and disseminates information about other agencies which cater to farm workers.

United Farm Workers Union of Washington State (UFWWS), founded in 1986, is the state's first recognized farm worker union in Washington. The union's headquarters is located in Sunnyside, Washington. The union also has a Seattle office to help with the union's efforts in the west side of the state. The UFWWS has been in the forefront of organizing farm workers and pressing for a variety of farm worker legislation. The UFWWS is an independent union. The UFWWS publishes the *"Si Se Puede"* newsletter. In early April of 1994, the UFWWS membership voted to become formally affiliated with the United Farm Workers of America. Some view this affiliation as benefiting both organizations but particularly the UFWWS' struggle against Chateau St. Michelle, a major winery in the Northwest and based in Washington state.

Washington State Migrant Council, incorporated in 1983 , is a multiservice non-profit agency serving 24 communities in Washington providing family and child care services. WSMC provides services ranging from health care, AIDS education, prevention of substance abuse and drop outs, to housing and related educational services to migrant and/or seasonal farm workers. WSMC"s main administrative office is located in Sunnyside, Washington. WSMC's 10th annual report highlighted its 1992 funding budget of $15,327,493.00.

The Evergreen Legal Services—established in 1976 provides legal services to low income clients. A majority of its clients are seasonal and migrant workers. The Evergreen Legal Services has two locations including Sunnyside in Eastern Washington and in Everett in Western Washington.

Yakima Valley Farm Workers Clinic, established in 1978, is located in communities with high number of farm workers. These locations include Yakima, Toppenish, Wapato and Grandview. The clinics serve as a service net providing health services to farm workers who have difficulty in obtaining these services due to a lack of funds. Many of its clients are children and expecting mothers. Some of its health services include child health care, primary health care, health care for women particularly prenatal services, dental lab work, x-rays, minor emergency care, nutrition information, and a host of other health services. The clinic also runs a WIC program at its various site locations. Health care cost is based on income level.

Washington Human Development Corporation, opened in 1984, has several sites in Washington. These include its headquarters in Seattle, Mt. Vernon, Moses Lake, Pasco, Sunnyside and Wenatchee. WHDC focuses on employment training for agricultural workers seeking non agricultural related work. Other services include adult education, vocational training, support services and family case management. WHDC will no longer exist after June 30, 1994. It's operations will be carried out by the Washington State Employment Security Office for the near future.

EPIC, incoporated in 1979, has its headquarters in Yakima and has about 16 field centers throughout the state including Yakima, East Wanatchee, Manson, Bridgeport, Ellisforde, Sunnyside, Toppenish, Wapato, and Selah. EPIC's primary services to farm worker families include child care, Head Start, and assessment and referral of family needs such as employment, housing etc. EPIC works closely with other agencies including the Employment Office, Department of Social and Health Services and others. It's funding sources include state and federal grants. In 1993, EPIC provided services to about 1,500 children.

Okanogan Farm Workers Clinic, founded in 1985 as a nonprofit health clinic, has recently become the Centro de Salud Familiar de Okanogan, provides primary care for families, particularly pre natal care and preventive health education. Dental care services will soon also be available. It service area includes Okanogan and Douglas counties. Even though the clinic has gone a name change it continues to provide health services to agricultural workers. Farm workers make up about 50% of its clients.

Other organizations include the Central Washington Migrant Health Project, Moses Lake; Migrant Friendship Center, Wenatchee; Okanogan Farm Workers Clinic; Okanogan and others.

◆ Agricultural Workers in Idaho

Agriculture, including agriculture related business, ranks as Idaho's number one industry generating receipts of close to $3 billion in 1991. Some 10.5 % of Idaho's jobs are agricultural related. Almost 17,000 individuals work in food processing. Another 32,000 work in farms and ranches.[21] Compared to Washington this figure is small.

Mexican/Chicano workers contribute much to maintain agriculture as Idaho's number one industry. According to Phil Bowman, Idaho Department of Employment there is a conservative estimate of about 25 thousand farm workers in Idaho.[22] The Idaho Commission on Hispanic Affairs cite that the bulk of these agricultural workers are Mexicano/Chicano or Latino.[23] This is similar to Washington and Oregon. Southern Idaho counties (Canyon, Ada, Owyhee, Twin Falls and others) surrounding the Snake River Plain employ the majority of agricultural and food processing plant workers. Idaho's Magic Valley is the most agriculturally dependent region in the state with agriculture production accounting for 45.3% of all regional products. Food processing accounts for an additional 32.1%. This pushes the Magic Valley's agriculture to a high 77.4 %. These areas produce various berries, vegetables, tree and vine fruits and field crops such as potatoes.

A survey conducted in 1990 by the Idaho Department of Employment Agriculture Labor Bureau and local Job Service offices provide insights about farm workers in Idaho. Seventy-one percent of all respondents were married and were accompanied by their spouse. Seventy percent are male whereas 30% are female. The average family size was four. Thirty-three percent cited Mexico as their permanent home. Forty percent identified three southwestern states including Texas, California, and Arizona as permanent home bases. Texas represented 27 % of the figure. In contrast, only 24% of those surveyed indicated that Idaho was their permanent home. The survey revealed that interstate farm worker movement between Idaho, Washington, and Oregon was considerably small. Almost 50% of the respondents indicated that they resided in labor camps. Twenty seven rented in the open market. A very small percentage reported that employers provided housing.[24] The Idaho Farm Bulletin published by the Research and Analysis Bureau of the Idaho Department of

Employment reported in 1992 that some migrant workers were homeless and camping out in Canyon County area. The Department of Employment also reports that Idaho has a surplus of agricultural workers. A number of these findings are reflective of national trends regarding agriculture workers as reported in the National Agricultural Workers Survey (NAWS).

Even though Idaho is similar to Washington and Oregon in ranking its agriculture segment as a top revenue maker, Idaho's agriculture employment has been declining since the 1920's. Much of this decline has been attributed to production efficiencies bought by machinery and changes in the market niche as evident in the growth of trade and service sectors.

Issues Facing Agricultural Workers in Idaho

There are a number of significant issues confronting agricultural workers in Idaho. Most significant is that in contrast to Washington, Idaho does not have the organizational infrastructure critical in providing services and advocacy for agricultural workers. Even though the Idaho Migrant Council and other private non profit organizations exist, Idaho lacks the number and sophistication of organizations present in Washington which cater to agricultural workers. This became evident to me while visiting a meeting of the Idaho Farm Worker Resource Committee which was established to "improve agency coordination and collaboration to enhance education, services, and protective rights for farm workers and their families". It was interesting to note that only two non profit private organizations were represented. The bulk of the organizations present were state agencies including the Department of Employment, State Department of Education, Migrant Education, and other state agencies. The creation of the Resource Committee is reflective of an existing vacuum or dearth of community based organizations advocating for farm workers.

A second issue facing farm workers in Idaho is the absence of a labor organizing entity such as the United Farm Workers Union in Washington or Pineros y Campesinos Unidos Del Noroeste in Oregon. Idaho is the only state in the Northwest which has "right to work laws. This "right to work" status was legislated in 1986. An organization called the Idaho Farmwokers Association established in 1982 to deal with farm worker issues has not fully develop. In fact for several years it has remained dormant. Recently, efforts to reorganize and recharge the association have emerged. In speaking with Rogelio Valdez from Caldwell the hopes are to revive the association so it may become a key effort in the legislative and political sphere in Idaho.

The notion of the association becoming a fully developed farm worker union in Idaho is also invisioned.

A third issue facing agricultural workers is the dearth of state based legislation benefiting agricultural workers. Whereas agricultural workers in Washington and Oregon may benefit from workers' compensation or state laws, Idaho agricultural workers are exempted from State minimum wage laws, workers' compensation laws and unemployment insurance laws. Some have advocated for initiating a licensing and bonding requirement for farm labor contractors similar to that in Oregon. Much of the protection afforded to agricultural workers are based on federal laws which many criticize as being inadequate. Some believe that Idaho needs a complaint driven state enforcement mechanism and the creation of a state agricultural labor enforcement unit with jurisdiction over agricultural labor practices, such initiatives are seen by some as the only effective means of protecting workers' rights.

A fourth issue facing agricultural workers in Idaho is the dearth of research on farm workers in Idaho. Even though the NAWS research may be useful in identifying farm worker issues, the marginal level of state specific research in Idaho contributes to farm workers continuing to be a voiceless population in Idaho politics and policies. The Migrant Seasonal Farm Worker Survey conducted by the Idaho Department of Employment Agricultural Labor Bureau in 1990 was to ascertain some very basic information such as who makes up Idaho's farm workforce, where do they come from, where do they live and other demographic data. Research contributes to making a social issue visible and difficult to ignore. Research also contributes to assessing a social need and offers direction in addressing an issue. A continuing dearth of research regarding agricultural workers in Idaho perpetuates a status quo in the marginality of farm workers in Idaho.

A fifth issue facing farm workers in Idaho is the difficulty they experience in linking with key service agencies such the Idaho Department of Employment and others. The Farm Worker Resource Committee has identified the lack of bi-lingual staff in service agencies critical in providing services to monolingual Spanish speaking agricultural workers. The FWRC has established a Bilingual subcommittee to address the problem, identify specific area needing attention, and assist agencies find solutions. This is an important issue because it impacts access and issues concerning health, housing employment, education and other basic need areas.

A sixth issue which negatively impacts agricultural workers in Idaho is the availability of affordable and adequate housing. The Idaho Migrant Council, Idaho Legal Aid Services' Migrant Farm Worker Law Unit and the Idaho Department of Employment have all expressed the housing issue among Idaho's agricultural workers. The Idaho Migrant Council has documented this housing concern through several studies. The ILAS/MFLU's Winter 1994 newsletter included a graphic view of the housing issue among farm workers. Some labor camps are constructed with federal moneys others are privately build by farmers. The ILAS/MFLU evaluates public housing as decent to substandard, while grower housing is generally deplorable. During the winter when many labor camps close, farm workers who remain find it difficult to locate low income housing. Due to housing discrimination and the requirement of a six or twelve month lease by private renters, farm worker find it a real challenge in securing affordable and adequate housing. Undocumented workers find it specially difficult as they are not eligible for public housing. The dearth of federal or state funding to build year round housing contributes to a continuing housing concern for agricultural workers in Idaho.

Accessing health services is also a significant issue for agricultural workers in Idaho as in other Northwest states. Issues of language, cost, unfamiliarity with the maze of medical services which are primarily staff with anglo service providers, and other similar concerns present barriers to agricultural workers seeking health services.

The Terry Reilly Health Services, a nonprofit health provider in southern Idaho, is an example of a health service organization providing outreach health services to agricultural workers Terry Reilly Health Services has four clinics including Nampa, Homedale, Marsing, and Boise. Elena Rodriguez serves as the clinic's farm worker service coordinator. As the clinic's farm worker service coordinator she visits the numerous farm worker housing camps in Canyon and Owyhees counties including the Chula Vista labor camp located in Wilder, Idaho.

These and other issues confronting agricultural workers in Idaho present significant areas that need to be reviewed to successfully establish priorities and strategies in addressing the needs of farm workers in the Gem state.

Organizations Serving Agricultural Workers in Idaho

The following is a selective inventory of organizations providing services to agricultural workers in Idaho. This selective listing will better inform us as to the various services and strategies being used in Idaho.

Concilio Migrante de Idaho or the Idaho Migrant Council, founded in 1972, has six area service offices located in Blackfoot, Caldwell, Twin Falls, Burley, Caldwell and Idaho Falls. The IMC provides a variety of supportive services including health/medical, emergency services including food, rent and transportation, AIDS education, ESL classes, employment and job training. IMC fulfills a significant advocacy role for farm workers.

Idaho Legal Aid Services; Migrant Farm Workers Law Unit, established in 1974, provides legal assistance to low income migrant and seasonal farm workers. Its four offices serve farm workers in Caldwell, Twin Falls, Pocatello, and Idaho Falls. Employment, housing and other basic living issues involving legal concerns are the type of cases this agency works on.

Farm Worker Resource Committee, established in 1992 under the direction of the U.S. Department of Labor, consists of representatives from federal, state, local, public and private organizations which interact with farm workers and their families. The FRC was fully recognized by Governor Cecil Andrus in 1993 as an authorized advisory committee to the governor. The FRC's mission is to improve the agency's coordination so that farm workers have equal access to health, educational and public services available to all; collect data on farm worker issues and provide information and analysis to the governor and other state office; and engage in educational and outreach activities regarding farm workers. IMC and ILA farm worker law unit are involved in this committee.

Terry Reilly Health Services, founded in 1971 as a primary care service non profit agency, provides services to low income families including farm workers. The Terry Reilly Health Services includes a network of four clinics located in Nampa, Homedale, Marsing and Boise. As mentioned earlier Terry Reilly has a staff position of a farm worker service coordinator for outreach purposes. Elena Rodriguez who serves in this position is constantly on the road visiting Idaho labor camps and providing health prevention information and assisting mono Spanish speaking farm workers become familiar with health services in the area.

Beyond these few organizations which provide services to agricultural workers there are the standard federal and state offices such as the Idaho State Department of Education-Migrant Education Program, Idaho Department of Employment, Health and Welfare, and others. One quickly recognizes that the organizational infrastructure directly providing services to agriculture workers is significantly less developed in Idaho in comparison to Oregon and Washington.

◆ Agricultural Workers in Oregon

Agriculture is Oregon's second largest industry with a grossing farm sales of over $2.6 billion a year. Oregon's agriculture product mix is diverse. This crop diversity is reinforced by agricultural areas such as the Willamette Valley where more than 170 different crops are grown. It's agricultural products such as peppermint, hazelnuts hops, cherries, onions, strawberries and others maintain national level production ranking.[25]

Oregon maintains seven major farming areas. These include the Willamette Valley (which represents the largest agriculture area in Oregon), Grant Pass/Medford area, The Dalles/Hood River area, Redmond/Bend area, Klamath Falls area, Hermiston/Pendleton/La Grand area, and the Ontario area. These farming areas attract the bulk of agriculture workers to Oregon. Agriculture related work runs between April and November. The strawberry harvest which attracts the largest amount of workers peaks out in June. June and July represents the months attracting largest number of workers. An Oregon Employment Division (OED) publication titled "Agriculture Wages and Employment Information" issued in 1992 estimates that Oregon's seasonal farm worker population in 1991 was about 34,200. This particular publication has not been updated. Figures in other OED research and statistics report indicate a declining estimated number of seasonal workers in subsequent years. In 1992 statewide estimates dipped down to 26,870 and down to 25,106 in 1993. According to this report seasonal farm workers are categorized as local or migrant. In another report issued by the Agricultural Experiment Station at Oregon State University, Special Report 910 published in 1993 indicates that foreign labor is the backbone of Oregon's seasonal labor force. Mexican descent workers comprise the bulk of these workers. This is in contrast to the state of Washington where local agricultural workers represent the majority group.

This figure of 34,200 seems low in comparison to other figures which cite agricultural workers in Oregon numbering up to 128,564 as reported in the Atlas of State Profiles which Estimate Number of Migrant and Seasonal Farm workers (1990). These estimates are extremely difficult to reconcile since the estimate gaps are very significant. This estimation gap is also found in Washington. The methods of counting agricultural workers as stated earlier varies from source to source.

Based on data from the OED, agricultural workers in Oregon generally earn about $5.00 per hour. *Pineros y Campesinos Unidos del Noroeste* (PCUN), a agricultural workers union based in Woodburn, Oregon, concluded from a 1989 PCUN wage survey that workers involved in piece-rate work earn less than the minimum wage.

Oregon growers will continue to employ a consistent supply of agricultural workers. This labor need and supply create a number of issues critical for agricultural workers. It is important to recognize the numerous issues that impact the agricultural workers within this context of supply and demand of workers.

Issues Facing Agricultural Workers in Oregon

There are a number of issues facing agricultural workers in the State of Oregon in the 1990's. A significant issue facing agricultural workers in Oregon is the lack of collective bargaining legislation for agricultural workers. The absences of such legislation contribute to maintaining farm workers isolated, unorganized and exploited. In 1989 a senate bill was introduced but died in the Oregon senate. The battle to secure collective bargaining legislation will continue to be a future goal not only in Oregon but also in Idaho and Washington.

A second issue impacting agricultural workers in Oregon is the relatively low participation of agricultural workers in Oregon's only agricultural workers union, *Pineros y Campesinos Unidos del Noroeste* (PCUN) PCUN's fact sheet indicates its registered membership numbering 3,400 plus workers. Even though PCUN has spear headed an active and relative successful and progressive unionization initiative in Oregon, much of Oregon's agricultural workers fall beyond its membership. Additionally, PCUN's primary turf is restricted to the Willamette Valley. PCUN's influence is yet to have an impact in Oregon's other major agricultural areas. This may however be related to PCUN's brief 10 year existence, Oregon's climate towards agricultural worker rights and organizing, and the difficulty involved in organizing a mobile labor force. PCUN's leadership has worked hard in establishing the union as a substitive labor initiative in Oregon.

A third issue impacting agricultural workers in Oregon is the ever illusive illegibility for unemployment benefits. Related issues to unemployment coverage are concerns such as sick and/or vacation pay, overtime pay, and other benefits usually available to workers in other employment sectors. In Washington most agricultural workers do not obtain employment benefits because they don't work the number of required hours to qualify for eligibility. Attempts to secure employment coverage for agricultural workers in Idaho met with failure recently. Agricultural workers in the Northwest including Oregon view the unemployment coverage as issue needing attention.

A fourth issue facing Oregon agricultural workers is housing. This issue of housing transcends the entire Northwest. During the 1960's Oregon instituted minimal standards for labor camp housing. Some farmers upgraded their housing units others not wanting to make the expense discontinued or bulldozed their camps. While the number of agricultural workers increased, camp housing declined in subsequent decades. Many farm worker families sought out housing in the surrounding communities. During the 1990's the shortage of available housing in general and in particularly affordable housing has created overcrowding, sub-standard housing, rent gouging and housing discrimination in Oregon.

According to a housing survey produced in 1991 by CASA of Oregon entitled "Oregon Farm Labor Housing Survey," 30 of the 31 farm labor camps in Marion county that can house a maximum of 1,268 occupants only 10% met all OR-OSHA requirements for labor camps. Permanent farm labor housing in Marion county has recently been expanded by the Housing Development Corporation construction of the *"Nuevo Amanecer"* complex which houses about 48 farm worker families. This new housing complex is only the second complex built in Woodburn in the past two decades.

According to an assessment of farm worker housing completed in 1993 by the Oregon Housing Associated Services there is a need of 2,259 housing units for year round and local seasonal workers. The report also indicated that an additional 6,584 housing units were needed to serve Migrant workers. Suffice to point out the critical housing needs are reflected in a community located in the center of one of Oregon's major agricultural areas.

A fifth issue confronting Oregon agricultural workers is pesticides in the work place. This issues affects agricultural workers regardless of locale. Advocates of agricultural workers argue that workers should have adequate knowledge and training in handling and applying pesticides. It is critical that methods of documenting toxic poisoning of workers resulting from uninformed use of pesticide chemicals and inadequate protective clothing be implemented and enforced. It is equally important to view issues of pesticides from a health, legal, economic, consumer, and workers' perspective. It is critical to acknowledge that many of the chemicals used in agriculture have yet to be fully studied for their potential long term harm on workers. PCUN is active in pursuing initiatives to better inform workers regarding pesticides. In 1992, Marion Moses, a well known pesticide expert, provided information and training to PCUN staff and interested agricultural workers.

A sixth issue affecting agricultural workers in Oregon is the PCUN boycott against two food processors in Oregon, NORPAC and Steinfeld, begun in 1992 and still going strong in 1994. Numerous organization in Oregon and in the Northwest have given support to PCUN's boycott including the United Farm Workers of America and the United Farm Workers Union of Washington State. Much work has been done on this boycott front by PCUN.

These are a few selective issues confronting Oregon's agricultural workers. It is useful for the reader to be better informed about the organizations which advocate in the behalf of agricultural workers in Oregon. The following is a selective listing and brief discussion of some of these organizations. This listing is intended to be a representative sampling rather than exhaustive.

Organizations Serving Agricultural Workers In Oregon

There are a number of organizations in Oregon that agricultural workers seek out to meet a variety of needs. These include the following.

Pineros y Campesinos Unidos del Noroeste (PCUN) founded in 1985, is an Oregon union dedicated to organize farm workers, nursery and reforestation workers. The union's fact sheet cites that it has a membership of about 3,400. The overwhelming majority are Mexican or Central American. PCUN's headquarters is located in Woodburn, Oregon. This progressive union advocates on agricultural related legislation; organizes workers; produces a newsletter and a radio program (La Hora Campesina) which informs farm workers and supporters about PCUN's initiatives; and a number of other services to agricultural workers. PCUN was instrumental in overturning an Oregon anti-picketing law which was in affect for almost 30 years. PCUN is still a maturing union but it has clearly marked its commitment to empowering agricultural workers in Oregon.

Farm worker Housing Development Corporation, a recently founded organization formed in 1991 by a coalition of agencies and community people in Woodburn, Oregon, is striving to expand the availability of farm worker housing. Towards this end FHDC constructed a housing complex called *"Nuevo Amanecer"* (New Dawn) in Woodburn. This represents the first housing project for farm workers since the 1970's.

Oregon Human Development Corporation was established in 1979 in Oregon as an extension of the California Human Development Corporation founded in 1969. This agency is presently in operation in California, Oregon, Washington and Hawaii. The Oregon Human Development Corporation has its headquarters in Portland, Oregon and has field offices in Hillsboro, Woodburn, Klamath Falls, Ontario, and Meford. OHDC's main work focuses on employment training of farm workers striving to leave agriculture work. OHDC also provides job placement, life and basic skills, and other support services. OHDC networks with state agencies, emergency shelters, food banks, churches and other social service organizations providing assistance to farm workers.

Migrant/Indian Coalition was founded in 1971 as a private non-profit statewide organization with its headquarters in Woodburn, Oregon. MIC provides a variety of services. Some of its services are directly targeted to benefit agricultural worker families. MIC operates Migrant Head Start at eight locations including Woodburn, Hillsboro, Gresham, Hermiston, Ontario, Klamath Falls, and Parkdale near Hood River, Oregon. MIC is funded through the Children Services Division in Oregon and Federal migrant funds. Migrant

Head Start Initiative is funded for 1,600 child care slots throughout Oregon. MIC is also involved in providing Pre-School services, health and dental services, some parenting classes and Even Start, a family literacy program with the school district.

Oregon Legal Services-Farm Worker Unit, established in the mid 1970's, is a subunit that focuses on working with agricultural workers. OLS has twelve sites throughout the state but only has farm worker sub units in Pendleton, Ontario, Woodburn, Hillsboro, and Oregon City. The majority of the legal cases this organization deals with involves wage dispute cases where a worker has complained that the agreed wages in part or whole have not been paid. Some other issues that may be work related including housing or work recruitment issues are also dealt with by this organization. This organization is similar to the Evergreen Legal Services in Washington and the Idaho Legal Services Migrant Farm Worker Law unit.

There are a number of farm worker clinics in Oregon including *La Clínica de Salud* in Woodburn, *Clínica de Cariño* in Hood River, *Clínica del Valle* in Medford, and *La Clínica Virginia Garcia* in Hillsboro. These Clinics provide a variety of primary care health services to farm workers. For instance *La Clínica de Salud* in Woodburn, Oregon provides maternity, medical, and dental services. It also runs the WIC initiative. It makes referrals to other medical units. The Clinic has a staff that includes three mid wives, three doctors and about eight plus bilingual nurses. Most people pay on a sliding fee scale based on income. The overwhelming majority are farm worker families.

Hispanic Elderly Farm Worker Project or *La Fuente de la Amistad* is an interesting initiative established in 1990 in Hilsboro, Oregon under the Area Agency on Aging in Washington County. The project targets Latino elderly of whom the majority come from a farm worker background. The project tries to serve as bridge between the Latino elderly and the various organizations and agencies serving low income elderly. The project uses a cadre of elders who serve as peer mentors to clients. These mentors guide clients through the maze of service agencies including medical offices, food stamps, social security, and other critical services. The project serves about 200 elders most of them who are or have been agricultural workers. This is a unique initiative whose funding will soon run out in 1994. It is hoped that the mainstream aging agency will assume the services begun by the project. The project's uniqueness warranted documentation even though the project will formerly end later this year.

Beyond these Organization there exists state and federal agencies, churches and food banks that also assist agricultural workers.

Summary

Agriculture in the Northwest is a significant industry sector. Much of this agriculture is labor intensive. Farm worker labor in the Northwest consist of agricultural workers that live locally, workers that travel within the State to seek work; and workers that travel from out of state.

Throughout the decades, each of the Northwest states have spawn community base organizations and service base agencies

In spite of these organizations and agencies, farmworkers continue to face significant issues concerning, income levels, health, exposure to pesticides housing, absence of collective bargaining and other critical issues requiring attention and resolution.

Agricultural workers have historically been marginalized nationally and regionally, including the Northwest. It is critical that marginalized agricultural workers be afforded the opportunity for self improvement. It is ironic that the hundreds and thousands of farmworkers that toil in the fields and orchards to place food on the table for millions of Americans, have yet to be afforded a place at the table.

Agricultural workers throughout the U.S. including the Northwest seek to be self-determining. Like all Americans they seek to enhance their lives, work and contribute to the general community.

Endnotes

1. Idaho Department of Commerce, *Idaho Facts* (Boise, Idaho: Division of Economic Development, 1992), p. 51.
2. Oregon State University Experiment Station, *IRCA and Oregon Agricultural Industries Special Report 9*, 10 April 1993, p. 147.
3. Washington State Employment Security Department, *Agriculture, Forestry and Fishing Employment in Washington State*, July 1992, p. IV.
4. Patricia K. Ourada, *Migrant Workers in Idaho* (Boise: Boise State University, 1980), p. 9.
5. G. Thomas Edwards, *"Irrigation in Eastern Washington, 1906-1911,"* Northwest Quarterly Vol 72 No. 3 July 1981, p. 113.
6. Oregon State University Experiment Station, *IRCA and Oregon Agricultural Industries Special Report 9*, 10 April 1993, p. 148.
7. Lawrence A. Cardoso, *Mexican Emigration to the United States, 1897-1931* (Tucson: University of Arizona, 1980), p. 38.
8. Don S. Willner, "The Forgotten People," Greater Portland Commerce, October 1964, p. 15.
9. "U.S. To Open Extensive Migrant Anti-Poverty Program In Oregon," *Portland* (Ore.) *Oregonian* April 8, 1964, p. 12.
10. Governor's Migratory Labor Committee, *The Governor's Migratory labor Committee, 1955-1966* (Boise: Employment Security Agency, 1966), pp. 1-10.
11. Interview with Tomas Villanueva Sunnyside, WA 19 December, 1993.
12. "Migrant Union Due for Oregon," *Salem* (Ore.) *Capital Journal* May 16, 1968, p. 1.
13. "Chicano Unionization Campaign to Heighten," Salem (Ore.) Capital Journal September 25, 1970. p. 24.
14. PCUN Update Issue #7 August 1991, p. 8.
15. "Brown Says Farmers or Laborers Must Act to Quiet Disturbances," *Boise* (Idaho) *Idaho Statesman*, 15 June 1971.
16. Washington State Employment Security Department, *Agricultural, Forestry and Fishing Employment in Washington State*, July 1992, p. 10.
17. *Ibid*, pp. 8, 9,
18. *Ibid*, pp. 14,17.
19. United Farm Workers of Washington State "Fact Sheet" Granger, WA. n.d., n.p.
20. Office of Rural and Farmworker Housing "Housing Needs and Household Characteristics of Agricultural Worker Households Living Year-Round in Surveyed Areas" Yakima, WA., n.d. n.p.
21. Idaho Department of Commerce, *Idaho Economic and Business: Windows of Opportunity* Boise, Idaho 1993.
22. Interview with Phil Bowman, Idaho Department of Employment Boise, Idaho 17 July 1994.
23. Idaho Commission on Hispanic Affairs, 1993 Spring Quarterly Meeting; presentation and discussion on Workers' Compensation for Farmworker Twin Falls, Idaho April 17, 1993, n.p.

24. Idaho Department of Employment Agricultural Labor Bureau, "Findings: Migrant Seasonal Farm Workers Survey 1990" Boise, Idaho, p. 5.
25. Oregon State University Experiment Station, *IRCA and Oregon Agricultural Industries Special Report 9*, 10 April 1993, p. 148.

Bibliography

◆ Books

Cardoso, Lawrence A. *Mexican Emigration to the United States, 1897-1931.* Tucson, Arizona: University of Arizona, 1980

Gonzales, Juan L. *Mexican and Mexican American Farm Workers.* New York, NY.: Praeger Publishers, 1985.

Guither, Harold D. *Heritage of Plenty: A Guide to the Economic History and Development of U.S. Agriculture.* Danville, Illinois: The Interstate Printers and Publishers, Inc. 1972.

Ourada, Patricia K. *Migrant Workers in Idaho.* Boise, Idaho: Boise State University, 1980.

Valdes, Dennis Nodin. *Al Norte: Agriculture Workers in the Great Lakes Region, 1917-1970.* Austin, Texas: University of Texas, Press, 1991.

◆ Journals

Edwards, G. Thomas "Irrigation in Eastern Washington, 1906-1911." *Northwest Quarterly* Vol. 72. No. 3 (July 1981), p. 113.

Willner, Don S. "The Forgotten People." *Greater Portland Commerce* (October 1964), p. 15.

◆ Newspapers

"Migrant Union Due for Oregon." *Salem* (Ore.) *Capital Journal,* 16 May 1968 Pg. 1.

"Chicano Unionization Campaign to Heighten." *Salem* (Ore.) *Capital Journal,* 25 September 1970, p. 24

"Brown Says Farmers Or Laborers Must Act To Quiet Disturbances." *Boise* (Idaho) *Idaho Statesman,* 15 June 1971.

"A Movement Grows In Treasure Valley." *Boise* (Idaho) *Intermountain Observer,* 28 November 1970, p. 20.

"Toward a Pluralistic Society In Treasure Valley." *Boise* (Idaho) *Intermountain Observer,* 28 November 1970, p. 20.

"U.S. to open Extensive Migrant Anti-Poverty Program In Oregon." *Portland* (Ore.) *Oregonian,* 8 April 1964, p. 12.

◆ Government Documents

Governor's Migratory Labor Committee *The Governor's Migratory Labor Committee, 1955-1966.* Boise, Idaho Employment Security Agency 1966.
Idaho Department of Commerce. *Idaho Facts* Boise, Idaho Division of Economic Development 1992.
Oregon State University Experiment Station *IRCA and Oregon Agricultural Industries Special Report 9*, 10 Oregon State April 1993.
Washington State Employment Security Department *Agriculture, Forestry and Fishing Employment in Washington State* Olympia, WA. July 1992.

◆ Unpublished Materials

Idaho Commission on Hispanic Affairs 1993 Spring Quarterly Meeting; Presentation and Discussion on Workers' Compensation for Farmworkers Twin Falls, Idaho April 17, 1993.
Idaho Department of Employment Agricultural Labor Bureau. "Findings: Migrant Seasonal Farm Workers Survey 1990. Boise Idaho.
Office of Rural and Farmworker Housing "Housing Needs and Household Characteristics of Agricultural Worker Households Living Year-Round in Surveyed Areas" Yakima, WA., n.d. n.p.
United Farm Worker of Washington State "Fact Sheet" Granger, WA. n.d., n.p.

◆ Interviews

Bowman, Phil, Idaho Department of employment, Boise, Idaho Interview, 17 July 1994.
Villanueva Tomas, Sunnyside, WA. Interview, 19 December, 1993.

5

An Educational Mode for Teaching Chicano Students in the Pacific Northwest

Ricardo Garcia ◆ *Anita Ordonez*

Chicano students attend school for ordinary reasons to learn what it takes to be an American and to learn to use English. Some hope to be on the volleyball or football team, to act in a school play, to raise a lamb for 4-H Club, and to make friends. Chicanos are whole human beings who attend school with naive ideas about the world, fears about the present, and hopes for the future. Like most people, they want to be happy, live a good life, and make a contribution to the family or community that succors them. Education for Chicano students in the Pacific Northwest should empower them to be fully participatory in their communities, the nation, and the world. Empowerment to be a viable adult should not come at the price of cultural alienation. There is no justifiable rationale for denying these students the chance to speak Spanish and English. There is no inherent contradiction between being Mexican and American in culture. There exist numerous studies and reports highlighting the critical educational status and problems Chicano students face in our schools.

On the National level, reports such as "Resolving A Crisis In Education" produced by the Thomas Rivera Center, a national institute for policy studies, located in Claremont California, points out some of the national realities of the status of Latino education. The report cites that nearly 12% of the nation's Latinos do not complete fifth grade. Almost half do not finish high school. Fewer than 10% complete a B.A. or higher degree. The report goes on to detail other facts about Latinos in education in the 1990's.

The National Council de la Raza, (NCLR) a national Latino advocate organization based in Washington D.C. also lament the educational status of Latinos in it's Bulletin Educational Network News and its National report entitled "Hispanic Education: a statistical portrait, 1990."

In the Northwest, similar reports point out the poor educational status of Chicanos/Latinos in the region. These include the "Report of the Task Force on Hispanic Education" (Idaho); "The Master Plan for Improvement of the Education of Hispanic Youth" (Washington State); and the Oregon Commission on Hispanic Affairs' Biennial Report 1991-93. Each of the reports cite and detail the inadequate educational status of Chicanos/Latinos in the Northwest.

Acknowledging the poor educational status of Chicanos/Latinos highlighted by the aforementioned reports, it is critical that educational proposals be developed to address the educational issues and needs of Chicanos/Latinos in the Northwest.

This chapter lays a foundation for educating Chicano students in kindergarten through the twelfth grade in schools throughout the Pacific Northwest—Idaho, Oregon, and Washington. Even though the educational experiences of Chicanos in colleges, universities, and other institutions of higher learning are important, we believe the K-12 academic foundations of Chicano students must take the highest priority. Without a thorough K-12 academic foundation in the traditional academic disciplines, Chicano students can hardly hope to take full advantage of the many opportunities that will be made available to them, especially in our current era of rapid technological innovations.

Operational assumptions appropriate for the education of Chicano students in the Northwest are described in this chapter. Aspects of the student's cultural heritage and social context are interwoven within the chapter which ends with a discussion of strategies and methodologies useful for providing Chicano students an empowering educational experience.

Educational Aims for Chicano Students

The education of Chicano students in the Pacific Northwest should provide the full panoply of knowledge, skills, and attitudes essential for full participation as politically active, culturally viable, and economically prosperous citizens within the United States and the global community. Educational empowerment should not coerce Chicanos to surrender all aspects of their home cultural values, beliefs, and languages. Rather, the schools should assist Chicanos in the development of biculturalism, synthesizing the best of Mexican and American cultures and enabling students to function within the broader Latino communities of the world as well as within the mainstream communities of the United States. We believe that full bilingualism and full biculturalism are desirable educational aims paramount for the growth and development of Chicano students.

Empowerment aims for Chicano students correspond to the historically validated aims of education elucidated by notable leaders and educators, such as Donaciano Vigil, George I. Sanchez, Horace Mann and John Dewey. Horace Mann is credited as the individual responsible for the implementation of the American common schools, the roots of our public school system. He believed if education of the youth were left entirely to the resources of parents, only the children of the rich could be educated (circa the 1840's), creating a society ruled by the wealthy. Mann proposed the idea—a free, public education should be the birthright of every American for equity reasons:

> *Education . . . is the great equalizer of the conditions of men the balance wheel of the social machinery . . . . This idea . . . gives each man the independence and the means by which he can resist the selfishness of other men (Noll and Kelley 1970).*

In the Southwest, the first governor of the Territory of New Mexico, Donaciano Vigil (1847) echoed Mann's philosophy in his first address to the territorial, legislative body in January of 1847:

> *The world generally is progressive and how can we avail ourselves of the advancement unless the [Chicano] people are educated? (Vigil, 1847).*

Education as the *great equalizer* is a vision of education as a liberating force which empowers individuals to take advantage of opportunites. Educated individuals can often create their own opportunities and control their fates to a larger extent than the uneducated. Education allows a person, or a group, to mold and shape their destinies. The expression, "knowledge is power" is more than a flippant cliché.

The idea that education should be a liberating force in the lives of Chicano people is reflected in the works of the highly respected Chicano educator George I. Sanchez. Dr. Sanchez was a pioneering proponent of quality education for Chicanos. He worked tirelessly for the improvement of schools and development of programs responsive to the needs of Chicano students. His book, *Forgotten People*, is the first book in the United States that directly addressed the educational needs of Chicanos. The book places educational needs within the context of the sociocultural realities of Chicanos in Northern New Mexico of the 1930's. Sixty years later, his words still ring true:

> *The curriculum of the educational agencies becomes, then, the magna carta of social and economic rehabilitation; the teacher, the advance agent of a new social order (Sanchez, 1940).*

Sanchez viewed schools as agencies of empowerment and teachers as one of the most important factors for the empowerment of Chicanos. Chicano educators have not waivered from the vision that quality education is the only kind of education acceptable for Chicano students. But, quality education does not mean more of the same old stuff. Here quality education refers to teachers and programs providing Chicano students an array of full literacy in American English and Mexican Spanish.

John Dewey extended the notion of education for individual empowerment to include education as political empowerment. Education is not only necessary for the benefit of individuals, but it is necessary for the survival of democratic societies. In *Democracy and Education* (1916) Dewey explained the interlocking nature of democracy and education. Democracy without education, cannot exist. For the people of a democracy to rule, to be in control of their government and their institutions, they must be educated, a thesis summarized in Thomas Jefferson's saying that if " . . . a nation expects to be ignorant and free . . . it expects what never was and never will be" (Padover 1946).

An educated citizenry is crucial for the perpetuation of a democratic society. Just as education benefits individuals, it benefits and empowers individuals to be politically active citizens within their communities, states, the nation, and the world. Democratic communities operate on an implicit social contract—individuals enter into an unspoken agreement but nonetheless binding agreement with their respective communities. As children, we come to expect to be given the protection of the adult community. Along with protection, the adults prepare their youth to take their place in the adult community. The contract has a *quid pro quo*—social responsiblity. As adults, the erstwhile children, should provide the next generation the same empowering skills for adult living and protection provided to them, which is possible only when adults are socially responsible.

Chicanos are an integral part of the human communities of the Northwest and need to be incorporated into the social context. Education is one of the key answers to incorporation. The basic education of Chicano students should empower them to be 1) capable of life long learning, 2) able to lead their lives in directions they desire as culturally viable individuals, and 3) able to act as literate and politically active citizens. As an educational aim, life long learning refers to the students' ability to learn a vocation or pursue further education at colleges, universities, or technical vocational institutes for economic gain and/or personal pleasure. The aim also pertains to the students' ability to teach themselves by utilizing libraries, museums, computer data banks, or any other knowledge depositories. Twelve years of schooling should provide Chicano students an education with breadth and depth in the traditional areas of languages, literature, mathematics, sciences, the social sciences, the fine or performing arts, health and physical education. Depth and breadth should be especially evident in the teaching of language, literature, mathematics, science, and the social sciences so the students are enabled to use these academic disciplines to enhance their lives in meaningful ways. The social sciences, in particular those areas that teach responsible self-government and political efficacy, should be permeated throughout the school's curriculum in all grades.

Self direction, the second aim, refers to the students' ability to exercise options after high school graduation. The desire here is to create persons who are autonomous and self sufficient, and self directed, able to initiate action to fulfill their life aims. Twelve years of schooling should provide Chicano students the ability to make a wide range of choices regarding a vocation as well as a vocation. Educational curricula and programs should be structured to include options that students as adults may select vocational, technical, or professional career paths as well as cultural orientations.

The third aim, political literacy and activism, is a crucial, fundamental educational aim within a democratic society. Students must know about the historical and political development of Chicano culture in the United States. The aim is especially pertinent to Chicano students because Chicanos, along with other Hispanic groups, are fast becoming a major demographic and political force in American life.

Do life long learning, self direction, cultural viability and political activism sound like idealistic, unachievable aims? The goals may be idealist, but they are achievable. All of education is idealistic. Education presumes that human beings are perfectable, that they can be molded and shaped to achieve beauty, harmony, love, and faith in the future. Public education in the United States functions on this idealistic assumption: all students are perfectable, they are educable, as in Adler's (1982) saying "[t]here are no unteachable children. There are only schools and teachers and parents who fail to teach them." What is a desirable education for students in one place in the country is desirable in other places, i.e., we reside in one country; the future citizens must all be prepared to assume the responsibilities of maintaining a democratic way of life. While lifelong learning, self direction, cultural viability, and political activism are idealistic goals, they are quintessential educational aims for future citizens—Chicano students, *también*.

◆ Uniqueness of Individuals

While there are many different opinions about the educational needs of Chicano students, there exists a fundamental consensus among Chicano educators—Chicano students are unique individuals. They should be viewed as unique. Like all students, some like schools, others do not; some are competitive, others are cooperative; some are sad or glad; some are tall, short, agile, clumsy, thin. Their bio-rhythmns are like most other people's—some are *night* persons, liking to work at night, others are *day* persons, liking to work or play by day. Some are curious or not too curious; some speak softly, others speak loudly; some are timid, others are assertive. They are not problems needing to be solved nor is the Mexican Spanish many speak a "foreign" language in North America, although at times, Chicanos are treated as foreigners in the Pacific Northwest.

Chicano students reside throughout the Northwest. They are found in population centers in the southern Idaho, and in eastern Washington, and in the Willamette Valley of Oregon.

Table 5.1. ◆ Idaho Statistics for Fall 1992-1993 Chicanos in School

School District	Total Enrollment	# of Spanish as Home Language	%	# of LEP
American Falls	1658	327	19.7	285
Blackfoot	4735	483	10	287
Burley	5494	610	11	157
Buhl	1624	152	.9	152
Caldwell	4732	1231	26	315
Jerome	2920	261	8.9	123
Marsing	682	171	25	123
Nampa	8139	425	5	395
Rigby (Jefferson)	4089	368	8.9	118
Rupert (Minadoka)	5411	1300	24	500
Twin Falls	7050	288	4	93

Source: Idaho State Department of Education

In 1992-1993, of the 182,792 total public school enrollment in Idaho, 9,587 reported Spanish as their home lanaguage. Of these 4,905 were assessed for English language abilities and 4,129 were found LEP. Out of the total enrollment in Washington's schools for the 1992-1993 year, 57,521 were identified as Latino, the majority being Chicano students. The Washington Department of Education provided the following data about the state's Latino students.

Table 5.2. ◆ Latinos in Washington's Schools, 1992-1993

County	District	# of Latinos	% of Latinos
Adams	Othello	1709	60.86
Benton	Paterson	12	19.05
Benton	Prosser	958	36.99
Chelan	Manson	314	51.82
Chelan	Lake Chelan	261	22.44
Chelan	Wenatchee	981	15.96
Douglas	Orondo	191	68.71
Douglas	Bridgeport	266	46.42
Dougals	Palisades	54	84.38
Franklin	Pasco	3536	46.38
Franklin	N. Franklin	682	38.90
Grant	Wahlukr	417	50.98
Grant	Quincy	765	40.48
Grant	Warden	420	50.12
Grant	Royal	379	39.94
Grant	Moses Lake	1208	21.40
Klickitat	White Salmon	138	10.53
Okanogan	Okanogan	113	11.44
Okanogan	Brewster	512	54.64
Okanogan	Pateros	59	19.67
Okanogan	Tonasket	136	12.29
Okanogan	Oroville	159	17.71
Skagit	Burlington Edison	351	11.70
Skagit	Mt. Vernon	894	18.43
Walla Walla	Walla Walla	1054	16.77
Walla Walla	College Place	256	32.28
Walla Walla	Touchet	67	32.84
Walla Walla	Prescott	80	35.87
Whatcom	Lynden	262	12.07
Yakima	Union Gap	127	24.61
Yakima	Naches Valley	149	10.70
Yakima	Yakima	3977	30.71
Yakima	E. Valley Yakima	278	12.87
Yakima	Mabton	697	84.18
Yakima	Grandview	1659	62.51
Yakima	Sunnyside	3062	67.62
Yakima	Toppenish	1995	66.02
Yakima	Highland	377	38.04
Yakima	Granger	782	70.13
Yakima	Zillah	238	21.42
Yakima	Wapato	1585	51.65
Yakima	Mt. Adams	191	16.65

Source: Washington Department of Education

Chicanos students are also concentrated in various school districts in Oregon.

Table 5.3. ◆ Latinos in Selective School Districts in Oregon, 1993

County	District	# of Hispanic
Hood River	Hood River	880
Malheur	Jordan	866
Malheur	Nyssa	620
Marion	Salem/Keizer	2,567
Marion	Woodburn	1,542
Multnomah	Portland	2,290
Polk	Central	604
Umatilla	Hermiston	736
Umatilla	Umatilla	270
Umatilla	Milton/Freewater	382
Wasco	The Dalles	265
Washington	Hillsboro	901
Washington	Forest Grove	803
Washington	Beaverton	2,389

Source: 1993-94 Summary of organization, students and staff in Oregon Public School

Before World War I, Mexican citizens were recruited to the Northwest to work on the railroads or farms as field workers. Others were brought here as a result of the *Bracero* Program of the 1940's. Some remained with their initial occupations as farm workers. Most have taken other lines of work. Contemporary Chicanos include "settled in" migrant families who work the fields and orchards throughout the Northwest but hold residence in one of the three Northwest states. Others are second and third generation Chicanos who work in a variety of occupations.

Because Idaho, Oregon, and Washington are located on the northern end of the agricultural migratory stream, there are some Chicano students whose residence is in other states. These students are highly mobile, appearing in Northwest schools during the early Fall and late Spring semesters. For the migrant elementary age children, summer programs are sometimes provided by the schools. Some of these students may not be U.S. citizens. The overwhelming majority of Chicano students in the Pacific Northwest schools—98%—are American citizens as are their parents who are thereby entitled to an equal educational opportunity. Under federal mandate, the small number who are not American citizens are still entitled to equal educational opportunities who should not be charged tuition to attend school.

The fundamental consensus that Chicano students are like most other students provides a teaching axiom: teaching Chicano students is no different than teaching other students. This does not mean Chicano students are exactly the same as non Chicano students. In fact, treating students as though they were all alike denies students their unique individuality. Good teaching requires that teachers understand and respect the individuality of all their students. To be effective, teachers need to be sensitive to the student's individual uniqueness which forms within a cultural context. The teacher must have an understanding of the student's culture and its attendant language. Genuine respect and understanding are not possible without a knowledge of the student's sociocultural background.

True understanding and respect do not come automatically when teachers are not members of the student's culture. Even when teachers are members of the student's culture, true understanding and respect are attributes that take much time and energy to translate into teaching behaviors. The best methodologies using the latest technologies are of little import without a true understanding and respect for Chicanos students.

◆ Cultural Bases of Chicano Students

Chicano students are all unique human beings who will develop their own unique cultural lifestyles, i.e., personal cultures. Of course, their personal lifestyles will be founded on the cultural bases of their homes and communities. Thus, we will be speaking of various characteristics regarding Chicano students in this chapter with the caveat that we the authors and the readers—must understand: the following comments about Chicano students are general descriptions and not absolute truths. We must not stereotype Chicano students. We must remember they are all unique individuals fully capable of learning anything taught in school.

In the past, Chicano students were sometimes described as *culturally deprived.* (Nieto,1992, 164) This prevailing attitude among educators was because some Chicano students did not exhibit behaviors of mainstream, Anglo students. They were deprived of a culture—what an impossibility! Human existence is based on culture. Life would not be possible without a culture. Now educators realize that exhibition of non mainstream behaviors is a function of cultural differences (García 1991). Chicano students are the progeny of one of the very oldest and most native cultures of North America.

They are the progeny of the *Indio-Hispanic* synthesis, i.e., the culture that evolved in Mexico as a result of Spanish colonization of the Aztec and other indigenous Indian tribes,1519-1821 A.D. The Spanish colonists attempted to impose their institutions and culture upon the indigenous people with the intent of transforming the indigenous people into Spaniards. The cultural resilience of the indigenous people their cultures had existed in North and South America for many centuries before the arrival of the Spaniards—overwhelmed the Spaniards and transformed them! Spaniards were transformed into cultural beings who combined aspects of *Indio* culture with aspects of the Spanish culture. McWilliams described the *Indio-Hispano* synthesis as "Indian in feeling, Spanish in plan." (McWilliams 1948: 72.)

The emergence of Mexican culture greatly influenced the development of what we call the American West—all the states residing west of the Mississippi River. Ranching and mining were the two major economic institutions of the early American West. Both of these institutions were fully developed by Mexican *vaqueros* (former African or Indian slaves turned cowboy) or *mineros* (miners) many years before the Americans migrated into the West. Anglo American pioneers found cattle ranching and mining fully developed by the Mexican people. The Americans simply took what they saw, translated the activities into English, and commenced to ranch and mine. (See Otis E. Young,Jr. *Western Mining* and William H. Dusenberry *The Mexican Mesta: The Administration of Ranching in Colonial Mexico.*)

Mexican culture also made its mark on western architecture, food, language, geography (place names) and laws regulating water usage. (See David Weber *The Spanish Frontier in North America*; Harold Bentley *A Dictionary of Spanish Terms in English.*) At least three distinctive architectual styles emerged from the *Indio-Hispano* synthesis for homes and buildings, these are the "Santa Fe" style, the "California Misssion" style, and the "Spanish Revival" style, and one other style for homes, the "Ranch" style. Examples of these styles can be found in most states. The Kansas City Country Club Plaza and Flagler College in St. Augustine, Florida are examples of the "Spanish Revival" style. The structure of the ubiquitous ranch style house, which probably can be found in most states, is based on the ranch houses built on 18th Century Mexican *haciendas*. The noted American architect,Frank Lloyd Wright, was known to have admired how the Santa Fe style homes blended with their ecology so much so he organized a school of architecture in Phoenix, Arizona to take full advantage of the desert mountain terrain of the Salt River Valley.

American English is replete with words introduced by way of Spanish. In Bentley's *A Dictionary of Spanish Terms in English*, examples are given of Spanish words from A-Z that have become adopted common American English terms. Here is a small sample:

barbeque	*coyote*	*jerky*	*mustang*
bonanza	*canyon*	*lagoon*	*patio*
bravo	*creole*	*mahogany*	*ranch*
corral	*hammock*	*mesa*	*tornado*

Also found in most states, are the place names of counties, towns, cities, and some states that reflect the *Indio-Hispano synthesis*. Here are some examples:

States	**Towns/Cities**
Arizona	*Lavaca, Alabama*
California	*Chula, Arkansas*
Colorado	*Orofino, Idaho*
Florida	*Isleta, Ohio*
Nevada	*Ribera, New Mexico*
Texas	*Mariposa, New York*

As a result of the *Indio-Hispano* synthesis, basic American foods were cultivated from indigenous cultigens, such as maíz (corn), beans, and squash. Also, European cultigens were imported and adapted for North America, such as peaches, melons, and water melons. These American foods typify cultural borrowing and fusion. All the examples discussed above regarding architectual styles, words, place names, foods, ranches and mines are the result of cultural contact, borrowing, and fusion between the indigenous, pre-Columbian Native Americans, the early Spaniards, and later North Americans. As these peoples came into contact with each other, they adopted and adapted from each other and thereby transformed their own culture as well as the cultures of the others.

Cultural borrowing and fusion, reflected in the *Indio-Hispano* synthesis, is the epitome of the American experience, a culture formed from the contact, borrowing and fusion of many different cultures. While often called a melting pot in which all cultures are homogenized into a standard, single culture, the American experience is much more like an ever evolving kaleidoscopic pattern—variegated, changing patterns always enriched with the addition of new cultures. The introduction of Chicano culture in the Pacific Northwest will continue the kaleidoscopic pattern, transforming and enriching the culture of the Pacific Northwest. Two cultural values pervasive among Chicanos that will enhance the culture of the Pacific Northwest pertain to *familia* and *respeto*.

Familia and *respeto* are interrelated, fundamental beliefs. They are at the core of Chicano culture. *Familia* refers to family values that involve more than the immediate, nuclear family. It refers to grandparents, cousins, nephews, brothers, and God-children—the extended family. Embedded in Chicano culture is a very strong family orientation. The family structure is organized on traditional, patriarchal lines where elders are held in high esteem. The father acts as head of the family. The mother plays a very important mediating role in the family. Her opinions and feelings are highly respected. Siblings are encouraged to think of themselves as members of the family. They are taught to share their things and to cooperate with each other while doing house chores. They are taught that all of their behavior casts light on the family. To save face within the family, they are encouraged to do good rather than bad deeds. Chicano siblings learn to think of themselves as team players motivated to think in terms of what is good for the family rather than as individuals in pursuit of their own self interests without thought about the greater good.

Respeto refers to a pervasive sense that persons should respect the rights of others. Built into this pervasive sense of *respeto* is the attitude that persons in authority—teachers, judges, parents, older brothers or sisters, etc.—are to be shown deference. Furthermore, just as one must respect one's elders, one must respect one's equals. Both the orientations toward cooperative, team playing as well as respect for the rights of others have an influence on the way Chicano students behave in school. For example, to Chicano parents, acting out in school or giving the teacher a difficult time are disgraceful behaviors that reflect on the family's reputation. Parents admonish their children to respect teachers, obey what they say, and never talk back to them. *"A sus órdenes,"* [upon your orders] is a mandate parents teach their children to follow in school.

When Chicano students appear to shy away from personal accolades or when they attempt to draw attention away from themselves, they are not merely passive and uninterested in what the teacher is doing. They may be acting out what they were taught at home in the family. "Get along with your brothers and sisters. Share your things, and above all, do not draw attention to yourself. Everyone is equally important in the family." The beliefs in *familia* and *respeto* provide teachers ideal learning behaviors. The students are ready and willing to learn from their teachers, and they will conduct themselves as team players who respect the rights of others. Teachers need only to buttress these beliefs with high academic expectations. Chicano students will learn up to these high standards. Historically, too many teachers have held low academic standards for Chicano students which has resulted in "dumbing down." Chicano students have lived down to the low academic standards held for them by their teachers, which has resulted in low academic performance.

◆ Learning Style Preferences

Good teaching requires teachers to respect and understand the individuality of their students. In the classroom, teachers are challenged to understand how each of their students learn. Because each student is unique, teachers can expect each student to learn in unique ways. Yet, an emerging field of research indicates there are general learning patterns people use, which are referred to as cognitive or learning style preferences. (Woolfolk 1992 128 129) The research emerged from the studies of how people organize and perceive information. Results of the research indicate variations or differences in the way people perceive and organize information rather than indicating or reflecting levels of intelligence. Some individuals may perceive information globally and thereby organize information globally, i.e., they have a field dependent learning style. Others may perceive information analytically and thereby organize information in separate parts, i.e., a field-independent learning style (Dunn 1987). For example, a field-dependent student would require an explanation of an entire math problem from formula to the answer to understand it well. In reverse, a field-independent student would need to be given parts of the formula separately and then separately develop the answer to the math problem.

Other types of learning styles are being discovered almost daily. One such style is referred to as impulsive or reflective. The impulsive student works very quickly but may make many mistakes while the reflective student works very slowly and may make few mistakes. Both impulsive and reflective approaches have distinct advantages and disadvantages. Teachers need to know about the growing area of learning style preferences and the belief learning styles may be linked to cultural backgrounds. Some of the research on the learning style preferences of Chicano students reports a preference for the field dependent style which require holistic, concrete, and social contexts for learning (Buenning & Tollefson 1987). Other studies report it is the cooperative, family structure that causes Chicano students to prefer cooperative learning within a social context (Vasquez 1990).

It is important not over generalizing about cognitive styles and cultural differences. This is a new, evolving area of research where there exists more questions than answers. The research coupled with experience shows that Chicano students—like all other students—learn differently. Teachers are challenged to be sensitive to the way(s) their Chicano students learn and to adjust their teaching styles to accommodate the students rather than expecting the students to adjust to the teacher's preferred teaching style.

◆ From Monolingualism to Bilingualism

Much confusion exists about Chicano bilingualism. In the past, Chicano bilingualism was viewed as a pathology that retarded the educational development of Chicanos. In Good's (1945) *A Dictionary of Education* bilingualism was described as "speaking of two different languages . . . believed by some authorities to complicate the development of language functions in the child."

The pathological view was based on faulty research revealing more about the researcher's prejudices than Chicano bilingualism. More recent research findings indicate that learning difficulties experienced by some Chicanos are a function of complex factors and should not be attributed to single causes, such as bilingualism (Cummins & Miramontes). In fact, bilingualism can serve to enhance academic achievement and learning in general. (Galambos & Goldin Meadow 1990: 1-56.)

There is a perception that all Chicano students are bilingual speakers of Spanish and English. Often Chicano students are referred to as *bilingual students* without regard to their actual language abilities. To some educators, the mere fact students have Spanish surnames implies the student is bilingual. Yet, there are Chicano students with Anglo surnames, such as Bird or McReynolds, who are Chicano in culture and who speak Spanish as well as English. The Anglo surnames occur for various reasons, such as marriage. Or, in Mexico, due to immigration from Ireland, Germany and some Asian countries, Mexican citizens retain their "foreign" surnames although they are Mexican in citizenship and culture. Often Chicano students reside in homes where Spanish is spoken more than English. The students may or may not speak in Spanish. In some homes the students serve as English interpreters for the parents and grandparents. In other homes, the parents choose to speak in Spanish to encourage their children to maintain their Spanish-speaking abilities. Other parents speak in Spanish but expect their children to speak in English as a means of developing English-speaking ability.

Federal and state policy serve to add to the confusion. Under the *Lau v. Nichols* Supreme Court decision, school districts must assess the language proficiencies of students who come from homes, where a language other than English is spoken, including may Chicano students. In the Northwest, students are asked to identify the language or languages spoken at home. If the student reports that Spanish is spoken more often than English, the student may be labelled "limited English proficient" (or LEP), especially if scores are low on some type of standardized test in English. The LEP designation then justifies special monies from state or federal sources which the school can request. But the LEP designation may say little about the student's actual knowledge of Spanish or English.

Some schools treat the LEP designation as a deficit in need of remediation rather than an asset useful as an academic building block. To prevent this, the state departments of education in Idaho, Oregon, and Washington employ LEP or ESL/Bilingual coordinators whose job is to assist school districts with the assessment and instruction of students for whom English is a second language. In Idaho, for example, the ESL/Bilingual coordinator conducts in service trainining workshops to help teachers and principals assess language proficiency. Idaho has adopted the LAS (Language Assessment Scales) which is a comprehensive language assessment that provides an overall profile of a student's language proficiency. Of course, there is no substitute for a teacher's knowledge of English *and* Spanish. With a knowledge of the two languages, the teacher is in a position to most accurately assess the language proficiencies of Chicano students so the student's bilingual background can be used as an academic asset rather than a liability.

It is critically important for teachers to understand the Spanish English capabilities of their Chicano students. Current research indicates that Chicano bilingualism can enhance a student's academic achievement when used properly by teachers (Willig 1985). *The student's bilingualism is not the root of the problem.* The root of the problem is *how* the teacher may *fail* to use the student's bilingual capabilities (Hakuta 1990).

Teachers need to assess the degree and extent to which their Chicano students are bilingual, i.e., to what degree do their students understand, speak, read, and write Spanish and English? And, which of the two languages is used the most by the student outside of school? Chicano students will fall somewhere on a language continuum ranging from Spanish-only to English-only monolingualism:

Spanish only——————Spanish & English——————English only

Students from migrant homes, or who are recent Mexican immigrants, may speak more Spanish than English. Students whose parents are second and third generation residing in the Pacific Northwest may speak more English than Spanish. Most of the students will fit neither extreme. Rather, they will be somewhat bilingual in both languages. However, the student's degree of bilingualism—degree to which student understands, speaks, reads, writes in Spanish and English—is dependent upon many factors, such as the student's age and prior educational opportunities.

Social Climate Within the Northwest

Understanding and respecting the student's culture and background requires a description of the social context Chicano experience in the Northwest. Northwest Chicanos are far removed from their root culture—Mexico—although most have linkages within Chicano communities through the Southwest. Unlike their relatives and friends from the Southwest, they do not have ongoing interactions with the people and culture of Mexico. Chicano students in the Northwest have fewer opportunities to interact with other Mexican and Latin American peoples compared to their peers in the Southwest.

The gap caused by geographic isolation needs to be filled by the school insuring that its environment embraces Chicano culture. There should be visible signs of Chicano culture throughout the school. Bulletin boards, posters, and classroom activities should be permeated with Chicano culture. When possible, Chicano adults of all kinds, including the disabled, should be invited to school to talk with all the students. Parents and grandparents should be used as integral parts of classroom instruction, perhaps by telling stories, relating experiences, or reading to students. The school should employ Chicano teachers, counselors, and administrators when possible to serve as role models. Non Chicano people in the Northwest are also affected by the isolation experienced by Northwest Chicanos. Most Anglo people have little contact or understanding of the rich texture of Mexican culture, because they have few opportunities to interact with people from Mexico and other Latin American countries. The isolation has caused stereotypes to form about Chicanos based on very limited data or contact with Chicano people. Regrettedly, the stereotypes have lead to prejudices and violent crimes against Chicanos (See Erasmo Gamboa *Voces Hispanas*).

While teachers cannot do much about the prejudices held by adults, they can do much to teach their non Chicano students about Chicano culture to counteract the prejudices and stereotypes they may learn at home or in the community. There are some very well developed programs available to teachers designed to reduce prejudice. (See the *Teaching Tolerance* video- and text kit produced by the Southern Poverty Law Center; the *Anti-Bias Curriculum* produced by the National Association for the Education of Young Children; the resource guide, A World of Difference, a prejudice reduction program produced by the Anti-Defamation League of B'nai Brith.) These kits, when used with discretion, can do much to reduce prejudice. Understand that sometimes teaching about prejudice directly causes defensiveness and may not serve to reduce whatever prejudice is held. But again, as with knowedlge about the Spanish language, there is no substitute for knowledge about Chicano culture. Simply teaching *all* students about Chicano culture through lessons in children's literature, through American literature, through research and writing projects about Chicanos, through the social studies (history, geography, anthropology, sociology), through lessons in Mexican Spanish and culture can do much to reduce prejudice *if done properly.*

The cultural isolation and regional prejudice experienced by Chicanos should not be allowed to penetrate the walls of the classroom. Rather, the classroom should be a sanctuary where Chicano students can learn about their cultural heritage and be shielded from the pervasive prejudices within the region. Remember that youth learn prejudices at home, among their peers, and within the community. These prejudices are brought into the school by students and are manifested in various ways, such as election of cheerleaders and school office holders, courtship patterns, name calling, and at times, fights. Teachers and principals need to be on the alert for the manifestations of prejudices and then act decisively to eradicate them from the classroom and school. Otherwise, Chicano students will find themselves segregated and marginalized within the school community much as are their parents might within their respective communities.

While the cultural differences of Chicano students should be understood and respected, social class differences may manifest in the classroom. Social class differences should also be understood but not necessarily accepted as viable attitudes or beliefs. We are now within a gray area. Cultural differences spring from values and beliefs that are universally accepted within the respective culture. These values serve to enhance and enrich the cultural group. Social class differences spring from class stratifications that form a sort of sub-culture within any group. The values and beliefs underpinning the sub-culture are not universally accepted by the group because they generally do not advance the interests of the group.

Willis's research with lower class boys in England shows they developed a resistance culture. They rejected what English schools attempted to teach them, standard British English, for example (Willis 1977). From their perspective, they were resisting the school's attempt to make them middle class. In the United State, Ogbu's research with lower class African American students reveals the same type of behavior. Being a good student, making good grades, cooperating with teachers, learning to read, speak, and write standard American English are perceived as the schools attempt to transform the African American students to "White." By refusing to learn what the schools offer, the African Americans are resisting the school's attempt to make them White (Ogbu 1987). Experience with some Chicano students shows a belief in resistance culture, i.e., schools and teachers are Anglo enemies which must be resisted. A belief in resistance culture may not be widespread among Chicanos. However, when it does manifest, educators should be aware that responsible Chicanos are not supporters of such beliefs, and in fact, look to the schools to educate Chicano youth. In fact, resisting teachers and refusing to cooperate run counter to a basic Chicano cultural value, as discussed above. Chicano students who are resisting what the school has to offer may be signalling teachers that what they are being taught is unrelated to their experiential background and may require changes in the content. The goals toward literacy should not be modified.

Social class differences manifested in the classroom may be rooted in the fact some Chicano families find themselves caught in the poverty cycle. Unable to break out of poverty, a philosophy of fatalism forms. Children from these homes may come to believe learning in school is hopeless, that they have little hope for the future, and that they should live each day as though it were the last without delaying gratification. Or, children from these homes may develop low self esteem, especially when they attend schools that reinforce and reward middle class children or they live in communities that harbor prejudices toward anything Chicano. Feeling of immediate gratification, of hopelessness, low self esteem, alienation and resistance may be based on the realities imposed by poverty. These feelings counteract and may neutralize the benefits of schooling. Learning is a gradual, developmental process that requires self discipline and perserverance, a willingness to delay gratification, and hope for a better future.

Teachers should be quick to recognize behaviors caused by poverty conditions and then enlist assistance of others (principal, counselor, school social workers) so measures can be taken to counteract the impact that poverty has upon learning.We should approach social class differences carefully. Many lower class parents value education and will go to any extent to insure that their children are educated. Others would help their children with school work if they had the time. Some simply need to know techniques they might use. (Ideas for working with parents are described below under *Parents as Teachers*.)

Educational Strategies

Educational strategies are broadly based approaches for teaching Chicano students. This chapter ends with instructional strategies that show promise for teaching Chicano students. The underpinnings of all educational strategies are the attitudes and effectiveness of teachers. Educational strategies are only as good as the teachers who use them. While educational strategies place emphasis on what teachers will do to students, what will the students learn as a result of the strategies? This is the question: teachers are encouraged to think in terms of results or outcomes—what will the students know or be able to do as a result of this or that strategy? We endorse the notion that students should learn to be responsible for their own learning so they can become self directed and autonomous, life long learners.

Effective educational strategies are easily thwarted by potent sociocultural forces endemic to American life, including the forces of poverty and racism. These forces pervade all sectors of American life and are found in all parts of the United States, including Idaho, Oregon, and Washington.

The Idaho Task Force on Hispanic Education conducted a comprehensive study of the educational status of Idaho's Chicano students. In its report to the Idaho State Board of Education, the Task Force reported six goals that schools and teachers could adopt to better meet the needs of Chicano students in Idaho. The goals are applicable to schools throughout the Pacific Northwest. For brevity, they are paraphrased here:

1. Maintain a school climate so Chicano students succeed at their own pace without losing self esteem.
2. Implement a culturally relevant curriculum pertinent to problems and issues Chicanos face now and in the future.
3. Use instructional methods to promote family like cooperation for working with above problems/issues.
4. Insure teachers, counselors, and administrators who are sensitive to Chicano culture and language work constructively with Chicano students and patrons.
5. Evaluate academic and vocational education programs to ensure they provide positive career options for Chicano students.
6. Employ Chicano teachers, counselors, and administrators as role models so Chicano students are encouraged to succeed and remain in school (Report of the Task Force on Hispanic Education 1991).

In September 1988 the Washington State Commission on Hispanic Affairs presented a report, "The Master Plan for improvement of the Education of Hispanic Youth" to the State Board of Public Instruction for the state of Washington. The report provided comprehensive, thorough recommendations in twelve chapters for the education of Washington's Chicano students. The report provided six broadly-based strategies designed to prevent eduational and academic problems before they emerge:

1. Meaningful encouragement and support should be provided at a personal level to Hispanic youth;

2. Knowledge gaps and voids in skill should be identified and dealt with before they develop into problems;
3. Parents should be given the information and taught the skills they need in order to support their children's educational experiences;
4. Non-traditional instructional methods should be used with Hispanic students who experience difficulty working with traditional school practices;
5. Success should be rewarded rather than failures being condemned;
6. The expectations of teachers and parents of Hispanic youths should be so high that student goals are transformed to match expectations (Master Plan for Improvement of Education of Hispanic Youth).

◆ The Strategy of Cultural Continuity

Teachers can use cultural continuity as a means of alleviating more basic problems. These problems—poverty, hunger, ignorance, and disease— are powerful enemies of Chicano students that can dissuade even the most optimistic teachers; these problems, especially those caused by poverty, may cast shadows over the better aspects of Chicano culture. Even though teachers have miminal control over the problems of poverty and its consequences, teachers have much control over their classrooms, the materials used in their classrooms, and the knowledge and skills learned in their classrooms. They can equip themselves with knowledge about Chicano culture, create classroom climates and environments that embrace Chicano culture, and serve as liberating forces in the lives of Chicano students while teaching the subject matter of their educational training.

Teachers can empower their students to use their own creative intelligence to break free from the ropes of poverty. To unleash creative intelligence, teachers should insure *there exists continuity between the culture of the home and the culture of the school* so that students can make a smooth transition between their lives at home and their lives in school. Teachers will need to acquaint themselves with the cultural backgrounds of their Chicano students if they are to make their class rooms and lessons culturally compatible. The students, their parents, and grandparents are important sources for insights into the culture. For example, the legend of the weeping woman, *La Llorona*, can be found in most Chicano communities in the Northwest.

The *La Llorona* legend has been traced to pre Columbian Aztec culture. As a mythological figure, *La Llorona* reflects a belief about the preeminent role that women play in the family. She also reflects the vagaries of human existence in an imperfect world. Throughout the Northwest, Chicanos have stories about *La Llorona*. The stories will differ from community to community. They have been adapted to reflect the geography and conditions of the various communities. Knowledge about Chicano oral traditions can also be learned by taking Chicano Studies courses in programs offered at some Northwest universities and colleges. Teachers can also checkout books from libraries, and with interlibrary loan systems, books about Chicanos from libraries all over the United States are available to teachers and their students.

Chicano culture should permeate the entire curriculum. It is acceptable to honor Chicano heroes, such as César Chávez, and to celebrate important Chicano holidays, such as the *Cinco de Mayo*, but it is more important that Chicano student experience their culture within the events of the classroom. Within most academic subjects, there are many places to incorporate Chicano culture. Here are examples: incorporate Chicano folklore and myths in children's literature in the elementary grades and American literature at the middle school and senior high levels; in the social studies the early explorations of the Spanish, which includes exploration of parts of the Northwest coastline, can be incorporated in geography and history lessons; in writing assignments at all grade levels, students should be encouraged to research topics about Chicano culture and then write a paper from which an oral report can be given.

Far better to incorporate Chicano culture into the regular curriculum rather than setting aside a day, week, or month to study Chicano culture. The additive approach implies that Chicano culture is an appendage to American culture rather than an integral part. By incorporating Chicano culture into the entire curriculum, teachers send the message that the culture is imporant enough to study all year long rather than just during certain days which are set aside.

Classroom experiences should be compatible with the students' learning modalities. Experience reveals that competitive learning modalities dominate in most classrooms. While competition plays a role in the academic development of students, cooperative learning modalities have been under utilized to the detriment of children who are not inclined toward competitive learning modalities. Yet, the research of Slavin (1983) and Johnson, et. al (1986) have yielded positive results when students were allowed to learn within a cooperative modality. Our experience indicates that using cooperative learning approaches can benefit Chicano students.Teachers should be careful about the use of either competitive or cooperative learning modalities. Students who are reared in extended, traditional families may be socialized toward cooperation rather than competition as a modality for action. But, this is not to say Chicano students are not competitive.

Teachers should keep in mind that the behavior of Chicano students may reflect orientations toward cooperation and competition depending upon their family envirnoments and socialization practices. This is why knowledge and understanding of the student's home and cultural background is so important.

◆ Strategy of Literacy at all Levels

Literacy generally refers to the ability to speak, read, write, and comprehend American English in the United States. But, literacy as here conceived refers to a complex of skills, attitudes, and knowledge hierarchically arranged in two languages, American English and Mexican Spanish. *Teach Chicano students to think creatively and constructively in the two languages.* At the lowest level is functional literacy referring to the ability to speak, read, write, and comprehend standard English and Spanish. Functional literacy also refers to the ability to read technical literature which entails an understanding of rudimentary mathematical and scientific concepts within the two languages.

At a second level is cultural literacy which expands functional literacy and refers to a knowledge of the literature, history and grand traditions of the core American culture, including major scientific and technological accomplishments. Cultural literacy also refers to knowledge about a person's ethnic or cultural heritage. It is important for Chicano students to know the values and beliefs of the core American culture as embodied in its literature and history; it is equally important that Chicano students be taught the content of their culture. Last, cultural literacy refers to an understanding of cultures and events on a global scale. While knowledge of the American core culture and knowledge of one's own heritage is basic to cultural literacy, global awareness and understanding of the peoples of the world is essential for the humanistic education of Chicano students.

At the highest level is critical literacy which refers to the ability to think analytically and creatively. Specific abilities here are:

1. to analyze and evaluate oral and written expression, including the ability to detect a writer's or speaker's biases;
2. with mathematics, rather than rote memorization of formulas, the ability to reason quantitatively with mathematical concepts and formulas is essential;
3. with areas of science, abilities to form research experiments, to form hypotheses and predict their outcomes, the abilities to examine the generalizability of experimental data and results, and to evaluate scientific theories in relationship to empirical data are basic;
4. with fine arts and the performing arts, abilities to understand and use the disciplined routines or forms used by artists to express ideas or emotions, or to produce desired affects are basic.

Critical literacy refers to the highest level of cognitive development because it requires that students learn to use the knowledge, concepts, and skills gained at the functional and cultural levels of literacy as tools for molding and shaping their lives. More than rote memorization of places, events, dates, names, formulas, and scientific maxims are required to achieve the aim of critical literacy. Rather, critical literacy requires students to analyze, synthesize, evaluate, and infer using data or other forms of knowledge in American English and Mexican Spanish.

◆ Developmental Bilingualism as a Strategy

Chicano bilingualism should be an educational asset which could be used to develop full Spanish English bilingualism. At the end of twelve years, Chicano students should be able to speak, read, and write in Spanish and English. As idealistic as this may sound, many students in schools throughout the world speak, read, and write in two or more languages. However, in the past, United States educators viewed Chicano bilingualism as an educational liability detrimental to the academic achievement of Chicano students. In Europe and Asia, knowledge of two languages has been the work of an educated person. In the United States, it has been the work of a language deficient person, in reference to Chicano bilinguals. The liability view was not based on valid research designs but rather the prejudices the researchers held about Chicanos. Since the 1970's, better designed research studies have reported that Spanish English bilingualism of Chicanos: 1) need not impede academic achievement in elementary school subjects; 2) need not impede the development of English; and 3) can serve as an advantage in some circumstances (García 1994).

Bilingualism need not impede academic achievement when the students are allowed to develop communicative and critical literacy competence in their stronger language. "Communicative" competence refers to the person's ability to use a language for normal, daily communications purposes occurring in a social context. "Critical literacy" competence refers to the ability to use a language for abstract thinking occurring when language is used to study most school subjects.

The ideal bilingual understands, speaks, reads, and write two languages with native like proficiency. Few bilinguals achieve ideal proficiency. Most favor one of the languages, especially for communicative competence. When the student begins school, s/he needs to continue developing communicative competence in the stronger language. Simultaneously, critical literacy development must occur in the stronger language. When the bilingual continues to develop communicative competence concurrent to the development of critical literacy, then his/her academic achievement should not be impeded. *To insure that the student's bilingualism does not impede her/his academic achievement, it is critical that the student be allowed to develop critical literacy with the use of the stronger language.*

Spanish English bilingualism need not impede the development of English. Dulay and Burt (1974) studied the English speech patterns of 145 bilingual children between the ages of five and eight. Their stronger language was Spanish. They were learning English. Dulay and Burt examined the speech samples for interference and developmental errors. Developmental errors are mistakes most infants make when they're learning English. Interference errors are mistakes bilingual persons transfer from their stronger language to utterance in their second language, such as the "Mexican" accent of some bilingual students when speaking English. Eighty five percents of the errors were developmental; ten percent were caused by interference. The remainder ten percent of errors were attributed to individual differences. In other words, *the errors made by the bilingual were the normal errors anyone would make while learning English.*

Bilingualism can serve as an academic advantage in some circumstances. In Peal and Lambert's research, Canadian, French English bilingual elementary students rated higher than monolingual students on standardized tests. The bilinguals benefitted from the semantic flexibility the two languages provided them (Peal & Lambert 1962). More recent studies with Chicano students corroborated the Peal and Lambert findings. (See Willig's study cited previously.) *Bilingualism can serve as an academic advantage for Chicano students.*

How can bilingualism be used as an academic advantage for Chicano students? There are no easy answers. *For optimal, academic results, Chicano bilinguals should develop communicative and critical literacy competence in their stronger language while studying the weaker language as a second language.* Once developing communicative competence in the second language, students should learn critical literacy competence in the second language. (The research on this approach supports its effectiveness. See previously cited studies.) Here's an example.

María and Mario are first graders. They favor Spanish over English. In class, their teacher presents most of the academic subjects in Spanish. Some subjects, like art and physical education, are presented in English. They also study English as a second language. During the second grade, they will continue to receive instruction with Spanish as the main medium of instruction. They will continue to study English as a second language. Sometime during the third grade, when Mario and María are able to communicate and think abstractly in English, they commence to receive instruction in more of the school subjects in English. Gradually, instruction in English replaces

Spanish as the medium of instruction. At this level of development, María and Mario should continue the study of Mexican Spanish and literature, which should continue much like English language and literature, through the 12th grade.

The strategy of developmental bilingualism is called *developmental bilingual education or maintenance bilingual education.* If María's and Mario's stronger language were English, then the above process would be reversed with English as the medium of instruction; Spanish would be studied as a second language.

Instead of using the developmental bilingual approach, what about using the English as a second language (ESL) approach? The ideal ESL approach isolates the students away from the regular class to teach them English at the communicative and critical literacy level. Done correctly, it would take two or three years to get the students to the level of communicative and critical competence needed to study academic subjects in English. In the meantime, the students will have fallen behind their English speaking peers in the regular school subjects. This ESL approach pulls the students out of the mainstream class and immerses them in English. While studying English, they are not studying the other subjects taught in school. They fall behind in those subjects.

A compromise approach between the developmental bilingual approach and the English-as-a-second language approach is called *transitional bilingual education.* The transitional approach makes a compromise by teaching the students academic subjects in Spanish for a short while, usually the first or second grades. Concurrently, the students are taught English as a second language. The approach's intent is instant fluency in English promoting a quick transition to English only instruction. *This approach can be effective if the students develop both communicative and critical literacy competence in English sufficient enough to succeed in an English only language environment.*

There is a high possibility the students will not develop full competence in English and will thereby be placed at a disadvantage in an English only classroom, dooming the student to semilingualism in which they do not develop full competence (communicative and critical literacy) in either language as well as hindering their development within academic subjects for the remainder of their educational careers. Semilingualism may partially explain the high attrition rates and the low reading scores of many Chicano students. Semilingualism is the result of poor instructional planning in which the developmental language capabilities of the students are not taken into consideration.

Semilingualism is very costly to everyone. To students, they are always in a position of having to "play catch-up" in most school subjects which may continually frustrate and discourage them from further studies. They are truly at risk of dropping out of school. To schools who are committed to teaching their students, semilingualism is costly also. Because the students have not developed full language competence in either language, the school must continually provide special remedial programs, detracting from the implementation of academic, enrichment programs. To society, semilingualism is costly in terms of loss of talent and human resources, especially within the area of bilingualism and biculturalism, talents greatly needed in an ever increasing interdependent global community.

For Chicano students whose stronger language is English, or who speak only English, language development should take a very different but conventional approach: *teach these students Mexican Spanish as a foreign language.* This approach is already being used in schools in Seattle, Washington, Portland, and Eugene, Oregon in elementary schools. This approach is not confined to Chicano students and includes any students whose parents want them to learn Spanish.

Whatever language development approach is used, there are some general factors to be considered. Students who are members of ethnic majority groups experience little difficulty acquiring a second language in elementary grades (Hakuta, Diaz & Ferdman 1986). For majority group children, learning a second language poses little threat to their ethnic identities. They will retain their majority group culture and identity. But, for Chicano students, learning English as a second language poses difficulties, including a possible threat to their ethnic group identity.

Chicano students may perceive that learning English is a threat to their ethnic identities if the school is using English only instruction to anglicize them. The perception is based on the truth. Practices in Bureau of Indian Affairs boarding schools for Native American students and public schools in the Southwest with high numbers of Chicano students used English only instruction to "Americanize" or "Anglicize" them. This practice is no longer lawful and is disallowed as a consequence of the *Lau v. Nichols* U.S. Supreme Court decision.

In the Pacific Northwest, schools face a dilemma. By teaching Chicano students in English only, by not teaching them Spanish and by not teaching the students about their Mexican cultural heritage, *the schools are in fact Anglicizing Chicano students*. Even though the school's intent may be to insure that the students learn English—an outcome we endorse—the students are placed in a position of learning English at the expense of losing Spanish, an outcome we do not endorse. The message received by the students is that their ethnic identity is to be changed—that their home language and culture are unacceptable in school. Although the school may not be consciously attempting to threaten the students' ethnic identity, the results are the same because the school is not developing the students biculturally in Spanish and English.

Motivation to learn English may also be impeded by community prejudices. Second language acquisition is easy when students are able to participate fully within the second language's culture. In the Northwest, Chicano students may be prevented from participating fully in their communities due to ethnic or social class biases. Consequently, their experiences communicating with native English speakers may be limited. To really learn a second language, students need to get plenty of experience using the language in natural settings, verbally interacting with native speakers. In communities with social class or ethnic prejudices against Chicanos, Chicano students may not be highly motivated to learn English since they have little opportunity, outside of school, to use English.

◆ The Strategy of Parents as Teachers

Teachers should not hesitate to call on parents to assist with the education of their children. Generally, Chicano parents are ready and willing to work with teachers and schools to assist with the education of their children. In the past, educators have tended to discourage Chicano parents from participation in school affairs. While not deliberately intending to exclude Chicano parents, educators have scheduled events for parental participation during the school day when working parents were unable to attend. More important, educators have not always communicated with Chicano parents about the progress their children are making while in school. Yet, educators have been fast to report problems to the parents so that the majority of communication between educators and Chicano parents have been mostly negative. Teachers need to report the good things their students are doing to the parents.

Teachers are encouraged to develop a partnership relationship with Chicano parents. They have in common the education of their Chicano students. As partners, teachers will need to schedule parent conferences in the evening or weekends. Principals should confer with the employers of Chicano parents so the parents could be allowed free time away from work to visit their children's classrooms during the school day.

When Ordóñez taught in Southern California she formed a Chicano parent's group entitled, Padres Unidos. This group met monthly to learn how to continue the education process at home, how to make learning games. It also served the parents as a support and advocacy group. The entire family was invited to participate in these meetings with babysitting provided by the elder children and videos and popcorn provided for the youngsters.

A weekly newsletter, Un Momentito, written in Spanish was sent hom to inform the parents of what was going on in the school as well as in the district. Notes from teachers were translated so that parents would undertand requests and concerns by the teachers. When these kinds of efforts, attendance at parent conferences by Spanish speaking families was 98%!

Once gaining parental trust, teachers can show parents how they might serve as teachers at home not only with homework but also with recreational activities that stimulate creative and critical thinking. Even simple card games can be used to teach arithmetic; and viewing television can assist with reading. For example, while watching a murder mystery such as *Murder, She Wrote*, parents can be shown how to direct their children's attention to important details, to understand the causes of events, to anticipate outcomes and consequences, and to arrive at resolutions without detracting from the enjoyment of solving the "who done it?" puzzle. With cable television, there are Spanish language programs that could also be put to use for educational purposes. Help with homework need not be negative nor intrusive. Parents should be shown how to demonstrate interest in the children's products, made at home and in class. By sending the products home with the teacher's remarks and asking the parent's to make corresponding remarks about the products, students can gain a sense of confidence and pride in their work.

Parents need to know that their involvement in the learning activities of their children is extremely important. They also need to know that their values are shown in what they do rather than what they say, i.e., parents need to know how to model their belief in education. When parents stress the importance of education with their children by reading to them or telling them stories, the children see that their parents value learning. García's parents always made him and his brothers and sisters listen to the evening news on the radio before supper. (There was no t.v. back then!). At supper, both parents moderated a discussion on the significance of the news, how the news was related to past events, and what consequences the news held for the future. Ordóñez makes it a practice to read to her three year old daughter every evening to imbue a love of reading. At the same time, she gives her daughter the opportunity to retell stories and/or to act stories out by taking on the roles of the various characters. At bedtime, children's musical song cassettes are played to soothe her daughter to sleep. Creativity boxes filled with all kinds of paper, glue, stickers, ribbon, glitter, etc. are part of a play area where her daughter has the opportunity to paint and create her own designs. Ordóñez supports the development of her daughter's imagination by providing numerous opportunties for her to exercise her mind.

Important Factors for Teaching Migrant Children

The children of migratory workers will pose special challenges in the classroom. Important factors to keep in mind are the children's mobility, poverty, health, and language development. Migratory workers are seasonal workers who must work in different areas depending upon the crops. They tend the fields or orchards, and when the crops are ripe, they harvest them. Then they move to another area for another crop. While they are situated in an area, they send their children to schools in nearby communities. During the school year, the students may attend two or three different schools, starting in the fall in one school, transferring to another in the winter, and then again to another in the spring.

The parents' jobs depend on their ability to move from area to area, i.e., mobility. Educational programs depend on an uninterrupted line of progression, i.e., continuity. As the students move from school to school, their educational progression is constantly interrupted, making it difficult for them to learn. The student's academic file follows the students as they go from school to school so that teachers can assess where the student should be placed. Because most states do not have statewide curricula which each school must follow, much variability exists in educational programs. Each school must develop very specific educational programs for each student depending on his or her educational status.

The continual interruptions of the students' educational growth and development caused by their mobility are exacerbated by the parent's socio economic status. Migrant workers function on a pay as you go economy. Their wages are low; they often are paid in cash and are not provided health or medical benefits. At times, they are forced to sleep in their cars or in outdoor camps. Health concerns, such as adequate diets or preventative medication, are deferred for a future date. Of course, poor diets and poor health care interfer with educational attainment. Teachers need to be sensitive to their students' health and nutrition needs. Assistance is available through local, state, and federal government agencies. School officials are aware of the services and can be of assistance to the teachers, but it is the teacher's responsibility to notify the officials about their students' health or dietary problems.

Chicano children from migratory families will most likely speak Spanish and English. There are no easy generalizations about the extent of their bilingualism. The students may speak and understand both languages well; others may be proficient in Spanish, i.e., they may be able to understand and speak Spanish quite well. Their English may be very functional, enabling them to communicate at a very basic level, but it may not be sufficiently developed to use as a learning tool in school, which may be evidenced when they attempt to use common English idioms, such as "pulling my leg" => "pushing my leg." Or, when they struggle to read children's stories unrelated to their cultural experiences. It is incumbent on teachers to develop a working knowledge of Spanish so they can assess the student's language development in Spanish as well as English.

Children from migratory families do pose a special challenge to teachers. But, teachers need not despair. They need to be sensitive, understanding and have high expectations. There are many stories about successful students whose family were migratory workers. For example, the late Dr. Tomás Rivera was born in Texas and travelled the migratory stream throughout the Midwest. He became interested in writing, recording his experiences as a son of migratory parents. His parents and teachers encouraged him to write in Spanish and English. He became a noted Chicano writer, whose novel, ". . . and the earth did not part" won the Quinto Sol literary award for 1970. Along the way, he earned a teaching degree and taught school. Later, he earned a Ph.D. in Spanish literature becoming a professor of Romance Languages at the University of Texas in San Antonio where he served as Vice President. At the time of his death, he was serving as President of the University of California in Riverside. Dr. Rivera's success story was due to his own hard won efforts and the encouragement of parents and friends. Yet, without sensitive, caring teachers who were committed to teaching him to a high level of expectation, Dr. Rivera may have never written that book or believed in himself enough to go the extra miles. Good teachers make a difference.

Summary

Demographic trends show that the Chicano student population is growing in the Pacific Northwest. More and more classrooms of students and teachers will have the opportunity of getting to know these students on a personal basis. This can be a positive learning experience for all involved. While teachers help Chicanos adjust to American life and society and the English lanugage, Chicano students can share their Mexican culture and Spanish language. All of those involved in the school can be learning new and exciting concepts at the same time.

While many Northwest schools are located in isolated, monocultural communities, our lives are enriched daily by the influence of Mexico on our language, our food and our architecture. Welcoming Chicano students into the classroom and community can help teachers to grow professionally, to appreciate the richness of Mexican culture and to break down stereotypes about the Mexican people. The challenge to our schools is to support the development of bilingual bicultural future world citizens who are not ashamed of their native lanagugae and culture and who can be successful in both of their worlds. Culturally sensitive teachers who develop warm, caring learning environments and infuse cultural concepts into their curriculum will nourish this population of untapped talent and help create future leaders for our interdependent world.

References

Adler, M. 1982. *Paideia proposal.* New York: Collier Books, 8.
Anti-bias curriculum. 1990. Washington, D.C.: National Association for the Education of Young Children.
Bentley, H. 1973. *A Dictionary of Spanish terms in English.* New York: Octagon Books.
Buenning, M. & Tollefson, N. 1987. The cultural gap hypothesis as an explanation for the achievement patterns of mexican-american students. *Psychology in the schools,* 14, 264-271.
Cummins, N.L. & Miramontes, O.B. 1989. Received and actual linguistic competence: A descriptive study of four low achieving Hispanic bilingual students. *American Educational Research Journal,* 26, 427-443.
Dewey, J. 1916. *Democracy and education.* New York: Macmillan.
Dulay, H.C. & M.K. Burt. 1974. Natural sequences in child second language acquisition. *Language Learning,* 24, 37-53.
Dunn, R. 1987. Research on instructional environment. *Professional school psychology,* 2, 43-52.
Dusenberry, W., 1963, *The Mexican mesta: The administration of ranching in colonial Mexico.* Urbana: University of Illinois Press.
Galambos, S.J. & Goldin-Meadow, S. 1990. The effects of learning languages on metalinguistic development. *Cognition,* 34,1-56.
Gamboa, E. 1992. *Voces Hispanas.* Boise: Idaho Commission on Hispanic Affairs.
García, R. & Ahler. 1992. *Teaching Indian students.* Norman: University of Oklahoma Press.
García, R. 1991. *Teaching in a pluralistic society.* New York: Harper Collins, 22.
_____. 1994. Language,ethnicity, and education in Banks, J. *Multiethnic education: Theory and practice,* 3rd ed. Boston: Allyn & Bacon, 275.
Good, T. 1940. *A dictionary of education.* Bloomington: Phi Delta Kappa,
Hakuta,K. 1990. *Bilingualism and bilingual education.* Washington, D.C.: Clearinghouse for Bilingual Education.
Hakuta, K., Ferdman, B. & Diaz, R. 1986. *Bilingual education: A new look at the research evidence.* Los Angeles: Center for Language Education & Research University of California, 41-45.
Johnson, D., R. Johnson, and E. Holubec.1986. *Circles of learning: cooperation in the classroom.* Edina, Minnesota: Interaction Book Co.
Mann, H. cited in Noll, J. & S. Kelley.1970. *Foundations of education in America.* New York: Harper & Row, 213.
McWilliams, C. 1968. *North from Mexico: The Spanish speaking people of the United States.* New York: Greenwood Press, 72.
Nieto, S. 1992. *Affirming diversity.* New York: Longman,164.
Ogbu, J. 1987. Variability in minority school performance: A problem in search of an explanation. *Anthropology & Education Quarterly,*18, 312-334.
Jefferson, T. cited in Padover, S. 1946. *Thomas Jefferson on Democracy.* New York: Penguin Press, 88.

Peal, E. & Lambert, W. 1962. *The relation of bilingualism to intelligence.* Washington, D.C.: American Psychological Association.

Sanchez, G. 1940, *Forgotten People: A study of New Mexicans.* Albuquerque: University of New Mexico Press, 86.

Slavin, R. 1983, *Cooperative learning.* New York: Longman.

Task Force on Hispanic Education. 1991. *Report of the task force on Hispanic education,* Boise, Idaho: Idaho State Board of Education, 7.

Teaching tolerance. 1993. Montgomery, Alabama: Southern Poverty Law Center.

Vasquez, J. A. 1990. *Teaching to the distinctive traits of minority students. Clearinghouse,* 63, 299-304.

Vigil, D. 1847. *Address to the first legislative assembly of the territory of New Mexico.* Quoted in Sanchez, G. *Forgotten People,* 19.

Washington State Hispanic Ad Hoc Committee. *Master Plan for Improvement of Education of Hispanic Youth.* Olympia, WA: Washington State Commission on Hispanic Affairs., 2-3.

Weber, D. 1992. *The Spanish frontier in North America.* New Haven: Yale University Press.

World of Difference. 1986. New York: Anti-Defamation League of the B'nai Brith.

Willig, A.C. 1985. *A meta-analysis of selected studies on the effectiveness of bilingual education. Review of educational research,* 55, 269-317.

Willis, P. 1977. *Learning to labor.* Lexington, MA: D.C. Heath.

Woolfolk, A. 1992. *Educational Psychology.* Boston: Allyn & Bacon, 128-129.

Young, O. 1970. *Western Mining.* Norman: University of Oklahoma Press.

6

A Cultural Profile and Status of Chicanas in the Northwest

Luz E. Maciel Villarroel ◆ *Sandra B. Fancher Garcia*

Introduction

The purpose of this chapter is to provide a cultural profile and status of Chicanas in the Northwest. Included in this chapter are a brief history and cultural profile of Chicanas. The chapter will also provide a discussion focusing on the current status of Northwest Chicanas in regards to the lack of equal access to public services, education, health, employment, politics, and law issues. Additionally, the chapter will identify Chicana support groups in the Northwest.

Chicano origins can be traced to the pre-Columbian period. Mirande & Enriquez (1979, p.10),[1] indicate that the Chicano(a) origins are ancient. Some argue that the term Chicano is derived from the Nahuatl "Mexica". Others propose that the term Chicano evolved from Mexicano (Mechicano). These proponents further say that the "sh" sound evolved into "ch". The origins of the term Chicano are clouded. It is critical for us to understand the contemporary usage of the term Chicano rather than duel on the origins of the term. The word Chicano(a) is also rooted in the Chicano movement of the 1960's. The word describes a group of people involved in an ideological and political movement. Chicana(o) is a specific term which is self-selected. It identifies men and women with a certain political consciousness and awareness of the long historical discrimination Chicanos/as have endured.

Several publications refer to Chicanas as women of Mexican ancestry residing in the United States. However, Chicanas are not homogeneous. Chicanas are a diverse group. It is possible to assume that Chicano(a) identity is a dynamic identity still in process and evolution. Some Chicanos suffer self denial while others maintain an ethnocentric position. Some self identify as Mexican-Americans, Mexicanas, Latinas, Hispanas or Spanish. However, in regard to ethnic identity some classify themselves as Mexicanas or Americanas. Chicanas very seldom identify themselves as Indigenous or Mestizas. Our educational upbringing has not allowed us to identify with the other half of our rich indigenous cultural heritage rooted in the Pre-Columbian period.

Whether or not one identifies as Chicana usually has more to do with one's political perspective than the specificity's of one's Mexican roots. For instance, there are some women of Mexican descent born in the US who do not self identify as Chicanas, but rather, Mexican-American, Latinas, or the non-existent "Hispanic".

In contrast, there are some women who were not born in the U.S. but yet consider themselves Chicana because they live within the present day political borders called the U.S. Those Chicanas also identify with the political history of oppression experienced by Mexicanos living within the U.S. political borders. Therefore, this chapter will include issues pertaining to those women not recognized as U.S. citizens. These same issues may also impact those women who are citizens.

In order to understand the current status of Chicanas in the Northwest it is imperative that one reviews briefly the history of Chicanas and their cultural profile. The roots of Chicana history are based on the culture of the pre-Columbian era, the colonial period of the sixteenth, seventeen and eighteen centuries and the Anglo occupation in the nineteenth century. These Spanish and Anglo colonial experiences have contributed to shaping the identity of Chicanas and suppressed the cultural heritage of Chicanas. Thus, Chicanas are products of the pre-Colombian culture and the two colonial periods which collectively have conflicted with the development of the Chicana identity.

Chicana Cultural Profile and History

The roles of women during the pre-Columbian period were dictated by a rigid moral code. The societies were stratified in terms of class. Strict codes of behavior were imposed on people according to their status. Standards of behavior were based on strict compliance to stereotypical female roles, such as being brave and fertile. All women participated in society in the areas of domestics, religion and the military. Aztec mythology consisted of a realm of male and female spheres. Reproduction was sacred and each girl learned her designated role based on being a female.[3]

In the Aztec religion women were considered spiritual and mythological figures not only on earth but also in other worlds. Aztec women played two very important roles: one as warriors and the other as participants in religious rituals. As warriors they had a partnership role with their male counterparts. They carried the supplies and cooked. In religion, they participated in rituals as priestesses, midwives and as healers. They received education in embroidery and sewing in order to participate in making clothing for the priests and idols.

During the Colonial Period, 1521-1821, the Spanish culture and the Indigenous culture clashed violently. The Indigenous and Spanish realities were two worlds, two perspectives, and two political systems. These two distinct realities clashed and elements of both cultures merged into one. A new mestizo nation emerged in the context of the New Spain viceroyalty political structure.

Within this new reality, Indigenous and Mestiza women became invisible and their history and their struggles became hidden behind a male-dominated society. However, when analyzing history from a Chicana perspective it is clear that women for five hundred years have struggled to resist colonization and slavery, and fought to maintain their family and culture.

Further reading on this resistance may be found in Irene Blea's book, La Chicana.[4] During the Spanish colonial period, Europeans introduced and put in place a Euro-male superiority ideology, reinforced by racist beliefs. Indigenous women and later African women were viewed as prey for the Euro-male colonists. Indigenous women were used to fulfill the sexual pleasure/gratification and domination needs of the Euro-male and were considered "impure". The children born of European and Indigenous unions were also considered inferior and impure.

The woman's role in the American continent was violated during the conquest. Her role was relegated to a subservient position in society. In religious ceremonies, she no longer participated in rituals. Her role in the family, was degraded to an inferior nature. She lost the right to own land and society no longer gave her the "matrilineal right." The new Euro-male superiority and patriarchy-based society prevented the indigenous woman from gaining access to power and rights. The division of labor based on gender and the status of women in society disempowered indigenous women. The male-dominated power structure was based on the ideology that females were inferior. This ideology benefited men in all facets of society including the church hierarchy and the mercantile class.

In summary, Indigenous and Mestiza women held one of the lowest social positions during the Spanish colonial period. During this period they suffered cultural destruction. Dominating forces were used to assure that women would maintain the submissive role benefiting the colonizers. Their roles were rigidly defined by cultural expectations and social class. The close and intricate Aztec family system, which was the main responsibility of the Aztec woman's domestic life, was replaced by the institutions of the encomienda, repartimiento and haciendas.

During the Independent Period and the U.S. occupation of México during the 1800's, México suffered the loss of half of it's territory to the U.S. California, Arizona, New Mexico, Texas, Colorado, Nevada and others areas became part of the U.S. These annexed territories were invaded with a different political belief system, religion and culture.

The Anglo takeover transformed Mexicanas/Chicanas to a colonized group of people. The political, economic, social and cultural power shifted from the Mexicans to the Anglo-Americans. Chicanos/as became landless, impoverished and exploited politically, socially, culturally and economically. The Anglo takeover perpetuated the loss of Chicana's right to own land.

This disempowering historical background has contributed to the Chicanas' current status in education, employment, health, and politics. It is evident that the economic, political and social oppression which Chicanas have experienced and survived for over five hundred years, is the main reason "Latinas are lacking in all social economic areas"[5] (Canales, J.; MANA, 1992)" at the national and regional level.

The Status of Chicana Women in the Northwest

In conducting this research it is evident that there is a lack of informational and demographic statistical records specifically relating to Chicanas in the Northwest. This chapter is not about statistics but about issues and concerns impacting the Chicano community. Several publications have focused on Hispanics at the national and at the state levels yet none have focused specifically on the Northwest. The lack of Northwest regional data about Chicanas confirms the need to publish documents such as this anthology. The fact that the Chicano(a) population is increasing at a very fast rate further indicates the urgent need for Chicanas/os to lead the way in gathering such data. It is also important that Chicanas/os interpret this data so that an accurate profile and current status be generated. This data will be helpful in developing an agenda to improve the general status of Chicanos(a) in the Northwest region.

Most of the information presented in this chapter is from personal interviews and autobiographies collected at Oregon State University in a class titled, Mexican-American Women: Chicana Feminism, oral history interviews and information gathered through an informal questionnaire which addresses several issues including discrimination, employment access to public services, education, health, law, higher education and support groups. Over one hundred Chicanas responded throughout the states of Washington and Oregon. The information was gathered in an oral interview format. This information is very valuable because it includes rural, urban, U.S. born, new immigrants and Chicanas transplanted from other states.

◆ Discrimination

Chicanas in the Northwest and at the national level, like Chicanas of the colonial periods, have endured social, political and cultural structures which have discriminated against them based on race, class and gender. Judy Canales, President of the Mexican-American Women's National Association indicates that the MANA report, "In Search of Economic Equity" reveals that "Latinas are lacking in all areas." She dramatically points out the need for our country's leaders to begin to replace rhetoric with action on a realistic social and family policy that provides opportunities for Latinas as well as Americans, who work to earn a decent wage, and to provide the basic needs for their families.[5]

Chicanas as a group in the Northwest continue to experience cultural, political and economic oppression and discrimination. The economic exploitation, oppression, and discrimination experienced by Chicanas not only come from a relation with Anglo men and women, but also develop from a relation with Chicanos. According to oral interviews conducted in Washington and Oregon, women in the Northwest from urban or rural areas, young or old, light skin or dark skin, indicated having experienced discrimination based on race and gender. Although class was seldom mentioned, it is worth noting that the small groups of Chicanas actively involved in Northwest politics mentioned having experienced class discrimination (1993-1994 oral interviews and autobiographies conducted in Oregon and Washington).

The discrimination faced by Chicanas based on gender and race is mainly due to the fact that the majority of Chicanas are Mestizas, bilingual/

bicultural, with very distinct features and language accents. Most Chicanas interviewed fit the above description and indicated having experienced and endured discrimination based on gender and race.

Chicanas in the Northwest have and are participating towards eradicating discrimination and injustice through organized efforts promoting civil rights and the Women's movement. They have participated as leaders and as advocates in the United Farm Workers of America movement, Mexican American Women's National Association (MANA), *Mujeres Unidas, Mujeres de Oregon*, National Council for La Raza, Oregon Commission on Hispanic Affairs, Washington Commission on Hispanic Affairs, Oregon Council for Hispanic Advancement (OCHA), *Movimiento Estudiantil Chicano de Aztlan* (MEChA) and in other well known Chicano/a groups.

Among some of these great leaders and advocates are Carmen Palomera-Rockwell, Gloria Pardo, and Luz Maciel Villarroel who have served on the Washington State Commission on Hispanic Affairs. In Oregon's Hispanic Commission, several women have served as Commissioners. These include Maria de Jesus Garcia, Consuelo Lightner, Liliana Olverding, Nancy Padilla, Wendy Veliz and Annabelle Jaramillo. Jaramillo served as Executive Director of the Oregon Commission on Hispanic Affairs. Gail Castillo, who heads Hispanics in Unity for Oregon and Yolanda Hernandez, who heads the Mexican American Citizen's League also serve as examples of women leaders in Oregon. In Washington, Yolanda Gonzalez-Hains, Sandra Garcia Fancher and Dr. Villarroel, organized the Whatcom Hispanic Organization. Teresa Martinez with Centro Latino, and Esperanza Barboa with El Centro de La Raza are just a few of the many key leadership positions Chicanas hold in Washington.

Chicanas in the Northwest are also advocates of children's rights, women in prison, the homeless migrant bilingual education, justice in the law system, etc. The Oregon and Washington State Commission on Hispanic Affairs Directories list many of these Chicanas involved in various leadership and advocacy positions in the public and private sector.

◆ Chicanas not Homogenous

Chicanas in the Northwest share the same historical perspective and culture as other Chicanas in the U.S. but have differences as well. These differences are evident in Mexican immigrants, Chicanas transplanted from other parts of the U.S. and Chicanas born and raised in Washington and Oregon. The differences among Chicanas U.S. born and born in México are many. Some of the key differences are cultural identity, language, cultural values and often times economic status. *Mujeres* from México often will identify themselves as Mexicanas and will speak English with an accent, especially if they migrated to the USA after the sixth grade. Their values are more tied to the Mexican way of life, which means having strong family bonds and responsibility of helping the family back in México. Often times due to emigration status they do not qualify for public services and college assistant programs. This sets them in an economic disadvantage status compared to U.S. born or naturalized Mexicanas/Chicanas. Chicanas who are born in the U.S. or who are transplanted to Oregon and or Washington are more likely to be bicultural, bilingual and have a combination of Mexican and U.S. values. Economically they are better off because they qualify for many of the services that a non citizen does not. For example we met many non-citizen Chicanas who wanted to pursue a higher education degree and were not able to because they did not qualify for Financial Aid and other scholarships and special programs.

In general there are differences among Mexicanas/Chicanas that contribute towards Mexicanas/Chicanas experiencing discrimination, isolation, and lack of economic gains. Within Washington and Oregon, as elsewhere, there are also differences between urban and rural Chicana issues. The differences are based on access to services and quality of services. In analyzing the resource directories for the state of Oregon and Washington, most services and organizations which specifically address women's issues were situated in the urban areas. *Mujeres* in the rural areas continue to be undeserved, undereducated and less likely to benefit from the public or private sector. Rural women are also less likely to transit into non-farm labor work and into higher education, unless migrant and educational opportunity programs assist them in the transition. Rural women are also more likely to be exposed to pesticides and more likely to drop out of school due to lack of role models and quality of education (Interviews with a group of Chicanas who dropped out in the Northwest).

◆ Lack of Material About Northwest Chicanas

When researching and reviewing over five hundred pieces of information, from local Spanish language newspapers: *El Goal Latino, El Mundo, El Sol, El Norteño, La Voz, El Mundo De Hoy, The Hispanic News, Oregon Migrant Education News*, articles, books and monograms, it has become evident that there is very little information written specifically on Chicanas in the Northwest.

Newspapers published in the Northwest which were analyzed provided very little organized information on the status and profile of Chicanas in the Northwest. In the last five years less than five percent of the articles in the newspapers address issues affecting women. In general the articles focus on community, immigration, employment, national news sports, international, and advertisement. It became obvious that Chicanas in the Northwest need to develop a voice which will address their concerns, issues, status and their profile in more organized and deliberate ways. Latino newspapers in the Northwest can be a great vehicle to gather and organize information about Chicanas throughout the Northwest.

◆ Women in the Media

Radio stations in the Northwest which air Spanish programming have increased in the last twenty years, however not at the same rate as the increase of the Chicano and Spanish speaking population. Listening to several Spanish speaking programs and gleaning information from interviews, it is evident that at least 95% percent of the programs that address *mujeres'* issues were women's voices. According to the Washington Commission on Hispanic Affairs Directory in Washington, of all the twenty five radio stations which air Spanish programs (Spanish surname) only two Chicanas were listed. In Oregon, of the fourteen radio stations listed four were directed by Chicanas.[6] The Oregon and Washington Directories only mention one television station which airs Spanish programming and is conducted by a Chicana.[7,8] This information about Chicana representation in the media indicates that there is an urgent need to encourage Chicanas to pursue TV, Radio and other media to assure that *mujeres* concern and issues are addressed adequately.

◆ Chicana Accomplishments Overlooked

Northwest writers and historians have not presented the accomplishments of Chicanas in education, employment, health and politics in spite of the barriers Chicanas have experienced in achieving their accomplishments. It is obvious that Chicanas are the ones that will write, research and document information for and about Chicanas. The lack of this research and information makes it very difficult to accurately state or write about the Chicano's current status.

The lack of written information and research does not reflect a lack of active participation of Chicanas at every level of political, social and economic private and public sector/institutions. Their participation goes unnoticed because traditionally, men have taken leadership positions, and women have primarily been confined to behind-the-scenes roles. On the national level Dolores Huerta of the United Farm Workers of America is an excellent example of Chicana leadership.

In the Northwest Chicanas who have made a difference in Washington include Margarita Mendoza de Sugiyama, Governors Office; Margarita Lopez-Prentice, State Senator; Carmen Zamora, Coalicion Pro Personas Mayores; Tina Mata, Immigration and Homeless Services; and Margarita Noyola, Hispanics for Youth. In Oregon, Linda Jaramillo, School Board, Forest Grove; Maria Estela Oliveros, Central High School Distric 135 School Board member; Eloisa Valverde de Chaudhary, School Board, Woodburn; Leticia Maldonado, Lobbyist, Portland Public Schools; Elvira Arce, President, Latin American Club, Woodburn; Luz Villastrigo, Occupancy Specially Housing Authority and is a member of City of Independance Cultural Awareness Committee. These are Chicanas who have contributed their leadership ability.

When Chicanas hold leadership positions, traditional male centered values undermine the leadership role and often times Chicanas are not taken serious (Interview information from women in leadership positions). Those Chicanas who have partnership relations in the Chicano(a) movement of the Northwest have often realized that their efforts continue to benefit men and the community, while women's needs and advancement are sacrificed or put on hold.

Interviewees expressed a feeling of being voiceless and experiencing some racism from white women. Some Chicanas who had been involved in the Movimiento Estudiantil Chicano(a) de Aztlan (MEChA) indicated having experienced chauvinistic attitudes and lack of sensitivity to *mujeres'* issues. Nonetheless Chicanas in the Northwest continue to provide leadership in the development of the Chicano community. The following examples of Chicana leadership reaffirm their active role.

In Oregon, Maria Solano, Coordinator Hispanic Cultural Center and Roxanna Perez De La Cruz Assistant Coordinator, OSU, Lilia Maciel Husen, Oregon State Penitentiary OSU Community Liaison, Maria Alanis, MEChA PSU Advisor, Dr. Luz Maciel Villarroel, MEChA WWO/OSU Advisor are a few Chicanas who have participated in the MEChA movement as advocates and activists. In Washington, Veronica Galvan of WWU, and Sandra Fancher Garcia organized the first farmworkers march for Whatcom and Skagit Counties. Chicanas who participated in the Anglo womens' movement indicated in their interviewies that race and class became intra-women issues.

◆ Lack Of Equal Access to Public Services

A national figure of 53.0 % (Oregon and Washington statistics were not available) of poverty rates of fatherless families/single-mother heads of households among the Chicanas quickly raises critical issues of equal access to public services by Chicanas with low income levels. Such public services include Aid to Families with Dependent Children (AFDC); Food Stamps; Medicaid and other public benefits distributed through the Department of Social and Health Services (DSHS); Family and Children Services, more commonly referred to as "welfare" programs including Women and Infants Care (WIC); low-income energy assistance programs; subsidized housing programs; and medical services, whether by private physicians, clinics, or hospitals.

According to the author's oral interview data, Chicanas in Oregon and Washington indicate that unequal access to services occurs as a result of various factors. Often services access is limited due to language barriers. Those language barriers result from the failure to recruit, hire, and retain bilingual, bicultural employees; a failure to hire, train, and certify qualified interpreters; a failure to provide translated written materials; and a failure to advertise the existence of the particular resource to the Spanish-speaking community in their dominant language.

Another factor is the alienation of the Chicano(a) community from the agencies which provide those services. This can occur because of the previously mentioned failure to communicate in their dominant language, or a failure to hire Chicanas or other people of color with whom Chicana clients can relate. Alienation can also occur if the agency is identified as being "part of the system" or aligned with powerful entities not readily trusted.

The latter comes into focus even more when the Chicana has no immigration documents, and is dependent on a male for her immigration status; is a recent immigrant, was born in Mexico to a United States citizen and therefore qualifies for derivative citizenship; comes from a family that regularly migrates or has migrated between the U. S. and Mexico, or otherwise has lived in a community where the majority of the people were always looking over their shoulders for the *"migra"* (border patrol) or other police.

Migrant farm worker women who travel to an unfamiliar area sometimes do not know how to drive a car or do not have access to a telephone, and if they did, they wouldn't know where to go or whom to call to secure needed services. Law enforcement officials often call the Border Patrol to act as interpreters, and invariably, they question the person about their immigrant status when they finish "interpreting."

◆ Educational Issues

The educational status and profile of Chicanas in the Northwest is often affected by barriers imposed by the dominant culture and not by so called cultural and language deficiencies of Chicanas. Inferior instruction, segregation, racism, classism, sexism and a lack of resources have traditionally been found to act as significant barriers to Chicana educational achievement. Zapeter finds that "terms such as cultural and language barriers are often used by the dominant culture to explain away minority students' failures and their unpreparedness for the labor market. In other words, the blaming of the victim approach becomes the norm in the schooling of our children. In order to break those barriers, There is a need to recognize and name what the barriers are and then address the sources that create these one by one" (Zapeter, B., Director of Education, H.O.P.E.; NHLA, 1992, Boston, Massachusetts).

In the Northwest, Chicanas have historically removed and continue to remove educational barriers on individual or group bases. According to the author's interview data, Chicanas' perceptions of the education system are not ones which nurture and embrace their unique qualities and contributions. Often they feel discouraged and neglected. The Chicanas interviewed indicated that the main areas of concern included language and curriculum, equal access, financing and resources, lack of role models at every level and parent school relations and communication. In addition many Chicanas feared that many children do not have access to quality education due to rural and poverty issues. Many are concerned that the schools' hostile environment is damaging their children, not only educationally but also socially, culturally and spiritually.

Several Chicanas indicated that they were never encouraged to go to college and that often they were told, "Why should you go to college, anyway you will probably get married and will have lots of children, why waste your time." One of the Chicanas who reported this comment is now the only Chicana pharmacist in the state of Oregon, Eloisa Valverde de Chaudhary. Some professional Chicanas interviewed also reported that often they were discouraged from speaking Spanish and were made to feel that their language and culture is of less value than others.

The Chicanas' perception of the education system is consistent with the results of the national educational statistic for Latino students. According to the 1992 National Hispanic Leadership Agenda Report, national statistics indicate a 56% high school dropout rate, only 6.8% graduate from college, and 15% are labeled illiterate by the traditional measure of literacy.[10] In the Northwest just like at the national level the number one issue in education is the drop or push-out rate. Rodriguez indicates that "the high school dropout rate for Hispanics is alarming and should tell us that these students are not dropouts but rather "push-outs"-pushed out due to institutional racism.[11] For example in Oregon, Hispanics make up four point six percent of the total student population, however the dropout rate is more that twice as high as the enrollment, it is fourteen percent.[12] The issue of pregnancy must be discussed in combination with the issue of education for Chicanas, given the high drop-out rates and high teen pregnancy rates at the national level. Past studies have examined the correlation between external versus internal controls and unplanned pregnancy rates. These studies indicate that women who cite external controls for life experiences have higher rates of unplanned pregnancy, whereas those citing internal controls have lower rates. Thus, those women who cite "luck," "chance," or "God's will" are more likely to become pregnant than those who cite personal preference or inattention as reasons. The bottom line is that, those women who do not believe that they have control over their lives or who have not learned that they can take control of their lives are the ones most likely to become pregnant. Many Chicanas interviewed lived under the above philosophy in spite of the fact that some were not Catholic.

Some of the Chicanas interviewed, who continued their education beyond junior high or high school indicated that they had to sacrifice their education in order to help their family. Many of these Chicanas ended up establishing their own family at a young age, and thus lost an educational opportunity. Many wished someone had talked to them about life and career options at an earlier age so they could have had choices. However, none of the Chicanas interviewed indicated that they would give up their children.

◆ Chicanas and the Abortion Issue

In the Northwest, a state pro-choice statute exists to legally protect a woman's reproductive freedom. Therefore, certain legal obstacles that exist in other states and which disproportionately effect teen women of color, such as parent notification requirements, do not pose a problem in the Northwest. However, once a Chicana becomes pregnant, there may not be ready support for alternatives to pregnancy, such as abortion. Access to abortions is directly related to rural and urban differences. Many parts of the Northwest do not even offer places where women can obtain information as to where the closest assistance is available.

Lack of money may deprive Chicanas from any effective choice, either because they have to travel far to obtain information and abortion services, or because they cannot afford the procedure. They may not be able to travel at all due to resistance from family members who may not respect their choice. If services are not available locally, it may be impossible to obtain an abortion in secret. The majority of the Chicanas interviewed were very hesitant to talk about abortion. Abortion is a very hush, hush issue in the Chicano community. For most Chicanas the main issue was not a matter of just a choice, but "is it a moral or immoral choice".

For others, motherhood may be a way to seek stature and the appearance of independence. Although, usually, it means going from being dependent upon parents to being dependent on a man or the welfare system. Many Chicanas preferred the embarrassment of being single mothers versus bearing the moral responsibility of getting an abortion. One Chicana indicated, "My child is a blessing and without him only God knows *como me hubiera ido si lo fuera abortado*." From several of the interviews it is obvious that abortion is not an option for many Chicanas. At the national level Chicana abortion is twelve (12%) percent verses fifty-five (55%) percent for White non-Hispanic, Thirty (30%)percent for Blacks/African Americans and Three (3%)for Asian Americans. Concrete data on Chicana abortions in the Northwest have not been distilled from national or regional data.

◆ Suspensions

School suspension was another issue of concern for many Chicana mothers and educators in the Northwest region.

For example in Oregon, 66.5 percent of the Hispanics who dropout did so because of "conduct" reasons, in other words due to "attendance and behavior". These students were really suspended rather than dropping out. (OPS, 1992-1994)[12] Indeed suspension is one of the major issues in education for the Northwest. Teachers, community leaders, parents and political leaders should be concerned with this issue if we want to address the low completion rate of Chicano(a) in grades one through twelve. Again we need to ask several questions: are Chicano(a) students dropping out or are they being "pushed out"? Is the school personnel trained to address Chicano(a) students' needs? Are Chicano(a) students being treated fairly and with dignity? Do we need to develop policies which address the suspension issue of Chicano(a)? What are the suspension rates among varying ethnic groups?

In spite of this gloomy picture in regard to education, Chicanas have and are actively participating at all levels of reforming the educational system. They will continue to face the challenge and positively impact the education system not only for Chicano children but for all children in the world. In the region there are several Chicana teachers and school administrators though not enough to be statistically documented. However, there are at least twice as many Chicana teacher aids who could become potential teachers. At the national level (2.9%) of all teachers are "Hispanic". In higher education (2.0%) of all faculty are "Hispanic". In spite of the low documented percentage of teachers at the national level, in the Northwest we found that there are many Chicanas involved in assuring that Chicano(a) children have access into the education system.

Chicanos/as in the Northwest reaffirm the national feeling that there is an urgent need to focus on the issue of teacher, administrators and faculty training. Many educators interviewed in Oregon and Washington indicated that this is one of the top ten issues in regards to Chicano(a) education. Many indicated that Chicano(a) students in the Northwest need teachers that can relate to them culturally, need role models, and teachers who care and value Chicano (a) students.

Some Chicanas in the Northwest are contributing to making educational institutions responsive to Chicanos/as. In Washington, there are several Chicanas, the following are just a few who are advocating and reforming the educational system for Chicano(a) children: Estela Ortega, Director, El Centro de La Raza; Irma Perez, School Teacher, Kent; Amelia M. Garza, Migrant Education Services, Yakima Valley OIC; Jeannette Morales, Administrator, Yakima Public Schools, Ginny Moncada, Moses Lake Head Start. In Oregon Tina Garcia, Project Coordinator, Migrant Education; Esther Puentes, President, Interface Network, Inc.; Maria Ruiz, Instructional Support Program, Salem Keiser School District; Dalia Torres, Director, Special Projects, Migrant Program; Gloria Rodriguez-Montgomery, Hispanic Resource Specialist, Portlant public Schools, and Olga Acuña, Coordinator of Special Education Support Services, Glenco High School.[13]

When researching for statistical data it became very obvious how critical it is for the Chicano community to gather its own data not only for statistical purpose, but also in order to develop community plans of action in order to address the issues affecting the educational attainment of Chicanos(as). The need to establish a Northwest Chicano(a) research center became very obvious. This anthology is a step in the right direction.

◆ Chicanas in Higher Education Making a Difference

Exploring the Chicano/a network in the Northwest colleges and universities we found that Chicanas are making a difference in higher education. We found that there is at least one Chicana at each institution of higher education in Oregon and in Washington. Many are in special programs while others are in entry level positions. The following is a listing of Chicanas contributing to Chicano/a higher education in the Northwest. In Washington, Dr. Margarita Marin, Sociology, Gonzaga University; Bertha Ortega, Dean of Students, Heritage College; Dr. Faviola Cuevas, Heritage College, in the Yakima Valley; Cleo Molina, North Seattle Community College; Jovita Guillen Lopez, Librarian/English Instructor, Skagit Valley College; Dianne Rodriguez, Student Advisor, Skagit Valley College; Dr. Guadalupe Friaz, American Ethnic Studies, University of Washington; Sonnya Arevalo, Admissions Coordinator, Western Washington University. In Oregon, Dora Alvarez, Nueva Ley Program, Chemeketa Community College; Irene Farrera, Minority Student Program, Southern Oregon State College; Mary Gallegos Oliver, Western Rural Development, Oregon State University; Linda Herrera, Minority Student Success Specialist Student Life, Chemeketa Community College; Bertha Herrera Martell, Office Coordinator, Office of Public Relations, Portland State University; Connie Mesquita, Coordinator, Multicultural Center, Lane Community College; Narcedalia Rodriguez, Assistant Director, College Assistance Migrant Program/CAMP, Oregon State University; Dr. Mary Romero Associate Professor, Sociology and Ethnic Studies, University of Oregon; Maria Alanis Ruiz, Assistant Director, Office of Admissions, Portland State University; Guadalupe Ramirez, Professor, Willamette University; Maria Ruis, Coordinator, Hispanic Clearinghouse Admissions, Southern Oregon State College; Margarita Rivera, Office Specialist, Office of Community Colleges; Dr. Luz Maciel Villarroel, Associate Professor, Educational Opportunity Program and Women Studies/Difference Power and Discrimination Program.

Many of the Chicanas we interviewed identified several issues in regards to equal access to higher education. For many the top issues were lack of role models, lack of moral support, lack of a nurturing environment, and the need to struggle with low expectations from personnel. Many also indicated achieving inspite of a racist, classist and chauvinistic environment. Most Chicanas in the above expressed their commitment to assuring that other Chicanos(as) have the support and equal opportunity to an education. Many expressed their strong commitment not only to their students but also to their community. Many identify activities which go beyond their call of duty, i.e. establishing tutoring programs/ESL, serving on local boards, developing cultural dance groups, establishing women's support groups and initiating college recruiting efforts at the elementary level.

◆ Health Issues

Today there is insufficient data on the status of Chicana health. One can venture to state from observations, interviews, and autobiographies that the Chicanas health in general is in jeopardy. Traditionally the level of medical services available to Chicanas has been based on income available to them. Because of this income factor, medical services have seldom been affordable to Chicanas. Chicanas face more barriers to health services than men. However, women utilize services at a higher level due to needs related to childbearing. One of the main health issues affecting Chicanas in the Northwest is the lack of preventive health care available because of a lack of education, income and language barrier.

Historically Chicana health issues have been ignored by both public institutions and the private sector. Most research conducted in regards to health issues does not specifically focus on Chicanos, let alone Chicanas in the Northwest. Furthermore, little or no research is conducted as to why Chicanas are more likely to suffer from certain diseases, nor has adequate attention been given to the issue of how to provide quality care to all, specifically Chicanas rural/farm workers, poor urban Chicanas and non- English speaking Chicanas.

According to MANA's Economic Equity Report, Chicanas in general are less likely to obtain routine medical check-ups than any other group of Latina women. This decreases her chances of preventing cancer, diabetes, unwanted pregnancy, heart disease etc. Lack of insurance is one of the main barriers for health care. Chicanas do not have access to primary care routine health services. Preventive care is a luxury for those who have health insurance or are financially able. In Oregon and Washington this is true for most Chicanas, because a large number depend on farm labor and are most likely to be uninsured.

MANA's report indicates that "Hispanics", women in particular, tend to be employed in the service industries. These are industries that do not provide health insurance coverage (50%).[14] Chicanas interviewed who were still economically dependent on their families indicated that their mother or father could not provide insurance coverage due to the lack of insurance in their place of employment. Some also indicated that they did not qualify for public assistance due to their or their family's immigration status.

MANA's report indicates that the top four leading causes of death for Chicanas(os) include, heart disease, cancer, accidental injuries and chronic liver disease. In addition, homicide, AIDS, and prenatal conditions are among the top ten killers of Hispanics. Among other issues affecting Chicanas are birth control, sterilization, abortion, teen pregnancy and prenatal care. Interviews affirmed that Chicanas in the Northwest are also facing the same health issues faced by Chicanas at the national level.

The majority of the Chicanas interviewed indicated that according to their family health history heart disease, diabetes, cancer and birth control are the top four health issues affecting them and their families.

Chicanas currently do not have a structure which addresses their health issues. The issues or barriers that need concentration are preventive health, policies in regards to health care, research, and health care education for Chicanas. It is also important to mention that the Chicana health status and profile is affected by cultural values and language. The factors are critical because many older Chicanas do not speak English. Culturally they run the risk of misdiagnosis and inappropriate treatment especially in the area of mental health.

Furthermore, in general, Chicanas in the Northwest do not have access to quality health care in spite of the fact that there are several Migrant and non-Migrant health clinics. The Chicano(a) population is growing very rapidly and the demand is growing at a faster rate than clinics are able to expand. Chicanas also lack a network from top to bottom and are unaware of health issues affected by drugs and alcohol and environmental problems (e.g., pesticides food additives and preservatives). In general, the Chicana's health has been neglected, they have endured insensitivity, and they lack access to quality preventive and comprehensive medical treatment. Some Chicanas in the Northwest are continuing to reach out to traditional native medicine. Many mention herbs, certain foods, and *curanderismo* as an alternative medicine. Many also have relied on obtaining their health care when they travel back and forth to México.

Health care, including issues of children's health, has traditionally been addressed by women. This general rule remains true for Chicanas in the Northwest. Chicanas interviewed indicated that usually they were the ones who took care of the children when ill and we also found that most of the *curanderas* in the region were *"mujeres,"* a tradition that evolved prior to the Pre-Colombian era.

One of the critical areas of medical need for Chicanas in the Northwest remains, as in other parts of the US, the lack of medical care for farm worker women, particularly prenatal care. Some farm worker clinics exist around the region. In Washington, these include SeaMar Community Health Centers in

Mt. Vernon; Central Washington Migrant Health Project in Moses Lake; *Centro Medico Familiar* in Walla Walla; *El Centro del Pueblo* in Wenatchee; *La Clinica de Trabajo de Labor* in Okanogan; *La Clinica in Pasco*; Okanogan Farm Workers' Clinic in Grandview, Sunnyside, and Toppenish. In Oregon: *La Clinica del Cariño*, Hood River; *Virginia Garcia* in Cornelius; *Salud de la Familia* Medical Center, Woodburn, and *La Clinica del Valle* Family Health Care Center in Phoenix. Although there are seven health clinics in the region, the demand is greater than can be provided by these clinics. During the harvest season, the services of these clinics are further over extended.

In Washington State, the issue of unequal access to medical care was recently highlighted when farm workers were excluded from the state's new "universal" health care coverage in 1993. Under pressure from farm worker clinics, the farm worker union, and other activists, the state expanded coverage to farm workers a year later, leaving the details to be worked out by a commission created for that purpose.

Again, this coverage will be particularly helpful for Chicanas in the agriculture stream who need adequate prenatal and postnatal care, medical attention for pesticide exposure, and work related accidents.

In both rural and urban areas, funding is needed to deal with AIDS prevention and treatment among the growing numbers of Chicanas becoming at risk, increased medical and dental care for women on public assistance, and equal access to abortions for low-income women.

In summary, Chicanas in the Northwest, like Chicanas throughout the nation are more likely to encounter cost as a barrier to unmet health care needs. Chicanos(a) are more likely to be exposed to pesticides due to their large numbers being employed as migrant workers. In general, according to available data, Chicanas are more likely to suffer from an excess incidence of cancer of the stomach, esophagus, pancreas and cervix. They are also twice as likely to die from stomach cancer, as non-Hispanic/Chicanas. Chicanos also suffer twice as much as non-Chicanos from cervical cancer. Lung cancer is on the rise due to smoking. Chicanas also suffer from other high risk diseases such as tuberculosis, which is four times higher, and diabetes, which is three times higher than in other Chicano/Hispanic groups or other non-Hispanic groups.[15]

Employment Issues

It is important to note that the issue of employment in regards to Chicanas is also a critical problem. Employment issues affecting Chicanas in the

Northwest are also based on race, class, gender, and immigration status. In this area Chicanas have also endured the injustice of discrimination based on race, class and gender. Equity in this area is critical for Chicanas. On the national level, Chicanas historically have been employed in gender segmented jobs. Therefore, Chicanas are more likely to be underpaid and overworked. Chicanas are more likely to be employed in low skilled, low paid jobs and are grossly underrepresented in managerial positions (15.8%) compared to (28%) non-Hispanic women. Chicanas hold mainly menial and low paying jobs. Chicanas are at the end of the pay scale. They earned 56 cents for every dollar a white woman earns, whereas black females earn 62 cents for every dollar earned by white women. The lack of education has contributed much to this under-employment status.[16]

Many Chicanas interviewed indicated encountering a revolving door more often than a glass ceiling. Interview data reflects that Chicana employment status in the Northwest has been affected by a lack of access to quality education, job training programs, language programs and role models. Chicanas in general indicated that a lack of adequate education or job training more often held them back from career opportunities and high paying jobs. In Oregon (11.8%) and in Washington 11.0% of the Chicano population attain a high school education.[17]

Chicanas in service occupations rate almost 10% higher than all other women's groups. The rate for managerial and professional specialty occupations for Chicanas is less than sixteen percent (15.8%) (MANA, 1992).

Chicanas are more likely to organize and participate in labor unions for economic advancement. Those who participated in unions had better health care benefits, higher wages, pension plans and other benefits. At the national level Chicanas who participated in unions earn 37.9% more per week than those who were not members of a union or were not represented by a union.

In the Northwest there are several Chicanas in labor movements. Some of the ones involved in these movements are advocates for labor movements not necessary because it will benefit them but because they want to help *la causa* for other Raza. Among these women are Tina Mata, Rosalinda Guillen and Sandra Fancher Garcia who have dedicated their efforts to the farm workers labor movements in Washington. In Oregon there are Alice Dale, Executive Director for the Oregon Public Employees Union; and Yvonne Martinez, American Federal State and County Municipal Employees Union.

In the Northwest, Chicana employment tends to be concentrated in technical and service occupations. Approximately two thirds of these interviewed were employed in these two occupational areas. In the technical areas we found Chicanas working in clothes factories, food processing, and in nurseries. In the service occupations many are working in motels and hotels as maids, some are working as house keepers, in restaurants as hostesses, cooks, dishwashers and as child care providers.

Chicanas in the Northwest are still trailing behind other women in the job market, and are concentrated in certain services such as the restaurant and hotel industries, farm work, food processing, and other unskilled labor. While there are Chicana role models filtering upward, they are few and far from being equally represented. In Oregon Chicanas are making a difference through the church and special programs such as the migrant programs, and educational opportunity programs, such as the College Assistance Migrant Programs. From reviewing the 1993 Resource Directories for Washington and Oregon for the Hispanic Community it is encouraging to note that several Chicanas are listed in high level positions accross the employment field.[19] Again education is a major barrier in employment upgrading.

In Washington, there is now one Chicana state legislator, and one Superior Court judge both in urban areas. Oregon does not have any Chicana state legislator or elected judges. There are a few Chicanas in state and federal government positions, or in large companies. Far more work needs to be done in the area of job advancement.

Some labor and professional organizations indirectly advance the cause of Chicanas. These organizations strive to promote and serve all people of color and women. Nevertheless, these efforts are worth noting because more often than not, advancement is accomplished through coalitions or through grassroots organizations.

In Washington, Chicanas and Latinas have sought inclusion of gender issues in two employment groups on different ends of the spectrum, farm workers and lawyers.

The constitution of the United Farm Workers of Washington State provides as one of its goals: *"De promover la participacion completa e igual de las mujeres en todos los asuntos y actividades y posiciones de liderazgo de la Union."* (To promote the complete participation and equality of women in all matters, activities and positions of union's leader)

The United Farm Workers of Washington State has continued to promote the participation of women in its leadership. Taking vital positions on the board, they have sent delegations to women's conferences in Canada and the U.S. and developed the leadership and speaking skills of those women by sending them to speak at general labor conferences, as well as its own rallies. Rosalina Guillen, represents an example of Chicanas playing an active and important role within the United Farm Workers of Washington State.

The Bylaws of the Washington State Hispanic Bar Association state, "The Washington State Hispanic Bar Association and its members shall not discriminate on the basis of sex, race, color, creed, national origin, gender, sexual orientation, religion, handicap, veteran or other protected status. Washington State Hispanic Bar Association members shall endeavor to enhance the rights and opportunities of women. The member who violates this express policy of the Washington State Hispanic Bar Association is subject to expulsion upon proper notice."

While written statements such as this may not seem like much, they are important stepping stones for the evolution of such institutions. They also serve as useful tools for discussing the direction organizations take at the time the constitution and bylaws are being drafted.

◆ Politics

The political involvement and participation in the Northwest and throughout the nation again depends on access to equal opportunities. Several barriers have denied Chicanas full participation in the political system. One of the main barriers for Chicanas is the lack of educational opportunities which promote the importance of citizen involvement and participation in the political process. Chicanas are the least likely to be educated on voting rights, voter registration, civil responsibilities and how the political system works.

The naturalization process and language provisions are two major obstacles Chicanas face when attempting to participate in the political system. One of the main reasons Chicanas face naturalization problems is that the immigration and naturalization service has discouraged Latinos from pursuing citizenship. The application process is complicated and long. These obstacles decrease the number of eligible voters. Many Chicanas, due to language barriers and a lack of political awareness, refrain from vocalizing their political concerns. However, some do get involved at the local level with the Spanish speaking community.

Chicanas in the Northwest like Chicanas nationally, face voter registration and redistricting practices as two political barriers inhibiting participation and political involvement. Rules governing voter registration vary and are often manipulated to maintain the current political status quo. This issue is detrimental to the Chicano community. Unfair redistricting practices often dilute the political power the Chicana(o) vote could have. Often redistricting changes are made deliberately to diffuse not only the Chicana(o) political vote but also that of other people of color.

Chicanas in the Northwest like other Latinos at the national level are involved in the political system and register and vote in greater numbers than Chicano/Latino men. According to the 1990 census bureau slightly more than 53% of the Latinas/Chicanas who registered only 35% voted. In comparison 50.5% of Latinos/Chicanos who registered, almost 33% voted.

In the Northwest as at the national level, Chicanas are more likely to be elected to school boards than to any other political position. Chicanos, although not in large numbers, are also elected as municipal leaders, county officials, judicial posts and as special district officials. A number of Chicanas also get appointed to public office at every level of government, including commissions on the Hispanic Affairs, and other state commission and boards.

In Washington there is one Chicana Senator, Margarita Lopez Prentice. In Oregon there are no Chicana legislators. However Chicanas are involved in policy making, on school boards. Chicanas are also participating in voter registration drives.

Although the Chicano(a) population is growing, unfortunately this does not mean Chicanas will automatically get elected to political posts. It is important to realize that over 38% of the Latino/Chicano population are not eligible to vote due to non-citizen status. In addition, another 35% are under age 18 and are not eligible to vote. Furthermore, according to the census bureau, of the Chicanos registered to vote (53%) about 35% actually voted.

The important observation about Chicanas in the Northwest is that Chicanas are represented everywhere and almost at every level of the political scene. Their numbers are small, but they express strong commitment to their communities. Many want to make a difference and are making a difference in their own way. Main issues for Chicanas, in the Northwest include the need to organize educational programs to increase the voting population; hold federal and state agencies accountable to address laws which impact the Chicano/Latino vote; hold political parties accountable for their political election promises made to the Chicano/Latino community; and continue to identify and support Chicanas for political positions and appointments at every level. Chicana educational, health and employment status and profile will prosper and improve when the number of Chicanas committed to Chicana(o) community issues increases in the political arena. Chicanas have never given up, and they never will; they have endured, survived and flourished in spite of over 500 years of resistance to colonialism of every kind. Chicanas will continue to survive utilizing not only current vehicles but will continue to draw experiences from others including pre-Columbian ways of surviving.

◆ The Law

As the number of attorneys of color slowly grows, the legal community, such as the American Bar Association, has become increasingly aware of the lack of equal access to justice in this country for the poor and in particular, people of color.

As with access to public benefits, lack of access to the justice system occurs for many reasons. In 1987, the Washington Legislature and State Supreme court established the Minority and Justice Task Force, which was transformed into a permanent commission in 1990. The minority and justice commission's purpose is to identify and address issues of unequal treatment in the judicial system. Washington is one of the foremost leaders in the country among the dozen states which have formed similar task forces to deal with the administration of justice problems.

The Minority and Justice Commission has staged public hearings around the state. The most often cited complaints at these public hearings were related to unequal treatment by the police and a lack of qualified interpreters in the courts. The Commission has created subcommittees to conduct research on disparate treatment, the education of judges and court administrators. Another area of research has focused on the issue of increasing diversity among the work force in the justice system.

Studies of prison incarceration have shown that the race and ethnicity of defendants contribute directly to the fact that they are more often charged with serious and violent offenses, detained prior to trial, sentenced to prison, and, once there, held for longer proportions of their sentences. Studies have specifically found that Latinos are one-and-a-half times more likely than whites to be imprisoned for crimes. It concluded that "For some officials, being Black or Hispanic seems to be part of being "dangerous and bad". [Crutchfield and Bridges, 1986]

In January 1993, a Washington Minority and Justice study focusing on juveniles showed that youth of color are more likely to be detained prior to court appearances than white youth, and this detention in itself leads to tougher sentences.

In September 1993, another Washington Minority and Justice study focusing on exceptional sentences (those which are shorter or longer than the guidelines) found disparate treatment for Latinos and Latinas in many areas. It also found that judges in rural areas (where there are often large Chicano communities) are more likely to go outside the guidelines. The study showed that Latinos and Native Americans are more likely to receive aggravated (longer) sentences than others. Latinos were also least likely to receive mitigated (shorter) sentences. The study also showed that white female offenders are more likely than white male offenders to receive either an aggravated or mitigated exceptional sentence. Latinas and African American female offenders in comparison are more likely to receive mitigated sentences than their male counterparts but are not more likely to receive aggravated exceptional sentences. The study recommended a more thorough examination of some of the issues uncovered by the research, "particularly the substantial disadvantage experienced by Hispanic offenders in the use of exceptional sentences."[20]

Past studies show that Latinos are greatly underrepresented on the bench and bar, and in court personnel. These studies have not reflected the make-up of juries, but it is reasonable to assume that they are also not reflective of the community at large. Of course, the lack of Chicanos and Chicanas in the system which administers the law has a direct impact on equal justice, and the perception of unequal justice. In 1988-89, national figures indicated that nine hundred and sixty nine out of 43,323 bachelors law degrees conferred were "Hispanics" (Northwest statistics were not available). It is estimated that less than 1% to 2% of the attorneys in the Northwest are Chicanas. In the Northwest and at the national level disparate treatment is an important issue not only for defendants, but also for judges, attorneys court personnel, plaintiffs, and witnesses.

The number of Chicana lawyers is still quite low. The law school also has one Chicana, Sandra Madrid, Assistant Dean/Faculty. There are at least eight Chicana attorneys in the state of Washington, Sandra Fancher Garcia, Bellingham: and in the Yakima Valley, Myrna Trejo, Patricia Loera, Lisa Castilleja, Laura Contreras, Rosa Maria Cortez. In the Seattle area, Monica Fernandez and Georgia Trejo Locher. All eight Chicanas belong to the Washington State Bar Association. In Oregon, there are several Chicana attorneys listed in the Oregon State Commission Directory, Maria Parra, Hilda Galavis-Stroller, Irene Bustillos-Taylor, Appellate Attorney, Public Defender, State of Oregon, Carmen Calzacorta, Aida Iranzo, Washington County District Attorney. Significant efforts are being taken by the University of Washington Law School, whose Chinese-American dean became the first law school dean of color in the US. Approximately 30% of the law students are of color, and about 40% are female.

The Washington Supreme court also established a Gender Bias Commission to look at the issue of treatment of women. One conclusion was that women plaintiffs are being awarded smaller damage awards, apparently because judges and juries view their lives less valuable, and because women are still earning about 60 cents on the dollar compared to men. Again, the study did not specifically include statistics on Chicanas, but given the census data indicating a continued low-income level, it is reasonable to assume that the few Chicanas that are able to retain an attorney are receiving smaller awards.

Support Groups in the Northwest

There are few support groups focusing on Chicanas in Oregon and Washington. Most groups either focus on Latinas or Latinos. Aside from MEChA, none have been identified using the word Chicano(a) in the organizations name. An examination of formal groups around the Northwest identifies the following groups:

Hispanic Women's Network, Olympia.
Mexican American Women's National Association NW., Seattle
Mujeres Activas en Letras y Cambio Social NW, Seattle
Washington Association of Women & Minority Entrepreneurs, Yakima [21]

In the Hispanic Resource Directory 1992-1994, three Chicana/Latina women organizations/associations were listed for Washington and none for Oregon: Mexican-American Women's National Association (MANA), *Mujeres Activas en Letras y Cambio* and the Hispanic Women's Network.[22]

In the *Annuario Hispano* 1994 Hispanic Yearbook, there were no *mujeres* organizations/association listed in Oregon and Washington. However there were several Chicano, Latino, Hispano and Mexicano organizations/associations.

The 1993 Women's Information Directory included two Chicana organizations, three Latina associations, one Mexican-American women's association, and over ten organizations/associations of Hispanic women.[23] Yet, none were from Oregon or Washington.

Thus we find a void of support groups focusing on the Chicana experience in the Northwest. However, Chicanas are able to seek limited support through Latino, Latina, and women's groups (such as the Northwest Women's Law Center Women of Color Project). Chicanas are also able to sometimes work within larger organizations by bringing their issues for inclusion within the larger set of goals and objectives, such as with the professional organizations noted earlier, unions, the Rainbow Coalition, socialist and radical groups, and mainstream political organizations like the Democratic Party.

In Oregon there are several organizations which focus on Chicana issues but only one specifically focuses on Chicana/Latina issues: MANA: Mexican American Women National Association. However, several women's support groups have been established such as the ones at Oregon State University, Portland State University, and University of Oregon. In Washington there are two Chicana student support group including *Mujeres Unidas* at Washington State University and Raices at Eastern Washington University. In addition, there are several women's groups through the churches and other community agencies. Women or Chicano support groups are found in the traditional governmental system. The majority are very informal, however they are addressing issues which are not only pertinent to women but family as well, including political, language, immigration educational, health and other issues affecting the Chicano community.

Summary

In summary, Chicanas in the Northwest as at the national level have endured triple oppression of discrimination based on race, gender, class and immigration status. Due to their immigration status many Chicanas in the Northwest lack command of the English language, familiarity with the dominant culture, and are not aware of legal systems. Many, due to these issues, face pre-mature deportation, racial and sexual harassment, and are vulnerable to employee rights violations such as wages, hours, maternity, health and safety violations.

It is evident that until Chicanas have equal access to quality educational opportunities, and when they are no longer faced with triple discrimination, their status in the labor force will continue as it has. Chicanas in general will remain one of the more impoverished groups in the Northwest however Chicanas will continue to endure, survive and prevail the long struggle.

Chicanas in the Northwest are not any different from those at the national level. In general, when looking at employment issues, Chicanas are the least educated, are more likely to be employed in unskilled and or semi-skilled occupations specifically in technical and service occupations. Less than 1% work in skilled trades and very few are employed in managerial and professional occupations. Chicanas also are at the lowest end of the pay scale and most are employed in minimum wage positions and are more likely to be "poor". Chicanas constitute a large number of seasonal farm laborers who are the least protected group. They are more likely to incur health hazards due to potentially harmful pesticides and are more likely to lack health care and unemployment benefits.

Other issues affecting Chicanas are adequate and affordable day care, immigration discrimination, and access to health insurance. Last but not least, affirmative action efforts have been inadequate and ineffective regarding hiring practices pertaining to Chicanas. The Chicana's current status economically is due to a lack of equal access to educational and employment opportunities and due to federal and nonfederal policies and practices including discrimination practices in the private and the public sector at every level.

Endnotes

1. Alfredo Mirande and Evangelina Enriquez, La Chicana: The Mexican-American Women, The University of Chicago Press, 1979. p. 10.
2. Ibid., p. 19.
3. Irene I. Blea, La Chicana and the Intersection of Race, Class and Gender, Praeger, Westport, Connecticut, 1992, pp. 1-167.
4. The Mexican-American Women's National Association (MANA's) Report: "In Search of Economic Equity," Washington D. C., 1992, p. ii.
5. Ibid., p. ii.
6. Washington State Commission On Hispanic Affairs, Hispanic Community Third Edition, Olympia, Washington D.C., 1992, p. ii.
7. Marlita A. Reddy, Statistical Record of Hispanic Americans, Gale Research In., Detroit, 1993, p. 151.
8. Washington State Commission on Hispanic Affairs, Hispanic Community Resource Directory, Third Edition, Olympia, Washington, 1993, pp. 67-69.
9. Oregon State Commission of Hispanic Affairs, Resource Directory for the Hispanic Community, Corvallis, Oregon, 1993. pp. 66-68.
10. National Hispanic Leadership Agenda, Policy Summary Report, Boston, 1992, p. 12.
11. Narcedalia Rodriguez, Strategies For The Recruitment And Retention of Undergraduate Hispanic Students in Institutions of Higher Education (Master Thesis), Oregon State University, Corvallis, Oregon, June, 1994. p. 9.
12. Oregon Board of Education, Oregon Public Schools Dropout, Grades 9-12, Reporting Year July 1, 1992-June 30, 1993, pp. 1-4.
13. Washington and Oregon State Commissions on Hispanic Affairs, Resource Directories for the Hispanic Community, Olympia Washington and Corvallis, Oregon, 1993, pp. 1-79 and 1-105.
14. The Mexican American Women's National Association MANA's Report, "In Search of Equity," Washington D.C., 1992, p. 25.
15. Ibib., pp. 25-26.
16. Ibid., pp. 13-14.
17. U.S. Department of Education, Office of Educational Research and Improvement, Digest of Education Statistics, national Center For Education Statistics, October, 1993, pg. 22.
18. National Hispanic Leadership Agenda, policy Summary Report, Washington, D.C., 1992, p. 13.
19. Oregon and Washington State Commission on Hispanic Affairs, Resource Directories For The Hispanic Community, Corvallis, Oregon and Olympia, Washington, 1993, pp. 1-105 and 1-79.
20. Weis Crutchfield, Engen and Gainey (compiled by), The Washington Sta. Minority and Justice Commission, "Racial/Ethnic Disparities and Exceptional Sentence In Washington State, " September, 1993, p. 29.
21. Oregon and Washington State Commission on Hispanic Affairs, Resource Directories For the Hispanic Community, Corvallis, Oregon and Olympia, Washington, 1993, pp. 1-105 and 1-79.
22. Alan E. Schoor, Hispanic Resource Directory, 1992-1994, The Denali Press, Juneau, Alaska, 1992, p. 364.
23. Shawn Brennan, Women's Information Directory, Gale Research Inc., Detroit, 1993, pp. 252-254 and 221-224.

Bibliography

Annuario Hispano 1994 Hispanic Yearbook T.I.Y.M., Publishing Co., Inc. McLean, VA, 1994.

Blea, Irene I. La Chicana and the Intersection of Race, Class, and Gender. Westport, Connecticut, 1992.

Brennan, Shawn, Editor; Women's Information Directory; Gale Research Inc., Detroit, 1993.

Crutchfield and Bridges. "Prison incarceration report."

U.S. Department Of Education, Office of Educational Research and Improvement Digest of Education Statistics, National Center For Education Statistics, October, 1993.

Hispanic Community Resource Directory; Ethnic Heritage Directory; Washington State Minority & Justice Resource Manual; D.S.H.S. directory.

Mirande, A. and E. Enriquez. La Chicana: The Mexican-American Woman. Chicago: The University of Chicago Press, 1979.

National Hispanic Leadership Agenda, 1992 Policy Summary Report. Boston, 1992.

Oregon Commission on Hispanic Affairs, 1993 Resource Directory For The Hispanic Community; 1993, Corvallis, Oregon.

Oregon Migrant Education News, (all issues) 1992-1994, Oregon Migrant Education.

Oregon Board of Education, Oregon Public School Dropout Report, Grades 9-12, July 1, 1992, June 1, 1993.

Oregon State System of Higher Education; Fact Book, December, 1992; Eugene, Oregon.

Reddy, Marlita A., Editor; Statistical Record of Hispanic Americans; Gale Research Inc., Detroit; 1993.

Rodriguez, Narcedalia; Strategies for the Recruitment and Retention of Undergraduate Hispanic Students in Institutions of Higher Education, (Research paper for partial fulfillment of the requirements for a masters degree), Oregon State University, Corvallis, Oregon, 1994.

Schmittroth, Linda, Editor; Statistical Record of Women Worldwide; Gale Research Inc.; Detroit, 1991.

Schoor, Alan E.; Hispanic Resource Directory: 1992-1994; The Denali Press, Juneau, Alaska, 1992.

The Mexican-American Women's National Association (MANA) Report: "In Search Of Economic Equity." 1992, Washington, D. C.

Washington State Commission on Hispanic Affairs, Hispanic Community Resource Directory; Third Edition 1993; Olympia, Washington.

Crutchfield, Weis et al, The Washington State Minority and Justice Commission, "Racial/Ethnic Disparities and Exceptional Sentence in Washington State", September, 1993.

Hispanic Community Resource Directory; Ethnic Heritage Directory; Washington State minority & Justice Resource Manual; D.S.H.S. directory.

Mirande, A. and Enriquez. La Chicana: The Mexican-American Woman. Chicago: The University of Chicago Press, 1979.

National Hispanic Leadership Agenda, 1992 Policy Summary Report. Boston, 1992.

Oregon Commission on Hispanic Affairs, 1993 Resource Directory For The Hispanic Community; 1993, Corvallis, Oregon.

Oregon Migrant Education news, (all issues) 1992-1994, Oregon Migrant Education.

Oregon State System of Higher Education; Fact Book, December, 1992; Eugene, Oregon.

Reddy, Marlita A., Editor; Statistical Record of Hispanic Americans; Gale Research Inc., Detroit; 1993.

Stalche, Verina "Women: The conquest and the struggle." NACLA Report (Norte Americas. vol. XXIV, no. 5. 1992.

Schmittroth, Linda, Editor; Statistical record of Women Worldwide; Gale Research Inc.; Detroit, 1991.

Schoor, Alan E.; Hispanic Resource Directory: 1992-1994; The Denali Press, Juneau, Alaska, 1992. The Mexican-American Women's National Association (MANA) Report: "In Search of Economic Equity." 1992, Washington, D.C.

Washington State Commission on Hispanic Affairs, Hipanic Community Resource Directory; Third Edition 1993; Olympia, Washington.

7

Chicanos in the Pacific Northwest: A Bibliographic Essay

Estela Elizondo-Radovancev

Introduction

In the last thirty years, a great deal has been accomplished by Chicanos to further the cause of La Raza in this country. Extensive research sources are available on Chicanos across the country, especially in areas like the southwest, where a large percentage of Chicanos live. Large urban areas, like Los Angeles and Albuquerque, which have large concentrations of Hispanics, support large universities and extensive educational facilities where considerable research is being done. Thus, much academic attention has been focused on the problems of Chicano education, economic status, housing, immigration and naturalization, politics and cultural traditions. Yet much of this research may not be applicable to Chicanos in other areas of the country because of varying local conditions.

This bibliographic essay is focused on the Chicano experience in the Northwestern states of Idaho, Oregon, and Washington with the objective of providing the reader with a current listing of selected and useful materials on this important topic. It is intended as a contribution to the limited amount of source materials available on the subject of Chicanos in the Pacific Northwest. In the past, this sizeable ethnic group has been ignored or not considered a suitable topic for scholarly or general study by main stream researchers. However, given the current growth of the Hispanic population in the Northwest, increased attention is merited from educators, researchers, government personnel, social service agencies, business organizations, the media, and the general public. The contributions made to American society by this politically important minority group can no longer be ignored.

The basic purpose of the present work is to provide the reader with references having wide topical coverage and historical perspective. The intent is not to be all-inclusive; some titles have been excluded. Rather, an effort was made to select materials by or about Chicanos in the Pacific Northwest region which may be most useful, readily available, or unique. Obviously, the materials will vary in utility, depending on the researchers' topic of interest. This essay includes both primary and secondary works, such as books, theses and dissertations, government documents, general reports, newspaper and journal articles, audio-visual materials, and computer software. It must be admitted, however, that the pool of available research materials on Northwest Chicanos is limited at the present time.

This bibliographic essay is organized into general thematic areas in an attempt to provide the reader with bibliographic information in a readable and interesting piece. The themes are presented as follows: terminology; bibliographies and reference; CD-ROM materials; demographics; Chicanos in the Northwest; migrants and farm labor; political issues; education; religion; health services; gender issues; biographical accounts; art, literature, and music; audio-visuals and media; newspapers; and the multicultural movement. All types of print materials are included within their thematic subjects, while audio-visual materials are listed separately. A bibliography which lists complete citations of all works included in this essay is appended.

The master's theses and doctoral dissertations included are especially important, since much of the historical material, research studies, and information is not available in other publications. These materials are of great value because many of them portray the Mexican American experience accurately and often include real-life photographs, charts, or graphs to help illustrate the author's point of view. The reader will find that most of these studies include bibliographic references which may prove useful. Most master's theses are available to the researcher through interlibrary loan, and most doctoral dissertations are available for purchase from University Microfilms International.

◆ Terminology and Chicanismo

The reader should be aware that a certain amount of confusion exists on the use and misuse of self-referent terminology in regard to Hispanics. Terms such as Hispanic, Mexican, Mexican-American, Chicano, Latino, etc., are often used interchangeably in referring to members of this minority group. Both Anglo and Hispanic writers have used these descriptive terms in differing ways, and it is best to remain flexible and be aware of varying usage. The present bibliographic essay includes those works which reflect or include the Northwest Chicano experience, regardless of the variant usage of self-referent terms.

In seeking to understand modern-day Chicanos, it is important to appreciate the historical and cultural factors which make this group unique. As a take-off point, the reader may wish to review materials which attempt to define Chicanismo as an ideology, as a historical political movement, and in comparison to other Hispanic groups. Richard L. Nostrand's "'Mexican American' and 'Chicano': Emerging Terms for a People Coming of Age" is an excellent source to use in the identification of terms such as Mexican, Chicano, Spanish-American and other variations of self-referral. Nostrand traces the historical origins of these terms and follows their development through present-day usage. Theresa Aragón de Shepro, in her monographic work, *Chicanismo and Mexican American Politics*, provides an accurate definition of Chicanismo as an ideology as well as a modern political movement, and discusses the meaning of El Movimiento. Adelina Gonzales, in her short essay, "The Significance of the Chicano Movement in the 1990's" includes History, Culture and Pride as the three essential elements of the Chicano Movement.

Carlos B. Gil wrote a paper entitled, "The Many Faces of the Mexican-American; An Essay concerning Chicano Character" (ERIC No. ED255350) in which he attempts to define the differing facets of *mexicanidad especial* or the unique characteristics of Mexican people. This essay is a thorough review of Mexican traditions, language, and cultural values as these are transmitted from generation to generation and influence Chicanos in American society. Also recommended is the report, *Guide to Understanding People, Language, and Culture: Chicano*, prepared by Maria Viramontes de Marin under the auspices of the Office of the State Superintendent of Public Instruction in Washington State as a good introductory overview to Chicano culture and language.

◆ Bibliographies and Reference

Bibliographies and indexes are listings of materials on particular subjects and are used in basic research work. There are several important reference sources which are used nationally and include topics pertaining to the Chicano experience which should be mentioned. The first is *The Chicano Index* (which supercedes the *Chicano Periodical Index*) edited by Lillian Castillo-Speed, et al., and produced by the Chicano Studies Library Publications Unit at the University of California at Berkeley. This annual index provides citations of books, anthology articles, reports, and journal articles, by subject, author and title. Another well-known reference source is the *Chicano Anthology Index*, compiled and edited by Francisco García-Ayvens and published by the University of California at Berkeley. This work identifies 280 Chicano anthologies and includes approximately 5,000 essays and other creative works published about Chicanos from 1965 to 1987. Equally well-known is Matt S. Meier's *Bibliography of Mexican American History*, which includes historical works on Mexican Americans from 1848 to contemporary times, presented in chronological and topical divisions.

The standard reference work on Chicanos in the Northwest is Pat Matheny-White's *Bibliography of Chicano/Latino Art and Culture in the Pacific Northwest*. Though published in 1982, this continues to be a relevant listing of published monographs, reports, government documents, theses and dissertations, periodical and newspaper articles, audio-visual materials, and art works. Researchers may also use Matheny-White's companion volume entitled, *Bibliography of Chicano/Latino Art and Culture: National and International Perspectives*, which lists materials from other regions of the U.S. and provides a global perspective as well.

The Washington State Commission on Hispanic Affairs makes available an excellent reference publication entitled, *Hispanic Community Resource Directory*, which provides state-wide, current information on community resources of interest to Hispanics. This directory covers information on arts and entertainment, churches, community services, consulates, employment services, food banks and shelters, government services, health, Hispanic organizations, immigration resources, language translators, legal services, and women's groups. This is recommended as an invaluable resource for locating up-to-date information on agencies and business organizations.

◆ CD-Rom Materials

The advent of electronic information systems has made possible the production of subject specific CD-ROM materials. The "Chicano Database on CD-ROM" is a cumulative database containing information from selected reference works. It is an electronic database which was developed by the University of California at Berkeley to help students and scholars doing research on Mexican-American issues. The "Chicano Database" provides access to numerous bibliographic citations on Chicano topics.

Also potentially useful for researchers is the "Ethnic Newswatch" database on CD-ROM, produced by SoftLine Information Inc., which provides full text access to ethnic newspapers and magazines in the United States. Hispanic/Latino/Chicano newspaper and magazine publications are included with publications of other ethnic groups. This database currently includes 75,000 full text articles from 90 publications, and is a significant source of information on multicultural topics.

◆ Demographics

The U.S. Bureau of the Census makes available numerous publications on demographics, which are produced by the Government Printing Office. Several of these publications are well-known and contain very useful and up-to-date information on the Hispanic population. *The 1990 Census of Population; Social and Economic Characteristics* (by State) is a basic census publication which provides rural and urban population statistics for each state, including racial distribution. *The Hispanic Population in the United States: March 1992*, provides statistical information on the economic, educational and social characteristics of the Hispanic population. The report entitled *Hispanic Americans Today*, is a colorful, 48-page booklet which includes detailed information on Hispanics including language, labor force, health insurance, housing, business ownership, and voting registration. Also recommended is the publication, *1990 Census Profile: Race and Hispanic Origin*, which uses charts to illustrate comparisons between Hispanics and other races. *We the American Hispanics* is a publication containing general statistical comparisons of the Hispanic population.

Demographic in-state materials are also available, such as *Profile of the Hispanic Population of Idaho*, 1990 published by the Idaho Department of Commerce. This demographic and economic profile provides statistics on household characteristics and income, labor force status, educational enrollment, and population distribution by county. For basic statistics in the State of Oregon, the reader may refer to the report, *Persons of Spanish Origin by Race and Age*, compiled by the Center for Population Research and Census at Portland State University. This report provides racial distribution statistics by city and county. Annabel Kirschner Cook's edited report "Increasing Racial and Ethnic Diversity in Washington" in the publication *Washington Counts* provides statistical tables and county maps illustrating racial distribution throughout Washington State.

Another recommended source is Richard Slatta and Maxine Atkinson's article, "The 'Spanish Origin' Population of Oregon and Washington: A Demographic Profile, 1980" which was published in the *Pacific Northwest Quarterly*. This article profiles changes in the Hispanic population since 1970, provides statistical data, and discusses the regional implications for the growth of this ethnic group in Oregon and Washington. A second article which may prove useful is Annabel Kirschner Cook's "Diversity Among Northwest Hispanics" published in the *Social Science Journal*, which is an analysis of some Hispanic social and economic characteristics with comparisons to the Anglo population in the Northwest. Also of interest is a newspaper report on demographics that appeared in the Spokesman Review, "Hispanic Population soars on East Side", written by Rick Bonino, which provides useful information and statistics on Hispanics in Eastern Washington and Northern Idaho.

Chicanos in the Northwest

The Chicano population in Idaho is smaller in comparison to that of Oregon and Washington. However, they continue to grow in numbers and influence, and there are some source materials available to researchers. *Historia Verdadera del Chicano del Norte* [True History of the Chicano of the North] by David Herrera and Clifford E. Bryan is available as an ERIC document (No. ED104577) and outlines the plight of first, second and third generations of Chicanos in the Northwest. Herrera and Bryan also make some interesting comparisons between Chicanos in the Southwest and those who chose to settle in the Northwest. Patricia K. Ourada's chapter, "Mexican Heritage and Experience in Idaho," in *Interpreting Local Culture and History*, edited by J. Sanford Rikoon and Judith Austin, is recommended as a compact historical introduction to the Hispanic community in Idaho. Ourada examines the four distinct Hispanic groups in Idaho—Mexicans, Mexican Americans, Spanish Americans, and Chicanos—and discusses their contributions to the lucrative agricultural industry, the history of the bracero program, their deplorable living conditions, and the problems of prejudice.

A primary source on the subject of ethnic groups in Idaho is entitled *Idaho's Ethnic Heritage*, which was co-edited by Laurie Mercier and Carole Simon-Smolinski. This special project was co-sponsored by the Idaho Centennial Commission and the Idaho State Historical Society in recognition of Idaho's Centennial Celebration and includes extensive information on Mexican-Americans. Volume one is the "Resource Guide" and is especially useful since it provides a listing of sources, including published and unpublished materials, photographic collections, sound recordings, and pertinent historic sites and buildings. Volume two presents "Historical Overviews" and Mercier gives an outstanding account of the contributions of Mexican Americans in the evolving history of Idaho. Beginning with the Mexican miners of 1870, she goes on to describe the cowboys, the railroad workers, the farmworkers and the migrants, as well as the difficult working conditions and discrimination which they withstood. Mercier continues with contemporary history and discusses the Mexican-American struggle for civil rights, their endurance against racism and prejudice, and their increasing strength from the preservation of family, language, culture, and tradition.

Chicanos have been identified in Oregon as the fastest growing ethnic group in the state. There are some recommended materials which examine the status of Chicanos in Oregon. Richard W. Slatta is a leading historian who has written extensively on this topic. His master's thesis, "Chicanos in Oregon: A Historical Overview," which was completed in 1974 at Portland State University, is an outstanding research study which provides historical perspective to the presence of Chicanos in Oregon. This in-depth work includes an analysis of Chicano terminology, a history of Hispanic migration to Oregon, the farm workers' decision to settle, support for Cesar Chavez and the United Farm Workers Union, demographic characteristics, the influence of the Valley Migrant League, evolving political organizations, Chicano cultural activities, as well as media coverage. Slatta also discusses the schools, the bilingual programs, various educational problems of Chicano students in higher education, and the founding of Colegio Cesar Chavez, (Mt. Angel, Oregon) which was the first independent accrdited Chicano institution of higher learning in this country. Slatta's landmark study is highly recommended as a vibrant and readable account of the Chicano experience in Oregon.

Also recommended is a second study by Richard Slatta entitled "Chicanos in the Pacific Northwest: An Historical Overview of Oregon's Chicanos," which was published by *Aztlan*. This article presents an excellent historical review of the settlement of the Chicano population in Oregon and discusses their social and economic problems. In his monographic study, *Ethnic Genesis: Oregon's Chicanos*, scholar Doug Kupel has also provided an outstanding historical account on this subject. Kupel presents a historical introduction and goes on to discuss the various political, economic, and educational concerns of the Chicano population in the process of establishing itself in Oregon.

In the last few years there has been an increase in the number of historical materials on Chicanos in Washington State. Rodolfo Acuña's well-known book, *Occupied America: A History of Chicanos*, includes some references to Northwest Chicanos, especially to the migration of Texas-Mexicans to the Yakima area. Researchers should consult the work of Dr. Erasmo Gamboa, from the University of Washington, who has written a number of references on the history of Chicanos in the Northwest. His article, "Chicanos in the Northwest: An Historical Perspective," published in *El Grito*, provides historical information on Chicanos in Washington State, and discusses the social and economic problems of residents in the Yakima Valley. In addition, Bruce E. Johansen and Roberto F. Maestas have written a compact history of farm laborers in Yakima, an account of the Gallegos family, and the founding of El Centro de la Raza in Seattle entitled, *The Creation of Washington's Latino Community: 1935-1980*.

Special mention must be made of the Washington State Commission on Mexican American Affairs, which was established to improve the well-being of the state's Hispanic population and to assist in increasing the Mexican-American population participation in government, business, and education. Researchers are referred to ERIC No. ED254599 for a report entitled "Hispanic Strategies for 1984-85. A Planning Document," which outlines the responsibilities of the Commission on Mexican American Affairs, and focuses on issues of concern to Hispanics in Washington State. Basic, in-depth information and statistics are provided in the areas of immigration, employment and business development, education, voter registration, and services to the Hispanic elderly.

◆ Agriculture, Farm Labor, and Migrants

Agriculture is a major element in the economic well-being of the Northwest economy. Over the years, programs were developed allowing the growers to use migratory farm labor during the harvest season. An increasing number of studies have been done on farm laboring groups in the Northwest. Erasmo Gamboa, as mentioned earlier has written on the status of the Mexican

American community in the Northwest, especially in the Yakima Valley. His master's thesis, entitled, "A History of the Chicano People and the Development of Agriculture in the Yakima Valley, Washington," was completed in 1973 at the University of Washington in Seattle. This landmark work is an in-depth study which parallels the historical development of the agricultural industry with the struggle of Chicanos to achieve social and economic equality in the Yakima Valley.

Gamboa continued his studies of agricultural farmworkers and his doctoral dissertation, "Under the Thumb of Agriculture: Bracero and Mexican American Workers in the Pacific Northwest, 1940-1950," which was completed in 1984, was the result of many years of research work. This is an in-depth examination of the demographic shift of contracted Mexican braceros and Mexican American migrants to the Pacific Northwest to fill the labor shortage caused by World War II. In the process, they lay the framework of modern-day Chicano communities and brought their culture to this region.

"Braceros" is a Spanish term meaning workers who labor with their arms. During World War II, binational labor agreements allowed braceros to enter the U.S. to perform necessary farm work. Erasmo Gamboa, in his outstanding monographic work, *Mexican Labor and World War II: Braceros in the Pacific Northwest, 1942-1947*, covers the historic elements of the bracero program and the importance of Mexican migration to the Northwest. This book examines the farm labor crisis, bracero strikes, their social life, and the decision by many to settle in the Northwest. The stark illustrations show the drab camps, poverty, and hard labor which these men endured. Gamboa's book, the culmination of his graduate studies, is highly recommended as a basic source of information on Mexican American migrants and their exploitation.

There have been numerous studies on the mobility patterns of agricultural workers who migrate to the Pacific Northwest. In Idaho, they settled in the Treasure Valley region along the Snake River, in Oregon the majority settled in the Willamette Valley, and in Washington State, the majority of the migrant farm workers settled in the Yakima Valley. Farm workers comprise a large percentage of the Chicano population in the Northwest.

One of the most thorough studies on Mexican migrant laborers in Idaho is Patricia Ourada's study, *Migrant Workers in Idaho*, which was funded by a faculty grant at Boise State University. This historical account begins with the Pre-1900 period and traces in detail the historic development of Idaho's agricultural enterprise, its dependence upon domestic and migrant farm labor supply, World War II and the Mexican Bracero program, as well as subsequent problems with discrimination, living conditions, and health care. Ourada's study includes maps and descriptions of Idaho's farm labor camps, discusses the acute problem of undocumented aliens, efforts to improve the life-style of migrant workers, and current changes due to mechanization in the harvesting of crops.

An outstanding research work on Oregon's Hispanic migrants is Colleen Marie Loprinzi's master's thesis, "Hispanic Migrant Labor in Oregon, 1940-1990," which was completed at Portland State University. This historical study provides a general profile of the migrant, describes their contributions since 1940 to Oregon's agribusiness, their housing, health and working conditions, their overwhelming poverty and low wages, their attempts to use education to leave the migrant cycle, and the poor treatment they received from the growers and surrounding communities. External factors affecting migrants are also analyzed such as the role of the contractors, the Oregon economy, a profile of Oregon farmers and political actions which influenced their treatment of migrants, governmental policies and programs, and a chronology of union activism and labor resistance through the years. Loprinzi's thesis is an invaluable resource on the history of Hispanic labor in Oregon.

Another good source is Paul P. Koehler's independent study thesis entitled "Integration of the Mexican People in Woodburn, Oregon," which was completed in 1982. This is an engrossing account of the different groups which make up Woodburn's population—the large retirement community, the Mexican Americans, the Russian Old-Believers, and the established Anglo community. Koehler focuses on the large Mexican American population in Woodburn and discusses the farmworkers and undocumented aliens, the bilingual and Title I-M education programs, employment possibilities outside of agriculture, health care services, legal assistance services, and the lack of Mexican American participation in politics and the city government.

The earliest important study on migrants in Washington State was done in 1966 by the Consulting Services Corporation in Seattle, Washington, and is called *Migrant Farm Workers in the State of Washington*. This is a four-volume study, and includes a bibliography, economic and social characteristics, an analysis of working conditions, and recommendations for change. Though dated, this comprehensive state-wide study should be consulted as a basic historical source of information on migratory workers.

Two articles by Erasmo Gamboa which appeared in the *Pacific Northwest Quarterly* will be of interest to the researcher. "Mexican Migration into Washington State: A History, 1940-1950," is an insightful, historical study of Mexican migration to the Yakima Valley and includes statistical tables and illustrations of employed farm workers. Equally important is Gamboa's "Mexican Labor in the Pacific Northwest, 1943-1947: A Photographic Essay," which provides visual testimony to the hard labor, poverty, and bleak living conditions which farm laborers were forced to endure.

Local perspective is provided by Jerry Garcia's master's thesis entitled "The History of a Chicano/Mexicano Community in the Pacific Northwest: Quincy, Washington 1948-1993," which was completed at Eastern Washington University. This is an engrossing discussion on the history of migration, the Bracero Program, the importance of Grand Coulee Dam to the development of agriculture in the Columbia Basin, the expansion of the Mexican/Chicano population in Quincy, Chicano activism of the 1960's and 1970's, and the current lack of political representation of the Chicano community in city government. Garcia used oral interviews as a means of gathering information for this study, and presents a number of poignant biographical sketches which vividly portray the life situation of the Hispanic community in Quincy.

Fernando Padilla's article, "The Mexicanization of the Lower Yakima Valley," published by *Revista Apple*, is a succinct account of Chicano-Mexicano immigration to the Yakima Valley, the rapid population growth, and subsequent increase in cultural activities. Padilla uses a "push-pull" model to discuss the factors involved in mobility patterns of migrating farm workers. Also recommended is Anne Marjorie Brunton's dissertation, "The Decision to Settle: A Study of Mexican-American Migrants," which is a basic source of information on migratory patterns of Chicanos from the Walla Walla, Washington area. A different perspective is provided by Erick Howenstine's dissertation, "Misperception of Destination Encouraging Migration of Mexican Labor to Yakima Valley, Washington," which examines the hypothesis that migrants hold unrealistically high expectations before moving to the U.S. and subsequently experience disappointment after arrival. In addition, the reader may be interested in the article by Brad Knickerbocker, staff writer for the *Christian Science Monitor*, entitled "A Northwest Region's Family Ties to Mexico", which describes the lives of several families living in the Yakima Valley and their social ties to Mexico.

Felix Martinez has completed a thorough study on this subject from the perspective of education entitled "Migratory Patterns of the Migrant Child in the Yakima Valley." This master's thesis seeks to identify the migratory patterns of migrant children, the push-pull factors which influenced the family's move to the Yakima Valley, and their living conditions after arrival. Martinez discusses the history of migration and provides statistical tables on migrant families, enrollment of migrant children in schools, and length of stay.

Although in the past migrants have usually been considered as rural or farm laborers, this is no longer the case. Urban migrants who move from one urban area to another in search of work are an economic factor in American society today. Often, rural migrants move to urban areas seeking a different way of life. In 1973, The Washington Agricultural Experiment Station published

Spanish-Speaking Migrants in Seattle, Washington by Sergio Sepulveda and Ralph A. Loomis. This report is important because it examines the unique adjustment problems which Spanish-speaking migrants experience in adapting to an urban lifestyle.

Of special interest on the subject of urban Chicanos, is Carlos S. Maldonado's article, "Mexicanos in Spokane: 1930-1992", published in *Revista Apple*, which provides an account of regional and national factors influencing the development of the Mexicano/Chicano community in Spokane, Washington. Maldonado points out that urban Chicanos are engaged in a variety of occupations and discusses the current status of Chicanos in the eastern Washington area. A companion article is Maldonado's "Mexicanos in Spokane: A Photographic Historical Essay; 1940's-1950's" which serves to vividly illustrate the lives of this emerging ethnic group in this part of the Northwest.

◆ Political Aspects

In seeking a better life, Chicanos have become more involved with political issues and social action groups. The farmworkers struggle for better wages, working conditions, improved housing, and medical services continues as an on-going endeavor. The organization of the United Farmworkers Union led by Cesar Chavez has resulted in signed contracts for labor. The historical development of farmworker unions has been documented by José Manuel Romero in his master's thesis, "The Political Evolution of the Farm Workers," which was completed at the University of Oregon. This outstanding study is an in-depth examination of migrant labor, the powerful agribusiness conglomerate, and the formation of the farmworkers union. Romero presents a historical overview of Mexican immigration to the U.S., the Bracero program, undocumented alien workers, the agribusiness interests, the American Farm Bureau, farm labor legislation, growers' associations, farmworker unionization, and the use of strikes and boycotts to attain union goals.

Another excellent source is the thesis by Jesus Lemos, Jr. entitled "A History of the Chicano Political Involvement and the Organizational Efforts of the United Farm Workers Union in the Yakima Valley, Washington," which was completed at the University of Washington. This is an important work which identifies and outlines the struggle of the agricultural growers and the United Farm Workers Union and discusses El Movimiento and Chicano politics in Washington State. Lemos describes the grass roots union organization process, the option to strike in order to achieve certain goals, the influence of Cesar Chavez, and the Chicano struggle against economic exploitation.

Also recommended is Margaret Miller's thesis of 1991 entitled "Community Action and Reaction: Chicanos and the War on Poverty in the Yakima Valley, Washington," which is a close look at the pivotal role which Chicanos have played in anti-poverty programs and other more aggressive forms of social action resulting in increased ethnic leadership.

Two current newsletters are available which may be of interest for researchers. The first is *PCUN Update*, which is published by Oregon's farmworker union (Pineros y Campesinos Unidos del Noroeste - Northwest Treeplanters and Farmworkers United) and is headquartered in Woodburn, Oregon. This brief newsletter is published in English and covers political events, the status of political activities such as boycotting cases, editorial commentaries, and notices of activities which may interest its readers. A second newsletter, *Si Se Puede*, is published by the United Farm Workers of Washington from its head offices in Granger, Washington. This newsletter, also published in English, covers current political events, such as legislation and boycotts, reviews working conditions, and recommends political actions for its readers.

◆ Educational Issues

It is generally agreed that the educational success of minority students is critical to the future economic stability and survival of American society. In recent years, educational participation and achievement of Chicano students has become widely encouraged. The alarming drop-out rate (over 40%) of Hispanic students is a national concern and requires immediate attention. The growth of the Chicano population in the Northwest has meant an increase in school enrollments, and has prompted state governments to evaluate Chicano student participation in the school system and the equity education programs.

Doris Helge's Congressional testimony, delivered in 1991 to the National Commission on Migrant Education, and entitled "Problems and Strategies Regarding Reducing America's Migrant Student Dropout Rate" (ERIC No. ED340528) is recommended as a basic source of information on the migrant dropouts. Some problems identified by Helge include family dysfunction and abuse, teen pregnancy, low self-esteem, poverty, parents' illiteracy, and substance abuse. Another recommended source is "Ideas for Action in Education and Work: Helping At-Risk Youth Succeed" (ERIC No. ED296044) prepared by Tom Owens, et al., under the auspices of the Northwest Regional Educational Laboratory in Portland, Oregon. This document reviews programs in the Northwestern states which are concerned with reducing the number of youths dropping out of school or remaining unemployed.

José Licano Palma's dissertation "Characteristics of Mexican American High School Stay-Ins: The Other Side of the Drop-Out Problem," is an important contribution to research studies on Hispanic student motivation. Palma's work focuses on Mexican American high school seniors in a rural agricultural area in the Northwest and seeks to identify characteristics of high achievers and low achievers. Motivational attributes linked with high achievement are family involvement, positive attitude, established goals, good attendance, and participation in extra-curricular activities. Attributes linked with lower achievement included single parent households, chronic absenteeism, and little involvement in school activities.

The area of parent-school relations has come to the fore in the last ten years, since parents have pushed for increased involvement in school management and in the education of their children. Senon Monreal Valadez's dissertation "An Exploratory Study of Chicano Parent Perceptions of School and the Education of Their Children in Two Oregon Community Settings," is recommended as a basic study on Chicano parents' negative perceptions of the schools, the teachers, and their children's educational experience. Equally important is the dissertation by Carmen Cecilia Ramirez entitled, "A Study of the Value Orientation of Lane County, Oregon, Mexican American Mothers with a Special Focus on Family/School Relationships," which examines perceived differences between traditional Chicano family values and those of the schools which their children attend as well as the nature of parent-school interactions. In 1990, Beverly Brown McConnell, a leading supporter of bilingual education, compiled a report, "Parent Leadership Training Program. An Evaluation" (ERIC No. ED327370) which discusses a program designed to assist parents to be effective partners in their children's developmental and academic growth.

In 1991, the Board of Education in Idaho completed an evaluation of Hispanic education issues within its school system (pre-school through grade 12), which resulted in the bilingual publication, *Report of the Task Force on Hispanic Education*. This report addresses specific Hispanic education issues such as providing a relevant curriculum, promoting self-esteem, hiring bilingual professional role models, encouraging communication between parents, teachers and school administrators, providing comprehensive counseling programs to meet career and social needs of students, and eliminating prejudice and bigotry within the schools. The Task Force has established some goals and made specific recommendations for implementing change.

An excellent, up-to-date report which presents different aspects of the educational problems of minority students is *The Yakima Equity Study: The*

Conditions of Success for Migrant, Hispanic, and Native American Students in the Yakima Valley by Patricia Vadasy and Mary Maddox of the Washington Research Institute in Seattle. This report moves away from the traditional mode of education, recognizes the many social and economic problems that affect students' school performance, acknowledges that a child's cultural background is the basic foundation to which new learning is added, and makes strong recommendations for fundamental changes to foster educational equity and facilitate the move towards multicultural education.

◆ Bilingual Education

Bilingual education has been an area of contention on the national level for over twenty years. The pro-and-con issues have been researched and debated by many scholars. Several studies on the implementation of bilingual/ESL programs in the school systems in the Northwestern states may be of interest.

Bilingual education programs at the elementary school level was the focus of Rafael Angel Díaz's dissertation "A Descriptive Study of Current Spanish-English Title VII, K-3 (1978-1979) Bilingual Education Programs, State of Washington; with Emphasis on Teacher Preparation, Curriculum, Instructional Strategies, and a Projection of a Bilingual Program Model." This study covers a wide spectrum, from teacher certification to classroom materials and instruction, and provides a bilingual education model which addresses the components of a multicultural education program. Also recommended is Socorro Martinez's dissertation, "A Comparative Study of Attitudes of Mexican-American Students in Third Grade Bilingual and Non-Bilingual Classrooms," which assesses the attitudes of Spanish-speaking children toward basic skill subjects, toward the school setting, and toward the self. This research study was conducted in Yakima Valley, Washington, and indicates that language and culture are factors most frequently related to students' attitudes.

The provision of educational services to Hispanics in Idaho is explored in Richard Mabbutt's research report, *Hispanics in Idaho: Concerns and Challenges*. This report, which was sponsored by the Idaho Human Rights Commission, presents testimony by members of the Hispanic community reflecting their concerns on perceived discrimination in public education. The major issues raised by citizens testifying at meetings were the high drop-out rates of Hispanic students, educational services for limited English proficient students, educational achievement levels of Hispanic students, the perceived lack of bicultural awareness workshops for public school personnel, the need of scholarship programs for Hispanic high school graduates, and racial harassment in the schools.

Mary Eileen Smith's dissertation, "Equality of Educational Opportunity for Language Minority Students in Oregon: A Survey of ESL/Bilingual Education Policy in Local School Districts," is a penetrating study on ESL/bilingual policies and practices in Oregon schools to determine equality of educational opportunity for language minority students.

Beverly Brown McConnell's dissertation "Effectiveness of Individualized Bilingual Instruction for Migrant Students," was a study done with students in Texas and Washington State with results which indicate that a bilingual education program can produce academic gains for Hispanic-American children. The researcher may also refer to Beverly McConnell's "Long Term Effects of Bilingual Education. Short and Long Term Gains in Spanish and English and in Academic Subjects in a Bilingual Program; Plus a Follow-Up Study on Children One to Five Years Later." (ERIC No. ED206203). This is an evaluation of a bilingual program for preschool and primary grades, which is designed to meet the needs of migrant students.

◆ Migrant Education

Over the years, the education of migrant children has come under closer scrutiny by educators, government administrators, parents, and concerned citizens. Due to frequent mobility by the family in following agricultural crop harvest rotation during the year, migrant students face difficult educational problems transferring and adjusting to different school systems. Some source materials are available for educational researchers on this important subject.

Highly recommended is Joan Soderstrom's master's thesis entitled "An Investigation of Mexican-American Migrant Children Population in Idaho and the Educational Opportunities Provided by Selected School Districts," which was completed in 1967 and provides a historical perspective. This detailed study deals with the issues and problems of educating Mexican-American migrant children in Idaho, including family socio-economic status, mobility, language differences, loss of school time, and cultural disadvantages. Soderstrom discusses migrant mobility patterns, the relationship of migrancy to agriculture, and includes significant tables of labor camps and school districts.

Educators need awareness training to identify and work with the special problems encountered by migrant students. An excellent source to consult in this area is the "Cultural and Program Awareness Manual for Migrant Educators," (ERIC No. ED225743) by Merced Flores, which was sponsored by the Oregon Migrant Education Service Center and deals with Oregon's major ethnic groups, the Mexican Americans and Russian Old-Believers. This manual is intended for administrators, teachers, aides and other personnel working with migrant children. It covers the Title I-M program, migration patterns, ethnic and cultural backgrounds, English as a second language (ESL) problems and multicultural education. A second recommended source in Oregon was produced by the Jackson County Education Service District entitled "Jackson County Migrant Education. Migrant Education - Harvests of Hope," (ERIC No. ED212441). This is an awareness guide for teachers and discusses Public Law 89-10, major migration patterns and crops in Oregon, the Migrant Student Record Transfer Systems (MSRTS) plan, communication and learning problems of ESL children, the importance of personal identity, student/teacher interactions, as well as some classroom learning activities.

It is equally important for school administrators to be exposed to cultural diversity issues as part of their education program. Gail Chase Furman and Richard Sagor have written a paper on this topic entitled, "Washington State Administrative Certification and Cultural Diversity Requirements" (ERIC No. ED354626). This paper was presented at the 1992 Annual Meeting of the University Council for Educational Administration, which was held in Minneapolis. Furman and Sagor's report discusses school administrator licensure programs in Washington State and how these relate to cultural diversity issues.

Researchers may contact the State Department of Education Office in individual Northwestern states for up-to-date published materials on migrant education. The Idaho State Department of Education in Boise makes available annual overview reports on the status of migrant education. The report "Title I ESEA Migrant Education" (ERIC No. ED218041), produced in 1981 by the Idaho State Department of Education, includes information on the national and state goals of the migrant education program, suggests strategies for the attainment of specific objectives, and provides an overview of the instructional program. The report by Carolyn Reeves and Patrick LeCertua entitled "Chapter 1 ECIA Migrant Education Evaluation Report" (ERIC No. ED256542) is a discussion of the Idaho State, Migrant Education Program and provides basic information on budgeting, number of students enrolled, the MSRTS, the Migrant Education Resource Center, and interstate program cooperation.

Similarly, the Oregon State Department of Education makes available special materials, such as "Migrant Education Projects. Projectos de Educaciùn Migrante" (ERIC No. ED212440) which is a bilingual English-Spanish publication and provides a summary of the Title I Migrant project, the requirements for funding, and the implementation process.

The Office of the State Superintendent of Public Instruction in Washington State also makes available excellent reports on migrant education. Special mention should be made of Kathleen C. Plato and Alfred Rasp, Jr.'s work in compiling a number of annual reports entitled, "Washington State Program Evaluation Report for Migrant Children's Education" (ERIC Nos. ED218044, ED218045, ED218046, ED256541, and ED301394.) These reports cover the period from 1979 through 1987 and review the objectives of the migrant education program, describe the program components, and discuss the services performed during the year.

Educational researchers may be interested in locating information on special programs which provide opportunities for migrant students to attend school. The report by Rosendo Rivera and Carlos Treviño entitled, "State of Washington Migrant Education Secondary Credit Exchange Program," (ERIC No. ED258742) provides a description of the SCEP plan, which allows students to earn credits towards graduation following differing classroom time schedules. Also of interest is the Portable Assisted Study Sequence (P.A.S.S.) program, which allows migrant students to make up credit deficiencies and continue to accummulate credits as they migrate to other schools. The reader may consult ERIC Nos. ED281691 and ED330518 for a historical overview of the P.A.S.S. program, as well as student enrollment data for various states, including those in the Pacific Northwest.

◆ Career and Vocational Education

Appropriate counseling in career and vocational education is crucial in the life choices which students make. The dissertation by Ruth Ketchum Burns entitled, "Model for a Career/Life Planning Program for Mexican-American College Students," completed in 1973 at the University of Oregon, examines the need to develop an effective career/life planning program for Chicano students. Burns' study is recommended since it discusses some problems encountered in counseling students from different cultural backgrounds, the qualifications of counselors working with Mexican American students, the importance of group discussions in exchanging information, and other issues which are relevant today. Also recommended is the work done by Frank Garcia, Jr. and Melva Ybarra-Garcia entitled, "Strategies for Counseling Chicanos: Effects of Racial and Cultural Stereotypes," (ERIC No. ED278757) published by the Office of the State Superintendent of Public Instruction in Washington State. This manual is intended as an awareness guide for school counselors and educators in understanding the Chicano culture and in dealing with racial stereotypes.

Readers may also refer to "Choices for Migrant Youth," by Rosalind Hamar and Andrea Hunter (ERIC No. ED239801) sponsored by the Northwest Regional Educational Laboratory, for a description of the Experience Based Career Education (EBCE) program of career and vocational development to help high school migrant students stay in school.

In 1990, the State of Idaho, Division of Vocational Education, undertook a special survey of Hispanic student participation in vocational education programs, and published the report entitled, "Hispanic Youth - Dropout Prevention," which is available in Spanish and English. The Task Force which conducted this study identified goals to encourage Hispanic student success in vocational education programs. Recommended goals included the development of state and business associations interested in reducing the high drop-out rate of Hispanic students, providing role models, greater participation by the community and family in the education process, the elimination of discrimination and prejudice in the schools, and the provision of financial assistance for Hispanic students.

Equally important is the article by Teresa Wirsching and Laurie Sternberg, "Determinants of Idaho Hispanic Female Participation in Adult Vocational Education Programs," which analyzes factors that influence Hispanic women's decisions to participate in vocational programs. This study found that factors such as attitude towards women's role, degree of acculturation, and socio-economic status, influenced participation or non-participation in vocational education programs.

Also recommended is the work of Toshio Akamine and Cynthia Dillard, which was done at Washington State University at Pullman, entitled "Improving Access of Special Populations to Vocational Education in the Yakima School District," (ERIC No. ED281984) which examines the barriers to student enrollment in vocational education programs in the Yakima School District. This study identified significant barriers to be the inability to schedule classes, inadequate counseling, and lack of information on vocational education.

◆ Higher Education

Although Mexican-Americans are one of the largest ethnic groups in the Northwest, this is not reflected in college or university enrollments. Large numbers of Chicano students drop out during the high school years and never resume their formal education. High school graduates who do enroll in an institution of higher education often drop out before attaining the bachelor's degree. Thus, institutions of higher education have experienced recruitment and retention problems with Chicano students. Antonia Lejia and Tony Sandoval have written an excellent article, "Hispanics Still Underrepresented at Washington State University," published by *Revista Apple*, which concretely illustrates the problem and the need for change. Scholars may also refer to an article by Toma Sowa "Eastern Reaches Out to Chicano Students," which was published in the *Spokesman Review* in 1993, and discusses the recruitment and retention of the Chicano Education Program at Eastern Washington University. Other institutions of higher learning in the Northwestern states have had similar retention problems.

Some special programs have been instituted in higher education to accommodate and assist migrant or at-risk students. In 1992, the Chemeketa Community College in Oregon, under the auspices of the Beacon Project, produced an excellent guide entitled, "Collaborating to Help High Risk Students Succeed" (ERIC No. ED346926). This publication presents an overview of efforts undertaken by the Oregon consortium of the American Association of Community and Junior Colleges to help high-risk students to succeed.

Another special program is the College Assistance Migrant Program, better known as CAMP, which is discussed in the article by Katherine S. Mangan entitled "Defying Odds, Children of Migrant Workers Attend College with Help from Federal Program Offered on 5 Campuses," which appeared in the *Chronicle of Higher Education*. Mangan describes this federal education assistance program for migrant students, its availability at five sites around the country (including Boise State University and Oregon State University in the Northwest), the provision of scholarships and other funds for financial support, and the recruitment and retention process. Additional information on the CAMP program in Oregon is provided in the report by E. D. Duarte entitled, "Oregon State University College Assistance Migrant Program" (ERIC No. ED238647), which describes this outstanding program that was developed to recruit, assist, and encourage migrant students in higher education.

Some important studies have been done on the motivational factors which influence the success of Chicano students in the academic environment. Luz Maciel de Villarroel's dissertation, completed in 1986, "A Study of Self-Concept Among Mexican-American/Chicano(a) Students Attending Community Colleges and Four-Year Institutions of Higher Education in Oregon" is a comparative study of self-concept as a motivational factor for Chicano students in higher education, and includes some data on age and gender differences. The thesis by Rafaela Ortiz, completed in 1984, "A Profile of Mexican-American Students at Eastern Washington University" focuses on a survey of Chicano students and seeks to identify factors which hinder academic success. Also recommended is the thesis by Roberto Enriquez entitled "Finding Common Ground: Chicano History, Poetry and Oral Tradition in the Classroom," which deals with student perceptions of school curriculum versus cultural identity.

In Washington State, a basic source of information on minority student achievement in higher education is *The Status of Minority Students and Faculty in Washington's Higher Education System*, published in 1990 by the Office of Financial Management. This informative report includes educational demographics, recruitment, and retention procedures for students and faculty in higher education.

The abysmal, drawn-out failure of Colegio Cesar Chavez in the State of Oregon may be especially significant, since its name is symbolic of the Chicano struggle for survival in a discriminating society. Colegio Cesar Chavez was established in 1973 as the first independent accredited Chicano educational institution in the U.S. Courses of study at this unique institution included Chicano studies, bilingual-bicultural education, and the College-without-walls (Colegio sin paredes) program which moved away from traditional classroom methods and allowed students the freedom to explore any aspect of life and learning. Carlos S. Maldonado's dissertation, "The Longest Running Death in History: A History of Colegio Cesar Chavez, 1973-1983," is a piercing, insightful study on the social, political, and administrative factors which resulted in the demise of this institution of higher learning representing Chicano values and goals.

◆ Religion

Religion has always been an integral part in the lives of the Chicano people, whose depth of religious belief has helped them to survive hard work, poverty, and discrimination. A large percentage of Mexican Americans are Catholics, although this is beginning to change. Scholars interested in this subject are referred to a newspaper article by Nicholas K. Geranios, "Bishop wants to Reconcile Cultures," which was published by the *Spokesman Review*. This report introduces the Rev. Francis E. George, who was appointed as the Roman Catholic Bishop of Yakima in 1990. The article goes on to describe the diocese in the Central Washington area, which includes a membership of 60,000 Catholics, and Rev. George's plan to reconcile any differences between Hispanic/Anglo members.

A different perspective is provided by the doctoral dissertation written by Wayne R. Hawkins entitled, "Hispanic and Anglo Christians: A Model for Shared Life," which was completed in 1985. This perceptive study seeks to develop a theological base for a bilingual, bicultural (Anglo and Hispanic) congregation and a model which protects the uniqueness and integrity of both cultures. This study includes a history of colonialism in Mexico, the social dynamics of the discrimination of Mexican-Americans, the rigidity and insensitivity of the educational system towards Hispanic students and bilingual education programs, the activities of the Columbia Basin Christian Ministry, and the need for change in order to overcome the separation of cultures.

Paul A. Felver's dissertation places an emphasis on ethnic communication and is entitled "Intercultural Relationships: Blocks and Bridges among Hispanics, Blacks, and Anglos in Pasco, Washington, with Implications for the Pacific Northwest Conference of the United Methodist Church." This study is concerned with the improvement of intercultural relationships within the ideal global village concept and contends that the church should lead the way in this endeavor. Felver focuses on the ethnic groups in Pasco, and discusses prejudice, stereotypes, language and cultural differences and makes some recommendations for building intercultural relationships.

◆ Health Services

Health care in the Chicano community has received increased attention by researchers across the nation. Of particular concern has been the Chicano belief in folk remedies and their reliance on family and friends for assistance. A recommended source on this topic is Ardys McNaughton Dunn's dissertation entitled "Traditional Medicine Among Mexican Americans: The Role of Acculturation and Socioeconomic Status," completed at the University of Oregon, which seeks to determine which of two factors—acculturation or socioeconomic status—best accounts for the dynamics of health practices of Mexican Americans in the Portland area. This interesting study describes the relationship between culture and medical knowledge systems, *curanderismo*, or folk healing, as it is practiced in Mexico, the use of natural remedies and supernatural healing forces, the patterns of health behavior among Mexican Americans, and their selective use of modern Western biomedical health care.

In Washington State, other research work has been conducted on the health care behavior of the Mexican American population. Nadine Frances Nelson's thesis "Health Resources Utilized for Various Health Conditions as Reported by Twenty-Five Mexican-American Mothers in the Yakima Valley of Washington," completed in 1967, is a study of the cultural aspects of health and illness. Nelson examines the influence of cultural beliefs on health care practices in a sample of Mexican American women and discusses medical systems as an integral part of the culture in which they occur. A second recommended source is Joan Edna Uhl's thesis, completed in 1975, entitled "A Description of Lay Referral Networks and Health Care Seeking Behavior Among Mexican-American Families in Seattle: The Need for an Appreciation by Health Professionals," which concerns the transcultural health needs of Mexican Americans in a modern, urban setting. Uhl discusses the dual cultural traditions (Mexican/Anglo) of Chicanos, the effects of cultural duality on the seeking of health care, the use of folk remedies and healers, the kinds of contemporary medical treatment sought, and their satisfaction with available health care services.

Migrant and seasonal farmworkers experience health problems which may be due to environmental factors associated with farm work and socioeconomic problems. The children of farmworker families are susceptible to the same problems, since they live under the same conditions. Some special programs have been established to promote preventive health care practices and provide health care services for children of migrant families. One of these programs for children was developed in Hood River, Oregon and was called El Niño Sano/The Healthy Child. Linda Christie Barter's thesis, completed in 1993 and entitled "An Evaluation of El Niño Sano Program: A Strategy for Promoting Health of Migrant Seasonal Farmworker Children," reviews this program which provides community-based, culturally-sensitive services for children. In addition, some states provide low cost dental services for migrant children through the school system. William Hansen and Ignacio Resendez describe this type of dental program in Washington State in their manual entitled, "Operations Handbook for Migrant Student Dental Services" (ERIC No. ED211307).

Recently, the controversial use of pesticides on crops and the physical effects which these pesticides have on the farmworkers who must work in the fields and orchards to harvest the crop has come under question. One highly recommended source to consult on this topic is Sandra J. Ely's master's thesis, completed in 1991 at the University of Oregon, entitled "Migrant and Seasonal Farmworkers and Pesticide Exposure in Oregon: A Comparative Analysis." This thorough and interesting study examines the health aspects of farmworkers and pesticide exposure in the fields, adverse health effects subsequent to exposure, including cancer, the frequency of specific symptoms, the seeking of medical assistance, and time taken from work due to illness. Ely also discusses the Environmental Protection Agency's implementation of the Federal Insecticide, Fungicide and Rodenticide Act (FIFRA) in pesticide control, the state enforcement of FIFRA regulations, and concludes with specific recommendations for the protection of the farmworkers.

The adequacy of health services for Chicano elderly persons has also come under review. Juan Paz has conducted an outstanding research study on this topic entitled, "The Chicano Rural Elderly: A Study of Their Natural

Helping Networks and Help-Seeking Behavior" (ERIC No. ED222806). Paz describes a study of 110 rural elderly Hispanics in Central Washington, and discusses their socio-demographic characteristics, the natural helping networks of family, friends and the barrio, social agencies which provide support, and the coping mechanisms that they need for survival.

Researchers should also consult two important studies on the health care of the elderly Hispanic population in Oregon. The 1978 thesis by Olga Carmen Dominguez entitled "The Perception of Health Needs of Spanish Origin Elderly Living in Lane County, Oregon" describes some of the basic health needs of the Spanish-speaking elderly population. Dominguez discusses the financial, social, linguistic, and transportation problems experienced by the elderly, and their perceptions of community health resources. Especially recommended is the 1990 research study by Judith Ann Chambliss entitled "'Asi es la Vida' (Thus is Life): Health and the Experience of Suffering Among Elderly Mexican-American Women," which was conducted in Washington County, Oregon. Chambliss focuses on the lives of four elderly Mexican-American women and explores the extent to which the theme of suffering emerges as a central aspect of their lives and as a factor influencing their health behavior. This study provides an in-depth look at the use/underuse of health services by these women, their distrust of government agencies, their reliance on family and church as strong sources of support, the importance of love, trust and respect between generations, and the necessity for health care providers to develop an awareness of the Hispanic culture.

◆ Gender Issues

Traditionally, gender roles have been strictly identified within the Chicano cultural norms. The Chicano family has been stereotyped as a rigid, patriarchal social structure in which wives are passive and husbands are dominant and carry out their family obligations as they see fit. Some researchers contend that acculturation smooths the transition from a patriarchal structure to a more open, modern structure. Readers interested in this topic are referred to the dissertation by Maxine Baca Zinn, entitled "Marital Roles, Marital Power and Ethnicity: A Study of Changing Chicano Families," which examines three dimensions of Chicano family life—marital roles, marital power, and ethnicity. Zinn discusses the importance of social networks in the structure of Chicano families, marital power as it differentiates from authority within the family, power as it relates to economic resources, changes in the families of working wives, the cultural ideal of the father as authority figure, as well as ethnicity and its effects on family life.

The emerging Chicana/Mexicana women's movement is pushing forward in political, social, economic, and literary circles. In recent years, Chicanas have advanced in the literary world, making their voices heard and their experiences known. Readers may be interested in an article by Annette White-Parks, who is from Oregon, entitled "Where are the Chicanas?" which was published in *Revista Apple*. This article presents a good historical overview of the Chicana tradition in literature, and discusses the stereotypes of Mexican American women as weak-willed, the Chicana's ambivalent role as family caregiver/writer, the cultural duality of Mexican/Anglo roles, and the writer's dichotomy between the regional and universal appeal.

◆ Biographical

It is from the perspective of personal experience that we often get a true glimpse into the real-life situation of another individual. Scraps of information gleaned from biographical accounts are pieced together to form a more complete picture of the joys, fears, and struggles which someone experiences in life. It is precisely this type of information that we get in Erasmo Gamboa's current publication, *Voces Hispanas: Hispanic Voices of Idaho, Excerpts from the Idaho Hispanic Oral History Project*, which was a combined project of the Idaho Commission on Hispanic Affairs and the Idaho Humanities Council. The biographical narratives are a poignant testimony to the life experiences, good and bad, of a sample of Idaho's Spanish-speaking people. For example, there is Felicitas Pérez García, who was so poor that she made her own bed out of boards and the bedcover out of corn sacks; Vicky Archuleta Sierra, who taught herself to read English and to play the guitar; and Antonio Hernández Rodríguez, a self-made restaurant owner, who has worked hard to eliminate discrimination in the Nampa area.

A similar, deeply touching work is Olivia Gomez's *Testimonies*. In this book, Gomez has gathered numerous personal accounts from individuals, mostly Chicano(a)s, who are part of the Latin American Community in Olympia, Washington. The book includes narratives such as that of Maria Esparza, whose husband, father, and uncle were all killed by the same person on the same day; Faviola Perrea, who believes in folk medicine; and Trinidad Ruiz, whose school teachers forced her to stop speaking Spanish. These insightful accounts are often thought-provoking and disturbing to the reader.

Also of interest is the genealogical work by Bruce Johansen and Roberto Maestas titled, *El Pueblo: The Gallegos Family's American Journey, 1503-1980*, which follows the Gallegos Family's experiences in their northward migration from Mexico through Colorado and on to the Northwest.

◆ Art, Literature, and Music

Materials on Northwest Chicano art, literature, and music are gradually becoming more accessible. A few Chicano organizations have been established to provide multi-purpose services to the community, such as economic, cultural, and social roles. Exemplary organizations serving the Chicano community is the Centro Chicano Cultural in Woodburn, Oregon, and the Centro de la Raza in Seattle, Washington. An important function which they provide is the sharing and creating awareness of traditional Chicano culture, music, and arts.

For basic information on this subject, the reader may refer to the publication entitled *Living Treasures: Hispanic Artisans & Traditionalists of the Snake River Valley*, edited by Lori Rea and sponsored by the Hispanic Folkarts Survey Committee. This report is the result of an interstate cooperative effort between Oregon and Idaho to survey the wealth of Hispanic culture and traditions in the Snake River region, and documents traditional arts and artists including music, theatre, dance, folklore, and culinary arts.

Sid White and Pat Matheny-White have made a valuable contribution to the field of Chicano art in the Northwest with the publication of their article, "Chicano/Latino Art & Artists: A Regional Overview," which appeared in *Metamorfosis*. The authors toured the Chicano communities in Washington, Oregon and Idaho, viewed art works in various forms, and identified the artists for this regional profile. This study provides the reader with biographical sketches of eighteen outstanding artists, identifies their primary artistic medium, and includes illustrations and brief descriptions of their work. This report provides basic information for the study of Hispanic art in the Northwest.

In the area of literature, the Centro de Estudios Chicanos of the University of Washington has been at the forefront in publishing works by or about Chicano writers and artists. Their literary journal, *Metamorfosis*, is published twice a year and is dedicated to disseminating creative works primarily by Chicano writers in the areas of literature and the arts. In addition, scholars may refer to the Monograph Series, which is also published by the Centro de Estudios Chicanos, and consists of individual volumes of literature and poetry by or about Chicanos.

On the subject of music, the publication *Gritos del Alma: Chicano/Mexicano Music Traditions of Washington State* is recommended as a current source of information. Erasmo Gamboa wrote the text and Cathy Ragland wrote the performers' biographical sketches for this bilingual publication, which was sponsored by the Washington State Arts Commission, and provides basic information on Chicano music and musical groups in the Yakima Valley.

◆ Audio-Visual and Media Materials

Material in audio-visual format provide a different medium in the dissemination of information. Microfilm and microfiche have been valuable research sources for many years. Video adds the elements of sight and sound for the researcher. Currently, several videocassettes are available which may be useful to teachers, researchers, and students.

A Historical and Cultural Perspective on Washington's Hispanics, a video cassette produced by Highline College, is a teleconference presentation. "Nuestra Lucha: Our struggle for Justice" is a 22 minute video produced by PCUN (cited earlier) in Oregon. The video presents information and background about farmworkers in Oregon and the Union's boycott against two major Oregon food processors. This 120-minute educational production is in color, with black and white slide sequences, and includes a question and answer session.

Aqui se Puede is a shorter 15-minute program, produced by Moving Images, which was written and directed by Melissa Young and Mark Dworkin. This color presentation focuses on the Yakima Valley farm workers from the Chateau St. Michelle vineyards, who want to organize a union but have been unable to do so, resulting in the boycotting of the wine. Several Chicano leaders are featured, including Tomas Villanueva, President, United Farmworkers of Washington.

Counted In . . .? is a 30-minute videocassette written and produced by Mark Huessy, directed by Hubie Imhoff, and is a KSPS Public Television Presentation. This color presentation reviews the problems which the U.S. Bureau of the Census has in using language spoken and/or Hispanic surname to tabulate the Hispanic population count. In addition, the Census Bureau does not have a clear-cut definition of a migrant or a seasonal farm worker and there is no reliable data on this segment of the population. This presentation continues with a short history of Mexican labor, the Chicano entrapment in the farm labor seasonal cycle, and their current struggle against poor wages, lack of benefits, limited educational opportunities, and discrimination.

"Yo tambien, He Estado Aqui" is a 25 minute video produced by the Idaho Migrant Council in 1977. The video explores problems faced by Chicanos in Idaho, particularly in the Caldwell area.

The media of television and radio are an integral part of our modern lives in electronic communication. Jean Cecilia Powell's master's thesis entitled, "Entre Dos Mundos: Between Two Worlds—Empowering Oregon's Hispanics," which was completed in 1990, provides a current view of Oregon's Hispanic population and their experiences. Powell's discussion includes a short history of migration from Mexico, political and economic factors influencing the migratory labor force, the labor unions in Oregon, the work of La Clinica del Cariño and El Niño Sano health programs, and the influence of the Roman Catholic Church. Since Powell is a journalist, she describes the process of reporting on Hispanics in Oregon, media coverage of ethnic issues, the politics involved in news presentation and reporting local and national news. This is an invaluable study which provides a view of politics and the news media as they affect Hispanics.

Also recommended is the thesis, "Emerging Media: A History and Analysis of Chicano Communication Efforts in Washington State," by Ramón Chavéz, which was completed at the University of Washington and examines communication and media in relation to the Chicano experience. Chavéz reviews Anglo mainstream media, Spanish language media, and Chicano alternative media as these relate to the Latino community. He goes on to discuss the Chicano rural/urban population, the use of media to bring about social change, the transmission of cultural traditions and music over the radio, and the expansion of the Chicano communication system within the state.

◆ Newspapers Published

In recent years, a number of Chicano newspapers have emerged in the Northwest as a medium of communication with the growing Chicano reading public. *El Sol de Idaho*, published in Idaho Falls, prints stories in Spanish only and is an important channel of communication for the Hispanic community in southern Idaho. *The Hispanic News*, published in Seattle, prints reports in English and Spanish and appeals to the bilingual reading public. One of the most complete Spanish language newspapers is *El Mundo: El Periódico de la Vida Hispana en el Norte Central de Washington*, which is published in Wenatchee, Washington. This weekly publication is divided into various sections ("Internacional," "Religión," "Deportes," and others) and prints its news stories within the appropriate subject. It also carries a more extensive classified section in Spanish/English. ¡*Viva! Periódico Español del Valle de Yakima* is apparently "Washington State's oldest continually published weekly Spanish language newspaper" and began publication in 1984. It is published in Toppenish, Washington and is distributed locally. Of special interest is the bilingual newspaper, La Voz, which is published by the Concilio for the Spanish-Speaking in Seattle, Washington, and has a wide readership.

◆ Diversity and Multicultural Aspects

Print and electronic media of all types have served to make the modern world a smaller place. We have become aware of the important role each country plays in the global community and have come to appreciate the world's diverse cultures and languages. Within American society the old "melting pot" concept, under which all differences would disappear, has given way to the current "salad bowl" concept, with its acceptance of multiculturalism. The national trend toward multiculturalism has made mainstream Americans more accepting of diverse cultures. The importance of maintaining this diversity of cultural traditions, languages, and personal characteristics of all ethnic groups is now recognized.

One of the best-known publications on population diversity in Washington State is *Peoples of Washington: Perspectives on Cultural Diversity*, edited by Sid White and S.E. Solberg. This fascinating book includes a chapter entitled, "Washington's Hispano American Community" written by Carlos B. Gil, which covers the current status of the various Hispanic groups residing in the state.

Multicultural education is being taught in school systems throughout the Pacific Northwest, and special awareness materials are being made available for classroom use. Gary Howard's booklet "The Mexican American/Chicano Experience . . . A Special Report," (ERIC No. ED285715) was produced as part of the Project R.E.A.C.H. Ethnic Perspectives Series by the Arlington School District in Arlington, Washington. This booklet views events in American history through the eyes of Mexicans/Chicanos and examines their contributions to U.S. culture.

A final recommendation is a current newspaper article printed in the *Spokesman Review* entitled, "One Town, Two Worlds: Othello's whites, Hispanics seek common ground," which is a 10-page, profusely illustrated report, and describes how members of both cultures are working together for a better life in Othello, Washington. As Anglos and Chicanos learn to work and live together, as well as with members of other ethnic groups, the ideal concept of multiculturalism in modern American society may become a reality.

Bibliography

◆ Terminology and Chicanismo

Gil, Carlos B. "The Many Faces of the Mexican-American: An Essay Concerning Chicano Character. Working Paper Series No. 1." ERIC, ED255350, 1982.

Gonzales, Adelina. "The Significance of the Chicano Movement in the 1990's." Revista Apple 2, No. 1-2 (spring 1991): 6-7.

Marin, Maria Viramontes de. Guide to Understanding People, Language, and Culture: Chicano. Olympia, WA: Washington State Superintendent of Public Instruction, 1980.

Nostrand, Richard L. "'Mexican American' and 'Chicano': Emerging Terms for a People Coming of Age." Pacific Historical Review 42 (August 1973): 389-406.

Shepro, Theresa Aragón de. Chicanismo and Mexican American Politics. Seattle: Centro de Estudios Chicanos, University of Washington, 1971.

◆ Bibliographies and Reference

Castillo-Speed, Lillian, Chabran, Richard, and Garcia-Ayvens, Francisco (eds.). *The Chicano Index: A Comprehensive Subject, Author and Title Index to Chicano Materials*. Berkeley: University of California, Chicano Studies Library Publications Unit, 1967-.

Garcia-Ayvens, Francisco. *Chicano Anthology Index: A Comprehensive Author, Title, and Subject Index to Chicano Anthologies*, 1965-1987. Berkeley: University of California, Chicano Studies Library Publications Unit, 1990.

Matheny-White, Patricia. *Bibliography of Chicano/Latino Art and Culture in the Pacific Northwest*. Olympia: Evergreen State College Library, 1982.

Matheny-White, Patricia. *Bibliography of Chicano/Latino Art and Culture: National and International Perspectives*. Olympia: Evergreen State College Library, 1982.

Meier, Matt S. *Bibliography of Mexican American History*. Westport: Greenwood Press, 1984.

Washington State, Commission on Hispanic Affairs. *Hispanic Community Resource Directory*. Olymoia, WA:, 1993.

◆ CD-Rom Materials

"Chicano Database on CD-ROM." University of California Berkeley Chicano Studies Library Publications Unit: Berkeley, CA.
Ethnic News Watch." Softline Information, Inc.: Stamford, CT.

◆ Demographics

Bonino, Rick. "Hispanic population soars on East Side." *Spokesman Review*, 21 July 1991.
Cook, Annabel Kirschner. "Increasing Racial and Ethnic Diversity in Washington." *Washington Counts* (Cooperative Extension Office, Washington State University), No. 2, June 10, 1991.
Cook, Annabel Kirschner. "Diversity Among Northwest Hispanics." *The Social Science Journal* 23, No. 2 (1986): 205-16.
"Hispanic Americans Today." (Current Population Reports, Population Characteristics, P23-183) U.S. Department of Commerce and the Bureau of the Census. Washington, D.C.: GPO, 1993.
"The Hispanic Population in the United States: March 1992." (Current Population Reports, Population Characteristics, P20-465 RV) U.S. Department of Commerce and the Bureau of the Census. Washington, D.C.: GPO, 1993.
"1990 Census of Population, Social and Economic Characteristics: Washington State." U.S. Department of Commerce, Economics and Statistics Administration, Bureau of the Census. Washington, D.C.: GPO, 1993.
"1990 Census Profile: Race and Hispanic Origin." U. S. Department of Commerce, Economics and Statistics Administration, Bureau of the Census. Washington, D.C.: GPO, 1991.
"Profile of the Hispanic Population of Idaho." Idaho Department of Commerce. 1990
Slatta, Richard Wayne and Maxine P. Atkinson. "The 'Spanish Origin' Population of Oregon and Washington: A Demographic Profile, 1980." *Pacific Northwest Quarterly* 75, No. 3 (July 1984): 108-16.
"We the American Hispanics." U.S. Department of Commerce and the Bureau of the Census. Washington, D.C.,: GPO, 1993.

◆ Chicanos in the Northwest

Acuña, Rodolfo. *Occupied America: a History of Chicanos*. New York: Harper & Row, 1981.
Gamboa, Erasmo. "Chicanos in the Northwest: An Historical Perspective." *El Grito 6*, No. 4 (summer 1973): 57-70.

Garcia, Jerry. "The History of a Chicano/Mexicano Community in the Pacific Northwest", Quincy, Washington, 1948-1993. Master's thesis, Eastern Washington University, 1993.

Herrera, David, and Clifford E. Bryan. *"Historia Verdadera del Chicano del Norte" [True History of the Chicano of the North.]*, ERIC, ED 104577, March 1974.

Johansen, Bruce E., and Roberto F. Maestas. *The Creation of Washington's Latino Community, 1935-1980.* Seattle: El Centro de la Raza, 1981.

Kupel, Doug. *"Ethnic Genesis: Oregon's Chicanos."* Ph.D. diss., University of Oregon, 1979.

Mercier, Laurie, and Carole Simon-Smolinski. *Idaho's Ethnic Heritage: A Resource Guide. Vol. 1.* Idaho Centennial Commission, March 1990.

Mercier, Laurie, and Carole Simon-Smolinski. *Idaho's Ethnic Heritage: Historical Overviews. Vol. 2.* Idaho Centennial Commission, March 1990.

Ourada, Patricia K. "Mexican Heritage and Experience in Idaho." *In Interpreting Local Culture and History*, edited by J. Sanford Rikoon and Judith Austin, 155-163. Moscow, Idaho: University of Idaho Press, 1991

Slatta, Richard Wayne. "Chicanos in Oregon: An Historical Overview." Master's thesis, Portland State University, 1974.

Slatta, Richard Wayne. "Chicanos in the Pacific Northwest: An Historical Overview of Oregon's Chicanos." *Aztlan 6*, No. 3 (fall 1975): 327-40.

◆ Agriculture, Farm Labor, and Migrants

Brunton, Anne Marjorie. "The Decision to Settle: A Study of Mexican-American Migrants." Ph.D. diss., Washington State University, 1971.

Consulting Services Corporation. *Migrant Farm Workers in the State of Washington.* 4 vols. Seattle, 1966-1967.

Gamboa, Erasmo. "A History of the Chicano People and the Development of Agriculture in the Yakima Valley, Washington." Master's thesis, University of Washington, 1973.

Gamboa, Erasmo. *Mexican Labor and World War II: Braceros in the Pacific Northwest,* 1942-1947. Austin: University of Texas Press, 1990.

Gamboa, Erasmo. "Mexican Labor in the Pacific Northwest, 1943-1947: A Photographic Essay." *Pacific Northwest Quarterly* 73, No. 4 (October 1982): 175-81.

Gamboa, Erasmo. "Mexican Migration into Washington State: A History, 1940-1950." Pacific Northwest Quarterly 72 (January 1981): 121-131.

Gamboa, Erasmo. "Under the Thumb of Agriculture: Bracero and Mexican American Workers in the Pacific Northwest, 1940-1950" Ph.D. diss., University of Washington, 1984.

Howenstine, Erick, "Misperception of Destination Encouraging Migration of Mexican Labor to Yakima Valley, Washington." Ph. D. Diss., University of Washington, 1989

Knickerbocker, Brad. "A Northwest Region's Family Ties to Mexico." *Christian Science Monitor*, 14 August 1992: 10-11

Loprinizi, Colleen Marie. "Hispanic Migrant Labor in Oregon, 1940-1990." Master's thesis, Portland State University, 1991.

Maldonado, Carlos. "Mexicanos in Spokane: 1930-1992." *Revista Apple* 3, No. 1-2 (spring 1992): 118-25.

Maldonado, Carlos. "Mexicanos in Spokane: A Photographic Historical Essay, 1940's-1950's." *Revista Apple* 3, No. 1-2 (spring 1992): 126-31.

Martinez, Felix M. "Migratory Patterns of the Migrant Child in the Yakima Valley." Master's thesis, Central Washington University, 1989.

McCutcheon, Laurie. "Migrants to King County Outside Seattle: How Many Are Coming, Where Are They Coming From, and Who Are They?" Ph.D. diss., University of Washington, 1989.

Ourada, Patricia K., *Migrant Workers in Idaho*. Boise, ID: Boise State University, 1980.

Padilla, Fernando. "The Mexicanization of the Lower Yakima Valley." *Revista Apple* 2, No. 1-2 (spring 1991): 59-63.

Sepulveda, Sergio, and Loomis, Ralph A., *Spanish-Speaking Migrants in Seattle, Washington*. Pullman, WA: Washington Agricultural Experiment Station, 1973.

◆ Political Aspects

Lemos, Jesus, Jr. "A History of the Chicano Political Involvement and the Organizational Efforts of the United Farm Workers Union in the Yakima Valley, Washington." Master's thesis, University of Washington, 1974.

Miller, Margaret. "Community Action and Reaction: Chicanos and the War on Poverty in the Yakima Valley, Washington." Master's thesis, University of Washington, 1991.

PCUN (Pineros y Campesinos Unidos del Noroeste) Update: Northwest Treeplanters and Farmworkers United. Woodburn, OR.

Si Se Puede: The Newsletter of the United Farm Workers of Washington, an Independent Farm Worker Union. Granger, WA.

◆ Educational Issues

Baker, Scott K. "The Reliability and Validity of a Direct and Frequent Measure of English Reading Fluency for Hispanic Students Who are Bilingual." Ph.D. diss., University of Oregon, 1993.

"Colleges Face Challenge in Attracting Minorities" *Spokesman Review*, 23 March 1991.

Enriquez, Roberto. "Finding Common Ground: Chicano History, Poetry and Oral Tradition in the Classroom." Master's thesis, Evergreen State College, 1992.

Fuhriman, Jay Richard. "A Study of the Differences Between the Holt Basic Reading System Vocabulary and the Normal Speech of Selected Mexican American First Grade Pupils in Nampa, Idaho." Ed.D. diss., Texas A & I University, 1981.

Helge, Doris. *"Problems and Strategies Regarding Reducing America's Migrant Student Dropout Rate. Congressional Testimony Delivered in Reponse to a Request from the National Commission on Migrant Education."* ERIC, ED 340528, 1991.

McConnell, Beverly Brown. "Parent Leadership Training Program. An Evaluation." ERIC, ED327370, 1990.

Owens, Tom. *"Ideas for Action in Education and Work: Helping At-Risk Youth Succeed."* ERIC, ED296044, 1987.

Palma, José Licano. "Characteristics of Mexican American High School Stay-Ins: The Other Side of the Dropout Problem." Ph. D. diss, University of Arizona, 1990.

Ramirez, Carmen Cecilia. "A Study of the Orientation of Lane County, Oregon, Mexican American Mothers with a Special Focus on Family/School Relationships." Ph.D. diss., University of Oregon, 1981.

Rasp, Alfred, Jr., and Kathleen C. Plato. *"Program for Migrant Children's Education: 1987 Washington Evaluation Report."* ERIC, ED301394, 1988.

Rivera Ortega, Manuel Geoffrey. "A Content Analysis of the Mexican American in Elementary Basal Readers." Ph.D. diss, University of Oregon, 1974.

Sorenson, Eric. "School Tries Harder to Recruit Minorities." *Spokesman Review*, 14 January 1990.

State of Idaho Board of Education. *Report of the Task Force on Hispanic Education (Bilingual Report)*. Boise, ID, 1991.

Teresa, Judith S. "Increasing Self-Efficacy for Careers in Young Adults from Migrant Farmworker Backgrounds." Ph.D. diss., Washington State University, 1991.

Vadasy, Patricia, and Mary Maddox. *The Yakima Equity Study: The Conditions of Success for Migrant, Hispanic, and Native American Students in the Yakima Valley*. U.S. Department of Education, 1992.

Valadez, Senon Monreal. "An Exploratory Study of Chicano Parent Perceptions of School and the Education of Their Children in Two Oregon Community Settings." Ph.D. diss, University of Oregon, 1974.

"Washington State University: Hispanic Staff Concerns." *Revista Apple* 3, No. 1-2 (spring 1992): 112-17.

Willsey, Samuel John. "Hispanic Placement in Special Education: A Comparative Study of Comprehensive Test of Basic Skills Scores." Ed.D. diss., Seattle University, 1992.

Windishar, Anne. "Schools Put Dunce Cap on Minorities." *Spokesman Review*, 21 October 1990.

◆ Bilingual Education

Díaz, Rafael Angel. "A Descriptive Study of Current Spanish-English Title VII, K-3 (1978-79) Bilingual Education Programs, State of Washington; with Emphasis on Teacher Preparation, Curriculum, Instructional Strategies, and a Projection of a Bilingal Program Model." Ph.D. diss., University of Washington, 1981.

Mabbutt, Richard. *Hispanics in Idaho: Concerns and Challenges.* Idaho Human Rights Commission, 1990.

Martinez, Socorro. "A Comparative Study of Attitudes of Mexican-American Students in Third Grade Bilingual and Non-Bilingual Classrooms." Ph.D. diss., University of Oregon, 1983.

McConnell, Beverly Brown. "Effectiveness of Individualized Bilingual Instruction for Migrant Students." Ph.D. diss., Washington State University, 1980.

McConnell, Beverly Brown. *"Long Term Effects of Bilingual Education. Short and Long Term Gains in Spanish and English and in Academic Subjects in a Bilingual Program; Plus a Follow-up Study on Children One to Five Years Later. Final Evaluation,* 1979-80 Program Year." ERIC, ED206203, 1981.

Smith, Mary Eileen. "Equality of Educational Opportunity for Language Minority Students in Oregon: A Survey of ESL/Bilingual Education Policy in Local School Districts." Ph.D. diss., Portland State University and University of Oregon, 1987.

◆ Migrant Education

Akamine, Toshio, and Cynthia B. Dillard. *"Improving Access of Special Populaitons to Vocational Education in the Yakima School District. Final Report."* ERIC, ED281984, 1986.

Flores, Merced. *"Cultural and Program Awareness for Administrators, Teachers, and Aides."* ERIC, ED225743, 1982.

Furman, Gail C. and Richard D. Sagor. *"Washington State Administrative Certification and Cultural Diversity Requirements. Draft."* ERIC, ED354626, 1992.

Garcia, Frank, J. and Melva Ybarra-Garcia. *"Strategies for Counseling Chicanos: Effects of Racial and Cultural Stereotypes."* ERIC, ED278757, 1985.

Hamar, Rosalind, and Andrea Hunter. *"Choices for Migrant Youth. Ideas for Action in Education and Work."* ERIC, ED239801, 1983.

Hispanic Youth: Dropout Prevention: *Report of the Task Force on the Participation of Hispanic Students in Vocational Education Programs.* State of Idaho Division of Vocational Education. Boise, ID: 1990.

Idaho State Department of Education. *"Title I ESEA Migrant Education: State Annual Evaluation Report."* ERIC, ED218041, 1981.

Jackson County Education Service District (Medford, OR). *"Jackson County Migrant Education. Migrant Education—Harvests of Hope."* ERIC, ED212441, 1981.

Oregon State Department of Education. *"Migrant Education Projects. Projectos de Educacion Migrante. Oregon Migrant Education."* ERIC, ED212440, 1980.

Plato, Kathleen C. *"1979 Washington State Program Evaluation Report for Migrant Children's Education."* ERIC, ED218044, 1979.

Plato, Kathleen C. *"1980 Washington State Program Evaluation Report for Migrant Children's Education."* ERIC, ED218045, 1981.

Plato, Kathleen C. *"1981 Washington State Program Evaluation Report for Migrant Children's Education."* ERIC, ED218046, 1972.

Plato, Kathleen C. *"Washington State Program for Migrant Children's Education. 1983 Evaluation Report."* ERIC, ED256541, 1984

Plato, Kathleen C. *"Program for Migrant Children's Education: A National Profile."* ERIC, ED255353, 1984.

Reeves, Carolyn M. and Patrick J LeCertua. *"Chapter 1 ECIA Migrant Education Evaluation Report. Fiscal Year 1983."* ERIC, ED256542, 1983.

Rivera, Rosendo R. and Carlos Trevino. *"State of Washington Migrant Education Secondary Credit Exchange Program."* ERIC, ED258742, 1984.

Soderstrom, Joan. "An Investigation of Mexican-American Migrant Children Population in Idaho and the Educational Opportunities Provided by Selected School Districts." Master's thesis, Idaho State University, 1967.

Wirsching, Teresa. "Determinants of Idaho Hispanic Female Participation in Adult Vocational Education Programs." *Journal of Vocational Education Research* 17, No. 3 (1992):35-61.

◆ Higher Education

American Association of Community and Junior Colleges. *"Collaborating to Help High-Risk Students Succeed. Beacon Guide."* ERIC, ED346926, 1992.

Burns, Ruth Ketchum. "Model for a Career/Life Planning Program for Mexican-American College Students." Ph.D. diss., University of Oregon, 1973.

Duarte, E.D. *"Oregon State University College Assistance Migrant Program Performance Report for 1982-1983."* ERIC, ED238647, 1983.

Lejia, Antonia, and Tony Sandoval. "Hispanics Still Underrepresented at Washington State University." *Revista Apple* 3, No. 1-2 (spring 1992): 107-11.

Maldonado, Carlos S. "'The Longest Running Death in History': A History of Colegio Cesar Chavez, 1973-1983." Ph.D. diss., University of Oregon, 1986.

Ortiz, Rafaela. "A Profile of Mexican-American Students at Eastern Washington University." Master's thesis, Eastern Washington University, 1984.

Sisneros, Anthony, Phillip H. Duran, and Hiram Perez. "Washington State University: Hispanic Staff Concerns." *Revista Apple* 3, No. 1-2 (spring 1992): 112-17

Sowa, Tom. "Eastern Reaches Out to Chicano Students." *Spokesman Review:* 8 November 1993.

Villarroel, Luz E. Maciel de. "A Study of Self-Concept Among Mexican-American/Chicano(a) Students Attending Community Colleges and Four-year Intstitutions of Higher Education in Oregon." Ph.D. diss., Oregon State University, 1986.

Washington State, Office of Financial Management, Executive Policy Division. The Status of Minority Students and Faculty in Washington's Higher Education System. Olympia, 1990.

Windishar, Anne. "Schools Look Inward For Minority Teachers." *Spokesman Review;* 23 March 1991.

◆ Business Connections

Milkman, Raymond H.. Economic Adjustment Strategy for the Ida-Ore Area, Idaho. EDA / Publication Division, Project no. 07-29-02265: Washington, D.C., 1980.

Washington State Commission on Hispanic Affairs. Hispanic Community Resource Directory. Olympia, WA:, 1993.

◆ Religion

Felver, Paul A. "Intercultural Relationships: Blocks and Bridges among Hispanics, Blacks and Anglos in Pasco, Washington with Implications for the Pacific Northwest Conference of the United Methodist Church." D. Min. diss., San Francisco Theological Seminary, 1983.

Geranios, Nicholas K. "Bishop Wants to Reconcile Cultures." *Spokesman Review*, 7 October 1990.

Hawkins, Wayne R. "Hispanic and Anglos Christians: A Model for Shared Life." D. Min. diss., San Francisco Theological Seminary, 1985.

◆ Health and Social Services

Barter, Linda Christie, "An Evaluation of El Niūo Sano Program: A Strategy for Promoting Health of Migrant Seasonal Farmworker Children." Master's thesis, Oregon Health Science University, 1993.

Chambliss, Judith A., "'Asi es la vida' (Thus is life): Health and the Experience of Suffering Among Elderly Mexican-American Women." Master's thesis, California Institute of Integral Studies, 1990.

Hansen, William E. and Ignacio V. Resendez, *"Operations Handbook for Migrant Student Dental Services."* ERIC, ED211307, 1981.

Nelson, Nadine Frances, "Health Resources Utilized for Various Health Conditions as Reported by Twenty-Five Mexican-American Mothers in the Yakima Valley of Washington." Master's thesis, University of Washington, 1967.

Paz, Juan J. Jr., *"The Chicano Rural Elderly: A Study of the Natural Helping Networks and Help-Seeking Behavior."* ERIC, ED222806, 1982.

Reschke, Robert R., "An Epidemiological Descriptive Study of the Under-Utilization Phenomena of Health Department Services in Eastern Idaho Amon Mexican Migrant Aliens and Resident Mexican-Americans." Master's thesis, University of Texas Houston, 1980.

Uhl, Joan Edna, "A Description of Lay Referral Networks and Health Care Seeking Behavior Among Mexican-American Families in Seattle: The Need for an Appreciation by Health Professionals." Master's thesis, University of Washington, 1975.

Winch, Martin. "Hispanics and Multnomah County Services." Multnomah County Commissioner: Oregon, 1990.

◆ The Women's Movement

Gutiérrez, David G., "Significant to Whom?: Mexican Americans and the History of the American West." *Western Historical Quarterly* 24, No. 4 (November 1993): 519-539

Moraga, Cherríe, and Anzaldía, Gloria. This Bridge Called My Back: Writings by Radical Women of Color. Kitchen Table, 1984.

Salazar, David, "A Cross-Cultural Analysisi of Chicano(a) and Anglo Undergraduates' Perceptions of Sex-Role Characteristics: Masculine, Feminine, Androgynous, and Undifferentiated." Ph.D. diss., Washington State University, 1979.

Teel, Loretta Ann. "An Exploratory Study of the Association of North American Acculturation with the Risk of Domestic Violence Among Mexican-American Migrant Farmworkers in a Rural Washington County." Master's thesis, University of Washington, 1992.

White-Parks, Annette "Where Are the Chicanas?" *Revista Apple* 2, No. 1-2 (spring 1991): 64-74

◆ Biographical

Gamboa, Erasmo, Voces Hispanas: *Hispanic Voices of Idaho, Excerpts from the Idaho Hispanic Oral History Project.* Boise, Idaho: Idaho Commission on Hispanic Affairs and the Idaho Humanities Council, 1992.

Gomez, Olivia, *Testimonies/Latin American Community in Olympia: An Experimental Research Group; Interviews by Olivia Gomez*. Olympia: Evergreen State College, 1991.

Johansen, Bruce and Roberto Maestas. *EL PUEBLO: The Gallegos Family's American Journey, 1503-1980*. New York: Monthly Review Press, 1983.

◆ Art, Literature, and Music

Rea, Lori, (editor). *Living Treasures: Hispanic Artisans & Traditionalists of the Snake River Valley*. Nampa: Hispanic Folkarts Survey Committee, 1991.

Centro de Estudios Chicanos, University of Washington. *Metamorfosis*.

Centro de Estudios Chicanos, University of Washington. *Monographic Series*.

◆ Audio-Visual and Media Materials

Chavéz, Ramón, "Emerging Media: A History and Analysis of Chicano Communication Efforts in Washington State." Master's thesis, University of Washington, 1979.

Gamboa, Erasmo, *A Historical and Cultural Perspective on Washington's Hispanics*. Produced by Highline Community College and the Telecommunications Center for the Washington Community Colleges. 120 min. 1991. Videocassette.

Huessy, Mark and Imhoff, Hubie, *Counted In . . .?* KSPS Public Television Presentation. 30 min. Videocassette.

Powell, Jean Cecelia, "Entre Dos Mundos: Between Two Worlds: Empowering Oregon's Hispanics." Master's thesis, University of Oregon, 1990.

"Yakima Gets Spanish-Language TV Station." *Spokesman Review*, 18 February 1991.

Young, Melissa and Mark Dworkin. *Aqui se Puede*. Produced by Moving Images. 15 min., Videocassette.

◆ Newspapers Published

The Hispanic News. Seattle, WA.

El Mundo: El Periódico de la vida Hispana en el Norte Central de Washington. Wenatchee, WA.

El Sol de Idaho. Idaho Falls, ID.

Viva!. Periódico Español del Valle de Yakima. Yakima, WA.

La Voz. Seattle: Concilio for the Spanish-Speaking

◆ Diversity and Multicultural Aspects

Gil, Carlos B. "Washington's Hispano-American Community." In Peoples of Washington: Perspectives on Cultural Diversity, edited by: Sid White and S. E. Solberg, 159-193. Pullman, WA: Washington State University Press, 1989.

Howard, Gary, and Colleen Neal. *"The Mexican American/Chicano Experience . . . A Special Report. Project R. E. A. C. H. Ethnic Perspectives Series."* ERIC, ED285715, 1981.

Sorensen, Eric. "One Town, Two Worlds." *Spokesman Review*, 7 November 1993.

Winkler, Karen J. "Scholars Say Issues of Diversity Have 'Revolutionized' Field of Chicano Studies." *Chronicle of Higher Education*, 26 September 1990, pp. A4-A6.